ERRATA

Due to a production error, some page numbers in the Index of Authors Cited and in the Subject Index are inaccurate.

Reported page numbers 1–133: correct
Reported page numbers 134–205: incorrect

To derive the correct page reference for numbers above 133, add two pages to the figure (e.g., "139" should be page 141).

BEYOND OUTCOMES

Recent Titles in
Perspectives on Writing: Theory, Research, Practice
Kathleen Blake Yancey and Brian Huot, Series Editors

Assessing Writing Across the Curriculum: Diverse Approaches and Practices
Kathleen Blake Yancey and Brian Huot

Standing in the Shadow of Giants: Plagiarists, Authors, Collaborators
Rebecca Moore Howard

History, Reflection, and Narrative: The Professionalization of Composition, 1963–1983
Mary Rosner, Beth Boehm, and Debra Journet

The Ethics of Writing Instruction: Issues in Theory and Practice
Michael A. Pemberton, editor

BEYOND OUTCOMES

Assessment and Instruction Within a University Writing Program

Edited by Richard H. Haswell

Perspectives on Writing:
Theory, Research, Practice
Kathleen Blake Yancey and Brian Huot, Series Editors

Ablex Publishing
Westport, Connecticut • London

Library of Congress Cataloging-in-Publication Data

Beyond outcomes : assessment and instruction within a university writing
    program / edited by Richard H. Haswell.
    p. cm. — (Perspectives on writing : Theory, research, practice)
Includes bibliographical references and index.
ISBN 1–56750–618–6 (alk. paper)—ISBN 1–56750–619–4 (pbk.: alk. paper)
1. English language—Rhetoric—Study and teaching. 2. Report writing—
Study and teaching (Higher) 3. College prose—Evaluation. I. Haswell,
Richard H. II. Perspectives on writing.
PE1404.B49 2001
808'.042'0711—dc21   00–049564

British Library Cataloguing in Publication Data is available.

Library of Congress Catalog Card Number: 00–049564
ISBN: 1–56750–618–6
       1–56750–619–4 (pbk.)

First published in 2001

Ablex Publishing, 88 Post Road West, Westport, CT 06881
An imprint of Greenwood Publishing Group, Inc.
www.ablexbooks.com

Printed in the United States of America

∞™

The paper used in this book complies with the
Permanent Paper Standard issued by the National
Information Standards Organization (Z39.48–1984).

10 9 8 7 6 5 4 3 2 1

Copyright Acknowledgments

The author and publisher gratefully acknowledge permission to use the following material:

From the National Council of Teachers of English, for an earlier version of Chapter 2: Richard H. Haswell and Susan Wyche-Smith (1994), Adventuring into assessment, *College Composition and Communication 45(2)*, 220–236. Copyright 1994 by the National Council of Teachers of English. Reprinted with permission.

From Ablex Publishing, for an earlier version of Chapter 13: Richard H. Haswell and Susan McLeod (1997), WAC assessment and internal audiences: A dialogue, in Kathleen Yancey and Brian Huot (Eds.), *Assessing writing across the curriculum: Diverse approaches and practices* (pp. 217–236), Norwood, NJ: Ablex.

From Elsevier for parts of Chapter 5: Reprinted from Richard H. Haswell, Rubrics, prototypes and exemplars: Categorization and systems of writing placement. *Assessing Writing 5(2)*, 231–268, 1998, with permission from Elsevier Science; for an earlier version of Chapter 10: Reprinted from Richard H. Haswell, Multiple inquiry in the validation of writing tests, *Assessing Writing 5(1)*, 89–109, 1998, with permission from Elsevier Science.

From the National Writing Centers Association Press, for an earlier version of Chapter 3: Lisa Johnson-Shull, Susan Wyche and Brian Griffith (1998), The butterfly effect: A multiperspective narrative of the effects of assessment on a writing center, in Carol Peterson Haviland, Maria Notarangelo, Lene Whitley-Putz, and Thia Wolf (Eds.), *Weaving knowledge together: Writing centers and collaboration* (pp. 59–79), Emmitsburg, MD: NWCA Press.

Contents

List of Figures and Tables   ix

Acknowledgments   xi

Introduction: Why WSU?
        William Condon   xiii

Part I   Program History: Three Narratives   1

      1   The Continuing Program: A Retrospective View
            Richard Law   3

      2   Authoring an Exam: Adventuring into Large-Scale
            Writing Assessment
            Richard H. Haswell and Susan Wyche   13

      3   An Assessment Office within a Writing Center:
            The Butterfly Effect
            Lisa Johnson-Shull and Susan Wyche   25

Part II   Toward Outcomes   37

      4   The Two-Tier Rating System: The Need
            for Ongoing Change
            Richard H. Haswell   39

      5   The Obvious Placement: The Addition of Theory
            Richard H. Haswell   53

      6   Exploring the Difficult Cases: In the Cracks of
            Writing Assessment
            Galen Leonhardy and William Condon   65

Part III   The Circle of Assessment and Instruction   81

      7   Writes of Passage: Conceptualizing the Relationship
            of Writing Center and Writing Assessment Practices
            Lisa Johnson-Shull and Diane Kelly-Riley   83

8   Taking the "Basic" out of "Basic Writing"
Susan Wyche   93

9   Value-Added Studies: Defending the Circle
Richard H. Haswell   107

10   Validation: Part of the Circle
Richard H. Haswell   125

Part IV   Beyond Outcomes   141

11   Students as Stakeholders: Maintaining a Responsive Assessment
Jennie Nelson and Diane Kelly-Riley   143

12   Faculty Opinion and Experience: The Writing Portfolio
Fiona Glade, Diane Kelly-Riley, Susan McLeod, and William Condon   161

13   Working with Administrators: A Dialogue on Dialogue
Richard H. Haswell and Susan McLeod   169

Part V   Program Future: Eight Questions   187

14   Whither? Some Questions, Some Answers
William Condon, Fiona Glade, Richard H. Haswell, Lisa Johnson-Shull, Diane Kelly-Riley, Galen Leonhardy, Jennie Nelson, Susan McLeod, and Susan Wyche   191

Appendices
A   The Writing Program at Washington State University: A Time Line   206
B   Writing Placement Essay Prompts— Washington State University   212
C   Information Rating Sheet   214

References   215

Index of Authors Cited   223

Subject Index   226

About the Editor and Contributors   231

List of Figures and Tables

Figure 0.1   Flow Chart of Washington State University's Writing Assessment-Instruction Program   xvi

Table 4.1   Basic Features Distinguishing Tier-One and Tier-Two Rating Stages   43

Table 4.2   Percent of Placements at Tier One and Tier Two for the First-Year and the Junior-Year Examination   44

Figure 6.1   Five Scoring Sequences in Tier-One and Tier-Two Readings   69

Table 6.1   Placement Outcomes on the Junior Portfolio by Transfer and Language Status: 1993–1999 (N=12,424)   71

Table 6.2   Placement Outcomes on the Junior Portfolio by Transfer and Language Status: 1995–1997 (N=4161)   72

Table 6.3   Placement Outcomes on the Junior Portfolio by Transfer and Language Status: 1997–1999 (N=5778)   73

Table 6.4   Recirculation of Junior Portfolios Written by Humanities Students (N=14) Evaluated by One Science Reader and One Humanities Reader   76

Table 6.5   Recirculation of Junior Portfolios Written by Science Students (N=17) Evaluated by One Science Reader and One Humanities Reader   77

Table 6.6   Recirculation of Junior Portfolio Examinations Written by Science Students (N = 38) and Read by Faculty Evaluators from the Humanities   77

Table 6.7   Recirculation of Junior Portfolio Examinations Written by Humanities Students (N = 30) and Read by Faculty Evaluators from the Humanities   78

Table 9.1   Comparison of Pairs of Essays, One Written as a Freshman and One as a Junior, by Washington State University Students (N = 64)   113

Table 9.2   Longitudinal Data on Nine Measures of Writing, Comparing the Essays of Students Composed at Their First and Junior Years (N=64).   114

Table 10.1   Results of Freshman Composition (English 101) Midsemester Writing Folder with Placed Students   131

Table 10.2   Results of the Junior-Level Portfolio Examination According to Language and Transfer Status   131

Table 10.3   Credit Hours Earned When Taking the Junior
              Examination and Results   133
Table 10.4   Performance on the Junior Examination According
              to Declared Major   135
Figure 14.1   Three Principal Characteristics of Portfolios   199

Acknowledgments

Funding for the preparation of this monograph, including numerous research studies, was generously provided by the Basil and Ella Gerard Endowment Fund, the Humanities Research Center, the General Education Office, and the English Department, all of Washington State University, and by the Mary and Paul Haas Endowment to the English Program at Texas A&M University, Corpus Christi.

Introduction:
Why WSU?

William Condon

And so, the good book says, the last shall be first. We—the coauthors of this volume—thought that having the newest member of Washington State University's Campus Writing Programs write the introduction would be appropriate. After all, I came to WSU in the fall of 1996 with many of the same questions most of our readers probably have. I had read "Adventuring into Assessment" (Haswell & Wyche-Smith, 1994) and "Shooting Niagara" (Haswell, Wyche-Smith, & Johnson-Shull, 1994), and although I was certainly impressed with the program, those pieces served more to whet the appetite than fill the belly. I wanted to know more. I couldn't tell, from the published descriptions, exactly what happened to those junior portfolios—or even whether, in the long run, I'd really *call* them portfolios. I wanted to know more about the two-tiered rating system—how it worked, how one could test its reliability, whether it really had an impact on instruction. I wanted to know a lot more about the instructional context for the assessment, about the territory "beyond outcomes" (as our title puts it). How did the institution guarantee that students would have enough writing for a portfolio? How in the world did they recruit enough faculty—*faculty!*—to assess three thousand portfolios per year? As good as the articles were, they left me with more questions than answers.

In any event, my questions didn't begin to get at the real significance of what these people had done. As I worked my way into my new position directing the programs that these good people had built out of their sweat equity, I was able to answer my questions. But I was also able to see how inadequate my questions were. I had focused on the University Writing Portfolio, which, as it turns out, is only one part of an unusually systematic set of programs that move students from entry-level assessment through first-year composition and a writing-rich General Education Program; through the portfolio, which assesses writing at mid-career, into a writing-in-the-disciplines model of (WAC) Writing Across the Curriculum; and, finally, through end-of-program assessments in the students' home departments (see Figure 0.1). In other words, this place was much more complicated than I'd realized, the connections between assessment and instruction much more intricate. And so, in coming to WSU, I also found that my early experiences—like my reading of the articles—raised more questions than they answered.

Rich Haswell—who left WSU just as I was coming on board—was awfully nice to propose this volume, because it would answer all my questions. But I can't look at this project quite so selfishly. I am still relatively new, but almost all my questions have been answered. Instead, this volume addresses the kinds of questions you, dear readers, certainly have, not so much about WSU's writing programs (though you'll get your answers, too) as about the kinds of problems people here have faced and the ways they have worked to solutions. Those problems are far from unique; in fact, I suspect that most of you will recognize in this volume situations you face on your campuses. One of the products of our learning has been that all good assessment is local; therefore, we have not written this book so that others might copy what we have done. Instead, we have written it because we believe that we have faced, and developed locally workable solutions for, a wide variety of the kinds of problems that you face, too. Our intention here is to explore those problems, describe the processes involved in working toward our solutions, and, incidentally, provide for the first time a full description of the programs we developed in response to the problems we faced. In nothing that follows do we intend to present The Way. Our hope is that by recounting our own programs' rites of passage over the past decade and a half we can help others work through the same dilemmas—not by providing model solutions so much as by providing a kind of heuristic for finding solutions. And so, in that spirit, we begin.

By virtue of the fact that WSU has established three cross-curricular writing programs—Writing Center, Writing Assessment, and Writing Across the Curriculum—together with the fact that the programs have evolved in such a way that assessment is fully (if problematically) integrated with instruction, this volume contains material that we believe a wide range of teachers, administrators, and students will find interesting. WSU's experience incorporates a rich set of solutions to common problems. Though the principal reason for writing this volume is to deal with the process of finding solutions, WSU's individual writing programs do feature innovative models that are both adaptable and attractive to other institutions. The Writing Assessment Program has already drawn national attention, both in the form of articles about the program and citations of its innovative nature by major figures in the field of writing assessment—most notably, Brian Huot. It also earned WSU two commendations in our 1999 Northwest Association accreditation visit. The Writing Center pioneered the development of small-group tutorials that, when attached to a first-year composition course, provide an effective alternative to remedial English (a program cited by Peter Elbow, among others) and, when attached to a Writing in the Major [M] course, provide an effective way to extend and intensify that experience, boosting the effectiveness of the [M] course and providing a more powerful learning experience for the students. The WAC program has developed a "Writing in the Major" model so that students can focus on ways of knowing and writing in their home disciplines without the awkwardness or complications that often accompany the label *writing intensive*. Each program carries its own innovations, but perhaps the greatest innovation lies in the integration of these programs. Each shares personnel and resources with the others; each provides input to and support for the others; together, these three university-wide programs lend each other strength. This interconnectedness is best illustrated in Figure 0.1.

WSU's curriculum features an alternation between assessment and instruction, and the assessment is designed to flow from the instruction and, in turn, to support it. For example, raters come from the courses into which students are placed, and their experience as raters feeds directly into their own course designs. In addition, the Writing Portfolio reinforces the need to have a writing-rich General Education Program, and the teachers in that program receive aid and comfort from the portfolio's location at midcareer. WAC faculty judge the portfolios; as a result, students who are underprepared for upper-division WAC courses receive the support they need as they work through those courses. Students, by our estimate, must produce at least one hundred pages of finished writing (i.e., not counting revisions) during their career at WSU—interviews with students, however, suggest that the total ranges from two hundred to three hundred pages; therefore, WSU's emphasis on writing means that students are routinely asked to do more than the minimum. In that sense, writing reinforces itself. Finally, participation in these programs is strongly intertwined. The Writing Center is the centerpiece of WAC, and it was the original host for the assessment. Faculty raters are strong supporters of writing, and the knowledge they acquire by looking over and discussing so much student writing—and in setting the standards for that writing—makes these faculty valuable resources for their colleagues. These programs belong to the university to an unusual degree, in our collective experience. Faculty and administrators assert ownership and pride, primarily because they can see the results. Perhaps, in the end, if we can tell the story of that sense of ownership, of investment, that will make the book worthwhile reading.

This is not to say that the ownership has been always uncontested or the investment always bullish. One of the distinctive qualities of this volume is the way the chapters (including one I helped write) speak openly about the underside of the programs—an underside that is sometimes unseemly, sometimes outright disturbing, but always more complex and less digestible than the upside or public view of it. The confusions, conflicts, and missteps of WSU's system and the history of that system should not surprise (only the willingness of the participants to speak about it). A

USING ASSESSMENT TO SUPPORT INSTRUCTION

WRITING PLACEMENT EXAM
ALL ENTERING FIRST-YEAR STUDENTS

| ENGLISH 104+105 | ENGLISH 100+101 | ENGLISH 101+102 | ENGLISH 101/105/198 | EXEMPT FROM 101 REQUIREMENT |

GENERAL EDUCATION CURRICULUM
40 CREDITS. ALL COURSES PRESENT OPPORTUNITIES TO WRITE.

UNIVERSITY WRITING PORTFOLIO
MID-CAREER WRITING ASSESSMENT FOR "NATIVE" STUDENTS. ENTRY-LEVEL ASSESSMENT FOR TRANSFER STUDENTS.
CONTENTS:
THREE PIECES OF WRITING FROM CLASSES
TWO PIECES OF WRITING PRODUCED IN TEST CONDITIONS

NEEDS WORK → PASS → PASS WITH DISTINCTION

TWO [M] COURSES + GEN. ED 302

TWO WRITING IN THE MAJOR COURSES ([M] COURSES)

END-OF-PROGRAM ASSESSMENT (IN DEPARTMENTS)

ASSESSMENT
MATCHES STUDENT WRITERS WITH APPROPRIATE LEVEL OF INSTRUCTION

INSTRUCTION
PROVIDES GROUNDING IN COLLEGE-LEVEL WRITING & WRITING-RICH GENERAL EDUCATION CURRICULUM

ASSESSMENT
MATCHES STUDENT WRITERS WITH APPROPRIATE LEVEL OF INSTRUCTION AT MID-CAREER

INSTRUCTION
PROVIDES:
• FOCUS ON WRITING IN THE MAJOR
• TUTORIAL SUPPORT OR ADDITIONAL COURSEWORK IN WRITING FOR STUDENTS WHO NEED IT

ASSESSMENT
PROVIDES OVERALL ASSESSMENT FOR GRADUATION

READING PLACEMENT EXAMS HELPS ENGLISH 101 TEACHERS ANTICIPATE STUDENTS' NEEDS

WRITING LAB LENDS ADDITIONAL ASSISTANCE THROUGH OPEN LAB, OWL, ENGLISH 102:
TUTORS LEARN WHILE HELPING STUDENTSIN ENGLISH 101 AND GENERAL EDUCATION COURSES

FACULTY READ PORTFOLIOS, BENEFIT FROM DISCUSSING STUDENT WRITING, FACULTY EXPECTATIONS, AND SUCCESSFUL ASSIGNMENTS. FACULTY READERS CARRY INFORMATION ABOUT PORTFOLIO AND STUDENT WRITING BACK TO HOME DEPARTMENTS

PORTFOLIO REWARDS HIGH ACHIEVEMENT, MATCHES STUDENTS' NEEDS WITH APPROPRIATE INSTRUCTION

DEPARTMENTS EDUCATE THEIR OWN MAJORS ABOUT WRITING IN DISCIPLINES. WRITING LAB LENDS ASSISTANCE THROUGH OPEN LAB, OWL, GenED 302

DEPARTMENTS ESTABLISH AND ENFORCE COMPETENCIES REQUIRED FOR GRADUATION

TWO ESSAYS: ONE ARGUMENT/ANALYSIS ONE REFLECTION
(TIMED WRITING: TWO HOURS)

ENGLISH 101 STUDENTS PRODUCE AT LEAST TWENTY PAGES OF FINISHED WRITING (NOT INCLUDING REVISIONS)

GENERAL EDUCATION (I.E., CORE CURRICULUM) COURSES OFFER STUDENTS OPPORTUNITIES TO WRITE, SPEAK, AND DO LIBRARY RESEARCH. WRITING ASSIGNMENTS INCLUDE ESSAYS, PROJECTS, EXAMS, WEBSITES, JOURNALS, E-MAIL, ETC.

PORTFOLIOS AVERAGE TWENTY PAGES OF WRITING

THREE ESSAYS FROM CLASSES

TWO TIMED WRITINGS (TWO HOURS): ONE ARGUMENT/ANALSYS ONE REFLECTION

[M] COURSES AVERAGE TWENTY FINISHED PAGES OF WRITING PER COURSE (I.E., NOT INCLUDING REVISIONS).
ASSIGNMENTS FOCUS ON THE KINDS OF WRITING DONE BY PRACTITIONERS IN THE FIELD OF THE STUDENT'S MAJOR.

Figure 0.1 Flow Chart of Washington State University's Writing Assessment-Instruction Program

major contradiction here became, quite unintentionally, one of the messages of the book. The more an integrated writing and assessment program is effective and human, the more it is complex, intertwined, always growing, and, therefore, liable to human ailments and errors. A complex system that functions must be built of subsystems that have a certain autonomy, hence subsystems that must occasionally clash and interfere with one another. In a parallel fashion, these chapters are relatively independent and sometimes disagree, but they still speak with the common voice of people who function within a functioning system.

In short, this volume offers an unusually frank and scholarly look at the development, the structure, the problems, and the effectiveness of a robust, university-wide writing assessment program, in the context of an equally robust, university-wide set of writing programs. It also, I would argue in closing, presents a description of what Kathleen Yancey (1999) called "third-wave" assessment—and what Guba and Lincoln (1989) describe as a "fourth-generation evaluation." These programs involved stakeholders in the planning process, they have kept stakeholders informed about the outcomes of the programs, and they continue to involve stakeholders heavily in decisions. These factors may cause the sense of ownership mentioned above—at any rate, these factors, rather than the specific programs, are what we would promote as worthy of imitation. Whether readers adopt these programs as models or not is really beside the point. We do hope they make interesting reading.

Part I

Program History: Three Narratives

Fifteen years ago, Washington State University (WSU) did not have an entry writing-placement exam, nor a portfolio-based, junior-level placement exam articulating with the entry exam, nor a cross-campus corps of faculty readers for the exams, nor tutorial courses at lower-division and upper-division levels to assist at-risk students through required writing courses. It did not have an ESL sequence of courses coordinated with the placement exams and the regular writing courses, nor required writing components in lower-division, general-education courses and required upper-division writing courses in the major, nor a Writing Across the Curriculum program with frequent faculty workshops, nor a Writing Assessment Office. There was no Writing Center with its own budget line, nor a director of General Education, nor a director of University Writing Programs, nor a PhD in Rhetoric and Composition. Today it has all of these things. Fifteen years.

Therein, as they say, lies a tale, the tale of a university writing-and-assessment program initiative. No. Therein lies many tales, as many stories as there were and as there are individuals creating, implementing, developing, administering, and maintaining these things that, with a friendly stretch of institutional imagination, are called a program. The tale or the history of a program is the stories of the people in it.

The three chapters in Part I narrate the WSU program as four individuals experienced and understood it. Together, the chapters offer a truth about new assessment and writing programs that is central to this book's take on them. The essence of a program initiative is not the curriculum, the requirements, the exams, the offices, or the outcomes. It is individuals. That is why narrative—that literary marriage of the singular and the adventurous—is the most appropriate mode for this book's first part, indeed for much of the rest of the book as well. Narrative has been the most popular mode for other accounts of initiatives in writing-assessment programs (e.g., Anson & Brown, 1991; Condon & Hamp-Lyons, 1991; Roemer, Schultz, & Durst, 1991; Townsend, Werder, & Wyche, 2000).

The three chapters together, however, offer another truth, equally central to this book. Individual accounts of the history of a program will never quite match, and that is not only because everyone experiences and understands things somewhat differently, but also because academic programs are living, dynamic systems, whose parts have to differ to function. So, for instance, in Chapter 1 a director of general education presents an All University Writing Committee rather as a cohering and founding force, in Chapter 2 two teachers treat the Committee more as a mortmain that had to be escaped for them to create an innovative exam system, and in Chapter 3 a director of a writing center and one of the same two teachers (!) relate how that exam system nearly destroyed the academic unit. This is not Babel. This is the actual ecology, the essential synergy, the real history of a program that is evolving and surviving.

In their account of the university ecology of a writing program, Kim Kipling and Richard Murphy use the word "symbiosis" (1992). In her study of organizational storytelling, Charlotte Linde writes, "Institutions have occasions that permit the telling of certain narratives. Other potential narratives, the unspeakables, are often difficult to speak because there is no sanctioned public occasion for them" (1997, p. 287). Part I of this book—and elsewhere in the book—offers a sanction, or sanctuary. It should be noted, however, that all three of these chapters tell of ways that their accounts were told within the program. That is part of what Linde calls "the ecology of narratives in institutions" (288) and an important part of a program that is getting along.

I

The Continuing Program: A Retrospective View

Richard Law

My perspective as an administrator of and advocate for the Washington State University (WSU) writing program necessarily involves a degree of distance from the real action. While I was a member of the original All University Writing Committee (AUWC) and had a hand in formulating the overall program in which the writing exam plays a role, I had very little to do with fashioning the details of the program—least of all the exam. My concerns were that each piece of the program as it was implemented remained tied to the original "enabling legislature" of 1988 but reshaped sufficiently so as to meet the contingencies of the moment and to accord with other features of both the Writing and General Education programs. Beyond that, my operating principles as an administrator have been to give the expert faculty a problem to solve within a larger, hopefully rational context, provide a supportive environment (i.e., scrape up funds) to the extent possible, and then stay out of their way. It has been an exciting process, often a spectacle. From my perspective, there has seldom been a time in which the program was not going through a crisis or some bizarre rite of passage, and I have shared fully both in our occasional revels and our more frequent panics. That said, I want to acknowledge that the writing program as a whole, and the assessment package within it, constitute the most unqualified success of any initiative with which I have been associated.

A number of convenient benchmarks support this claim of success. One marker, very visible to administrators, is the program's independent status in the university with a budget of its own. A second is the visibility of the program in the scholarly literature (this collection describing the program and its history might be taken as exhibit A). A third is the recent commendation from the Northwest Association of Schools and Colleges (NASC) accreditation team (1999), which cited both the WSU Writing Program and the General Education Program as exemplary practices. A fourth is the extent to which WSU's Writing Program not only encompasses but also transcends the recent recommendations of the Boyer Commission Report (Kenny, 1998). The Boyer Report sets out a sensible but modest agenda for research universities, strongly recommending the integration of communications skills into the curricula. In comparison, WSU's program is arguably bolder, more comprehensive, and more far-reaching in its effects.

Let me add the word *visionary* as well, for the WSU program was implemented in a respectable but very modestly funded institution. In many ways it is a model of what can be done when slender resources are organized carefully toward a designated goal. The NASC commendation of the two related programs at WSU, General Education and the Writing Program, was based in part on the overall vision implicit in the program. Indeed, if we speak of the "ecology" of the writing assessments at WSU, I believe the overall policy environment—the design of the undergraduate program and the coherence of its learning goals—has given the writing assessments much of their power and credibility. The writing assessments are key functional parts of a larger system, and they work because of their role in that system.

The overall vision of the Writing Program is in large part the legacy of Professor Thomas C. Barton, who chaired the AUWC from its creation in 1986 to his retirement in 1990—years that coincided with the formative period of the program. The seven-part program recommended by the AUWC in 1988 under his leadership has formed the basis of Writing Program policy ever since.

The seven principles of the Writing Program are:

1. Entering students will be tested for writing ability, using direct measures or samples of their writing. Placement in appropriate course work will be mandatory. (This principle established the Writing Placement Examination.)

2. General education courses, and not just English composition, will have substantial writing assignments, including both formal, graded

assignments and informal, "writing-for-learning" activities. The kinds and numbers of assignments will be coordinated and monitored by a university-wide oversight body.

3. The university's freshman composition course will be upgraded. Support and supervision will be increased.

4. A writing qualifying examination will be required of all students at the end of the sophomore or the beginning of the junior year. (This examination evolved into the University Writing Portfolio.)

5. A significant amount of writing will be required in each major offered in the university. (This principle evolved into the Writing in the Major requirement implemented in 1993.)

6. Staff development programs and additional support will be provided for faculty and graduate students to enable them to handle the additional assignments relating to writing.

7. A support program, including tutorials and special courses, will be developed by the university to assist students to perform at the required levels. (This principle permitted expansion and development of the Writing Center.)

I cannot overemphasize that the writing assessment program developed within, for, and because of this package of policies. Of the seven principles, it is difficult even in retrospect to identify the one most crucial to the success of writing assessment at WSU. Item 7, however, which mandated a greatly expanded role for the small and precariously funded Writing Center, was an obvious prerequisite. The Writing Center suddenly grew and flourished, moving from a small, marginalized existence in the university to a central role. From this group of dedicated people and their practical experience in handling placements of hundreds of students developed a critical mass of expertise in writing assessment.

THE WRITING CENTER AND INSTRUCTIONAL SUPPORT

The Writing Center administers the Freshman Writing Placement Examination and the University Writing Portfolio and, on a smaller scale, provides logistical support for other aspects of the Writing Program, such as Writing in the Major. The Center works directly with instructors to design assignments and assist in evaluating student work. The central mission of the Center, however, is to support instruction in writing through tutorials, diagnostics, and counseling. Under the auspices of this initiative, the Writing Center has developed effective, multifaceted tutorial programs. The Center offers a walk-in service that is open to all students and provides special services for English-as-a-second-language (ESL) students. It offers a peer-facilitated seminar,

English 102, linked to the freshman composition course, which supports freshman writers, particularly at-risk students identified by the placement examination. More recently, it has developed and offered upper-division peer-led seminars that support Writing in the Major and the University Writing Portfolio. Together, these instructional activities serve several thousand students each year, and student demand is increasing faster than overall WSU enrollment. Student use is a good measure of success: over 50 percent of the enrollments in the English 102 tutorials are now voluntary. By 1997, the Center had approximately 25,000 student contacts annually. Exit surveys of WSU graduates indicate that over 90 percent of students who used the Center's services report satisfaction with the assistance they received.

The Writing Center has also been very successful in training graduate and advanced undergraduate students to work as writing tutors, peer facilitators, and examination readers. The Center manages to inculcate a consistent philosophy about the teaching of writing and responsible interaction with peers. The educational benefits to students who serve as peer facilitators and tutors in the Center are clearly among the important by-products of the writing initiative. Similarly, training faculty readers in the techniques of assessment has carried the initiative out into all the colleges and infused knowledge of writing assessment throughout the institution.

The ecology of writing assessment at WSU includes not only the Writing Program but also the General Education Program and, to a certain extent, the major programs. The General Education and Writing initiatives developed in tandem, and in a deliberately complementary way. A broad blueprint for reforming General Education and for creating a Writing Across the Curriculum Program was drafted in 1985 by a team of four WSU faculty members (including, incidentally, Haswell and Law) who attended the 1985 Lilly Foundation workshop on issues in liberal arts education at Colorado Springs. The first phase of comprehensive planning began the next year with the establishment by President Samuel Smith of an All University Writing Committee and the President's Commission on General Education. A new set of writing requirements and a plan for reforming the General Education curriculum recommended by those bodies were approved in 1988 and 1989, respectively. The effort to implement those plans conjointly has been in progress for over a decade. In 1993, according to this goal, responsibility for implementing the package of Writing Across the Curriculum measures was assigned to the General Education Office.

The two closely related blueprints for change signaled a new emphasis on quality in undergraduate education at WSU. The two proposals insisted, in effect, that the General Education curriculum must be coherent in itself as well as supportive of the major areas. It identified for the first time the broad purposes of WSU's General Education Program and stipulated a number of specific outcomes for students, while proposing the means to achieve those goals. One of the deficiencies of the previous program was a general lack of provision for evaluating what was being accomplished by the curriculum. By defining the goals of the program in some detail, both the Commission and the All University Writing Committee sought to make the outcomes of the curriculum accessible to evaluation. Since 1989, WSU has been implementing this broad plan for general education reform in stages, attempting at the same time to evaluate student progress toward the learning goals of the program. This, in a nutshell, is the context in which the writing exam developed.

INCLUSION OF WRITING EXPERIENCES IN ALL GENERAL EDUCATION COURSES

Under the new program guidelines, all courses approved as General Education requirements must have some appropriate writing assignments integrated into the material of the course. A sunset review of General Education courses in 1994 to 1995 was undertaken to enforce that stipulation. The process of routine course approval also emphasizes the writing components of new courses. The new Tier III courses, the program's only upper division requirements, are obliged to have significant formal writing assignments similar to those required for Writing in the Major courses.

The goal of this policy of infusing writing everywhere in the curriculum is to reinforce and extend the skills learned in composition courses through practice in many different contexts and for many different audiences. This strategy also reflects an important consideration: students mature in stages while attending college. The broad conceptual structure embodied in the three tiers of the General Education Program has allowed development of graduated or even sequential courses and assignments. There is an another important synergy here between the Writing Program and the General Education curriculum that involves the conscious use of writing as a tool for learning. According to Ernest Boyer, writing can be used to "help to develop student's capacity to weigh evidence, integrate knowledge, and express ideas with clarity and precision." That is, infusing writing assignments throughout the General Education curriculum is a means of assisting students to master the higher intellectual skills and to improve their writing skills.

INCLUDING SIGNIFICANT WRITING EXPERIENCES IN ALL MAJOR PROGRAMS

There is now extensive practice of writing skills in every undergraduate program at WSU in addition to what is required in the composition curriculum. The requirements mandate that skills learned in freshman composition are reinforced frequently in other courses, through practice and repetition in many different contexts, with more challenging assignments at higher levels of the curriculum. Through the writing exam and its spin-offs, we have developed the means of assessing progress in those skills at several points in students' careers.

At least two intensive writing courses in the major program must be taken by each student as a graduation requirement. Although this piece of the Writing Program is not technically within the purview of the General Education program, it is integrated conceptually with it. Along with the University Portfolio, Writing in the Major has been one of the ways by which writing instruction has become distributed across WSU's undergraduate curriculum; it is, in fact, the chief means by which the General Education requirements have been functionally integrated with the rest of the undergraduate curriculum.

The purpose of Writing in the Major is to teach students the stylistic conventions and the kinds of writing prevailing in their own fields and to ensure student competence in those conventions. Responsibility for verifying that competence is assigned to the major department, which specifies the assignments and evaluates student performances. Writing in the Major courses are designed and taught by faculty in the field.

Implemented during the 1993 to 1995 school year, this requirement has led to the development of over 250 "M" or Writing in the Major courses. Remarkably, this extensive curricular revision has taken place largely without new resources. Departments and individual faculty members voluntarily increased their workloads to implement it. According to information gleaned from a survey in 1996, most departments have fully incorporated writing standards into their performance expectations for majors. A few, on the other hand, have not. Overall, however, the level of faculty and program response to this requirement represents a remarkable good-faith effort to meet new standards during a period of financial constraints.

An important by-product of this new requirement has been its stimulus to faculty development. The need to learn about M courses has provided many occasions for faculty in the specialty areas to learn also about the overall goals for the undergraduate program and to modify their own classroom practices accordingly. Another valuable by-product of the requirement, though currently exploited by only a few departments, is the information provided by M courses for end-of-program assessments.

SUPPORT FOR FACULTY DEVELOPMENT

The Writing Program has generated a large and ongoing need for faculty and teaching assistant (TA) training. Implementation of Writing in the Major alone has affected every undergraduate program on campus. Instructors across the university have had to learn to respond to student writing in more efficient and pedagogically useful ways. To support this instructional effort, the Writing Program has offered frequent workshops on the effective uses of writing and faculty responses to it. These workshops have been attended by more than 500 faculty members.

In short, the seven principles adopted in 1988 have become prominent features of WSU's instructional program and are inextricably intertwined with the General Education and major curricula.

As I think about the large numbers of WSU faculty members engaged in exploring new pedagogies related to the use of writing-for-learning over the past several years, I feel compelled to add to my list of benchmarks of success that *the Writing Program has changed the academic culture of the institution.* In large part, this was a grassroots change, not a change imposed from the top. One of the NASC evaluation team noted in conversation with me that, to an unusual extent, WSU faculty had created the program and had defined its objectives and its mission. The faculty continues to be involved. This observation is true whether one examines the program as a whole or looks at the development of the writing exam itself. Working with a very general plan and a set of learning goals, individual faculty members and groups were freed to find creative solutions as problems and obstacles emerged.

WRITING ASSESSMENT—THE EXAM ITSELF AND ITS CONSEQUENCES

The WSU Writing Program was developed in response to perceived instructional needs, which were confirmed by a survey of WSU graduates and the employers of WSU graduates conducted in the late 1980s. Among the goals of the General Education and Writing reform was assessment for program improvement and student learning outcomes. The use of assessment for these purposes has continued to be a guiding principle of the Writing Program. A survey of compliance with policy in the Writing in the Major courses was conducted shortly after implementation in 1996 and led to improvements of the faculty development program and establishment of a listserv network among WSU's 150 major programs and the Writing Center. Qualitative studies of student experience with the Writing Portfolio are almost continually under way. Analyses of overall student performances and responses to the Writing Portfolio have resulted in significant changes in both office practices and overall policies.

A Writing Assessment Office was established in 1993 and assigned responsibility for administering the University Writing Portfolio and Writing Placement Examination. The Writing Placement Examination and the University Writing Portfolio represent WSU's most visible assessment activities. Together, the two represent WSU's primary response to the Washington State Higher Education Coordinating Board mandate to collect data about its students and their progress at several points in their careers, including entry level and midcareer. Although the University

Portfolio and Placement assessments presented formidable logistical problems, they have had important positive outcomes. Provided that they do not procrastinate in submitting the portfolio, students with problems are identified and given assistance in a timely fashion, while there is opportunity for improvement. The data being collected from these paired writing performances are a potential treasure house for research on student maturation in critical thinking and writing skills. The holistic scoring methods developed at WSU in conjunction with the Placement Examination and Portfolio have attracted national attention and are often cited as models in the scholarly literature. The University Writing Portfolio also supports the General Education curriculum by encouraging more attention to writing on the part of instructors, while assessing student progress through it.

The Placement Examination and the Writing Portfolio have already resulted in the creation of new assessment instruments and techniques that appear very promising and may have many potential applications in other areas of the curriculum.

Richard Haswell, using an instrument he developed for the purpose (1998a), conducted a longitudinal study of WSU undergraduate writing, comparing in a blind study student performances at the freshman (Placement) level with their writing as juniors (Writing Portfiolio). This study, to my knowledge, is the first to offer empirical evidence for the "value added" by a curriculum (Haswell, 2000). The study also shows promise of enhancing our understanding of how students mature intellectually. In this area of assessment, the Writing Program may play a significant pioneering role in increasing our understanding of how students develop as learners.

In another important spin-off of the writing exam, Susan Wyche, Darin Saul, and Gary Brown have developed and tested a rubric for assessing the use of critical thinking in samples of writing. This "Critical Thinking Rubric" is intended to measure student progress in achieving the higher intellectual skills over the course of their college careers. Because our program goals stipulate the achievement of higher intellectual skills, we obviously need a capability to estimate the levels of attainment of those skills and abilities. The instrument employs multiple criteria, based on the scholarly literature on critical thinking and on widely accepted models of the maturation processes that students go through in college. Our aim is to develop a capability for a fairly fine-grained diagnostic of student progress and, therefore, a greater ability to address problems. If successful, the Critical Thinking Rubric could have implications for evaluating student performance in the capstone courses in General Education and end-of-program assessments in the majors. Ideally, however, this instrument will also serve as a diagnostic tool for faculty to reflect on and revise their own assignments and teaching strategies. This project, although part of the university's attempt to respond to the legislature's accountability initiatives, grew directly out of the assessment of writing at WSU.

Currently, the state of Washington is considering a state-wide, end-of-program writing assessment to be used at the public baccalaureate institutions. WSU's success with its writing exam has been an influential part of those discussions. The writing assessment techniques developed here appear to be emerging as a state-wide model for assessing the writing abilities of graduates.

Similarly, in an October 1999 meeting of the assessment coordinators of Washington's public baccalaureate institutions on finding ways to evaluate information literacy and technological competence of graduates, WSU's experience with writing assessment formed an important component of the response to this Higher Education Coordinating (HEC) Board and legislative initiative. We are beginning to experiment with electronic portfolios to capture more of the process of student thinking and problem-solving on the way to a finished writing product. In short, the writing exam has positioned WSU very well in the ongoing conversation on assessment among our sister institutions in the state as well as in the national conversations on assessment.

As an officer of this institution, however, I am more concerned with the way the exam and the programs in which it is embedded have changed the academic culture of WSU. One of the most obvious successes of the Writing Program is that writing is no longer treated as just another academic specialty. Responsibility for student writing has been shared widely, rather than concentrated in one academic area. General skills pertaining to general audiences remain the province of the English composition program, while the specialized conventions of discourse used in the various professions are taught in those specialty areas. In the course of moving through the curriculum, WSU students' writing skills are evaluated successively by the English department, by an all-university committee, and last, by the faculty of the student's major field. In this way, the writing initiative has successfully integrated many of the changes envisioned in the reform of undergraduate instruction in an effective but conceptually simple way. In spreading responsibility for writing instruction and assessment across the institution, the writing initiative has involved the whole range of undergraduate programs at WSU. And although the faculty has spent years discussing curricular arrangements—the way the requirements were to be distributed, and so forth—the most significant source of coherence in the undergraduate experience is probably the writing requirements and assessments.

While we are still in an early stage of developing the kind of academic culture desired, the university is probably more self-reflective and data driven than it has been. The writing exam and its spin-offs accord very well with the research mission of the university, turning institutional research onto our own practice. The creation of the Center for Teaching, Learning, and Technology (CTLT) in 1996 is another indicator of that change. The CTLT has assumed many of the responsibilities for faculty development and assessment formerly carried by the General Education Program, with consequent increases both in the resources and expertise available for those purposes. The CTLT greatly improves WSU's capacity to support both pedagogy and assessment, and it shares a common aim of making them a routine part of academic culture at WSU.

Linking the reform of General Education and Writing with other university initiatives has been a conscious objective, so that implementing the program becomes a means of simultaneous advancement in other areas. The General Education and Writing reform has, therefore, been a vehicle for change in several areas. At the same time, other University initiatives arising independently of the reform have supported or extended its objectives. I see no reason for this to change in the future.

As I reflect on the efforts of the past 10 years, in fact, it appears to me that the combination of a clearly stated set of goals and some minimalist curricular structure is in fact a powerful engine for overall institutional improvement—provided that the goals can guide practice in the classroom and that some credible measures of student progress exist. A decade ago, at the outset of this initiative, when I had a similar opportunity to reflect on what we were attempting in our initiative, I posed a series of questions:

> To what extent can we begin to deal more effectively with the problem of student writing if we enlist the full support and resources of our academic institutions? What can we do differently if we assume collective responsibility for the problem of poor student writing and organize a common effort to solve it? In particular, what are the components of a supportive context of institutional policy, academic requirements, and administrative action within which the efforts of individual teachers of writing are not wasted like water poured into sand, but combined and organized, and their effects thus reinforced and multiplied? (Law, 1989)

Ten years later, the answers to those questions that have emerged are quite positive, even gratifying. So much so, that if I were rewriting this essay today (which, in a sense, I am) I would pose an additional and very different question: *To what extent can a university use a writing initiative to drive ongoing improvement of its undergraduate programs and its academic culture?*

Based on our experience at WSU thus far, I feel confident in answering my own question positively: we *can* improve our effectiveness in these matters with institutional effort; the whole is indeed greater than the sum of its parts. Moreover, colleges and universities *can* improve their programs across the board by engaging in a comprehensive writing initiative. Writing is fundamental to education, and efforts to improve it systematically provide a wonderful leverage point both in institutional structures and in individual faculty motivation.

2

Authoring an Exam: Adventuring into Large-Scale Writing Assessment

Richard H. Haswell and Susan Wyche

In the fall of 1990, with a writing-examination system poised over their heads, a system mandated from outside, Washington State University's (WSU) composition faculty found themselves in an unpleasant but not uncommon fix. Writing faculty have faced similar events at colleges and universities before and, no doubt, will continue to do so in the future. In brief, teachers suddenly find themselves ancillary to the political reform movements promoting assessment within their own institutions. They blink an eye, and some victor is nailing a manifesto right on their classroom door, directly affecting their programs and the lives of their students. The only recourse seems frustrated acceptance or angry protest.

But this is not how our story turned out. We discovered that the real site of writing assessment is not so much a corner franchise within already established spheres of influence as a territory open for venture and exploration. We learned that writing teachers will do well neither to accept passively nor to react angrily—but simply to act.

Our adventure and advice do not always match folklore and folk remedies. Our story is not a repeat of "teachers victimized by administrative interests." We will not tell of efforts coming too late to avert educational disaster. Basically, we will recount a success story, a tale of writing faculty reclaiming part of their university's writing assessment program. In the spirit of the rest of this book, however, we do not end with the offer of an assessment package ready for others to use. Our moral is that writing teachers should be leery of assessment tools made by others, that they should, and can, make their own. Our particular adventure into assessment was *sui generis*, as we believe all such ventures elsewhere might well be.

THE WAITING CALL

That fall of 1990 at WSU, the particular situation in which we found ourselves was neither entirely discouraging nor entirely encouraging (see Appendix A for a chronology of events). On the one hand, several university reforms were under way with excellent promise for writing instruction. Under the direction of a member of the English Department very sympathetic to current composition theory and practice, the University was revamping its general-education requirements, recommending the requirement of extended writing assignments in lower-division core courses and writing-intensive methods in upper-division courses for majors. The faculty senate had mandated a writing placement examination for all entering students, a change that we had to agree was needed, especially for second-language students. The senate had also mandated a "rising-junior" writing test, which could send a welcome signal that instruction in composition should carry on past the first year. The faculty had created an All University Writing Committee, chaired by a former director of composition but with members from across campus. Among other initiatives, this committee was developing a one-hour tutorial course (later named English 102) that, taken with the regular first-year writing course (English 101), would save many students from taking the basic writing course (English 100).

On the other hand, the reform was heading—at least from our perspective—in some worrisome, even reactionary directions. Most troubling was the way the writing examination system was shaping up. The entry exam had been piloted as a one-shot, sit-down, impromptu essay, graded holistically with rates converted to placements. Worse was the mandate for the "rising-junior" examination, because it was being conceived as a barrier test, a hurdle that had to be passed before a student could "qualify" to take upper-division, writing-intensive courses. It too had been piloted as a single impromptu essay. It was this first-year/third-year examination system that we decided we could not live with, at least as it was being developed. As it turned out, our target was well chosen, and, without knowing it, we would end up helping to alter an element of

WSU's reform package that would have a key impact throughout the University's writing program.

That fall the two of us were not really part of the official team. One of us was an ex-director of composition, turned teacher and researcher; the other an untenured, newly hired director of basic writing. We felt neither committed to a clean slate nor yoked to previous work. So we began by imagining an ideal examination system—ideal, that is, for the instructional writing program. If the entry exam was going to place students into our courses, it should reflect the content of the courses. If there were to be two examinations, entry and junior level, they should be linked, providing a way to evaluate not only individual student development but the lower-division writing program as a whole. If primarily teaching assistants were to be readers, at least for the entry exam, the rating system should use their expertise as teachers rather than just their obedience to a holistic rubric (only several years later did we hear of William Smith's "expert model" of placing students [Smith, 1992]). We didn't want the system to cost students a lot of money or to be labor intensive (we all had other things to do). And we wanted an assessment program that integrated with WSU's general education reform.

Having imagined an ideal that appealed even to us, we protested. We wrote memos and visited offices. Then came our first surprise. People listened. The people included the dean of the College of Liberal Arts and the vice provost of Instruction. We discovered the first truth about institutional assessment of writing: no one feels competent to do it. There was no cabal surreptitiously administering its own agenda behind our backs. Rather, the administration was delighted to find writing teachers who said they had an innovative plan and were eager to get a problematic task out of their own hands. The All University Writing Committee—captivated with the sound of a "cutting-edge" assessment—gave us the opportunity not only to redesign and run new pilots but also to administer the real thing. They put one of us in charge of a new testing subcommittee that included several other university officials who either liked our ideas or could provide logistical support. These committee members turned out to be crucial; their knowledge about summer orientation, registration, fees, data reporting, budget, and university policy shaped the assessment from the start. They also provided us with a vocal group of supporters when our plan finally went to the All University Writing Committee for permission to implement.

In retrospect, we see five rules of thumb that we believe will help writing faculty at any campus get an initial hearing and find their way through the labyrinth of practical and political demands. The first we have just discussed:

• Assume that administrators are eager to let English faculty create the institution's writing assessment.

The other four pertain to the process:

• Let the local scene shape the examination, not the other way around.

• Take ideas but not necessarily orders from the most recent literature on assessment.

• Let innovation beget further innovation.

• For help in constructing the assessment test, rely most on the people who will maintain it.

Though obvious, so far at WSU these premises had been disregarded by those in charge of the writing examinations. Our assessment program would have been largely imported from other institutions, with rating methods reflecting designs of a decade or more ago. There would have been little connection among the two examinations (placement and junior-level) and the curriculum they supposedly supported. Once in place, the system would have stayed form-locked, in all likelihood gradually stagnating until it would be tossed out to try a different system. Worst of all, the program would have been alien to the people faced with the real challenge, to keep it going year after year (maintenance is the Achilles heel of assessment innovation; see White, 1990a).

We do not offer these five guidelines, however, as theorems. We do not argue that they generate one kind of writing assessment (better) rather than another (worse). As we describe the WSU context, the literature we found most inspirational, the way one part of our program inspired other parts, and the people who were involved with our assessment program, we merely hope to start sketching a general terrain that may show faculty at other institutions how they can start mapping out their own assessment initiatives. Our main message—repeated throughout this book—is that the pressure on colleges to implement formal assessment can be converted by local faculty as a power to drive programs serving their own instructional ideals.

THE LOCAL SCENE

Especially with writing placement, local context should be the major shaping force. After all, students walk into an "entry" exam right off the street of the local scene. Just as national standardized tests are justly criticized for slighting regional groups, so institutional placement tests should be constructed around regional groups. "Constructed around," however, misconstrues our experience: we discovered less that we had to find an exam to fit local conditions and more that local conditions helped build the exam for us. The distinction is important and worth illustrating.

As a land-grant residential university in a rural location, with comparatively few nontraditional students, WSU matriculates few students who show severe writing problems. The "basic writers" at large, urban campuses have little in common with the "basic writers" in our program. At the other end of the spectrum, we knew that some students did not need freshman composition in any form, and that the entry exam could be used as evidence for exemption and advanced credit. The rub was that the exam would have to place students in between, into the newly proposed one-hour tutorial course (English 102), students who were not basic writers but still "at risk." The placement examination would have to distinguish these marginal students from the many sufficiently prepared writers and from the few underprepared writers.

Another given was the core course, English 101. In the last three years, it had been revamped to focus on academic writing, with emphasis on critical thinking, college-level reading and library skills, and computer literacy. It had also acquired a multicultural slant with its integration into the new general-education requirements. English 101 was conceived as a mainstream course for the great majority of freshmen. There they would face instructors, almost exclusively graduate teaching assistants, all using the same multicultural reader and giving three common assignments: responses to readings, critiques of cultural events on campus, and essays utilizing secondary sources. The placement exam would have to allow us to judge whether students were ready for such a course.

Our basic writing course, English 100, had its own distinct character. Instead of the more usual remedial course, it was an opportunity for underprepared students to work on assignments like those in English 101 but at a slower pace with greater opportunity for peer and instructor conferencing. Because the course was graded pass/fail, it offered an easier transition into college-level writing. Because its credits did not apply toward general undergraduate requirements, however, it also doubled the time students spent in composition courses. The placement exam would have to set writing tasks easy enough to give marginal students a fair shake yet difficult enough to identify accurately students for English 100.

Two other local conditions, not academic but logistical, helped shape the exam. First, nearly 60 percent of our incoming freshman were arriving on campus during the summer for one of six two-day orientation sessions. Because the university promised that students could preregister for fall classes during these orientations, tests would have to be administered on the first day and results be ready the following morning for advisors. Most of the remaining freshmen (over seven hundred) would take the exam during fall registration week and would need the same quick response. The exam would be given three more times during the academic year—a total of 10 times. The exam had to be manipulable for multiple sessions and readable within a 24-hour turnaround time.

The second logistical problem followed from the first. We needed to maintain a small group of readers, test administrators, and clerical staff throughout the academic year. Especially during the summer, we would have no guarantee that the same readers would always be available. We

already knew that the readers—with the exception of test administrators—would be graduate teaching assistants. We needed a relatively simple rating and administering system, one that would not require repeated
training to maintain reliability and validity from session to session.

At first these constraints seemed just that: constraints. Faced with local
situations equally eccentric, many writing administrators shut their eyes
and hope boilerplate exams will place their students with not too much
ill fit and ill will. We discovered, however, that our local constraints
exerted a liberating and even creative force. Their influence on the final
shape of our examination can be seen in one of our exam prompts
(Appendix B). For instance, we strove for topics that would be open
enough to allow basic and marginal students scope and, at the same
time, be challenging enough to distinguish the most accomplished writers. In keeping with our English 101 design, we also sought topics that
would encourage multiperspective thinking. Although the topic sheet
does not show it, we devised rating and recordkeeping procedures that
permitted a seven-slot placement within a 24-hour turnaround (see
Chapters 4–6). As we will discuss, the need to integrate the first-year and
the junior-year placement also proved fertile, influencing the frame-and-
slot design for the rhetorical tasks and their developmental level of difficulty and interest.

THE LITERATURE

The literature on assessment taught a similar lesson. Like the local conditions, it seemed formidable and constraining at first, but it proved liberating. For one to think that a local context sets current problems to
which solutions will be found in the literature of past assessment is a serious mistake. On that false assumption, teachers who fear the technical
specialization of the literature will soon despair and turn to readymade
exams. Teachers who persist will find that solutions reported for one
locale only occasionally match the problems of another, or that the solution promoted in one report will be questioned in four others. This does
not mean, however, that the literature is useless in constructing local tests.
It means its uses go far beyond solving problems, often freeing test con-
structors to be creative with options and insights rather than binding
them with set answers. It should not intimidate, it should intimate. (For
the literature that most influenced us, see Haswell & Wyche-Smith [1994].
Speck [1998] is a recent useful resource.)

The literature reinforced for us early an already known fact, that different placement-test methods place students differently. This is true of
different kinds of tests, direct and indirect, and also of different rating
procedures: general impression, holistic, analytic scale, trait measurement, paired comparisons. We needed a constant reminder of this truth as
we were designing our exam, became we weren't likely to see different

possible outcomes, which can only be shown through laborious empirical comparison of different testing systems.

Also early on, the literature reinforced some of our predilections. For example, we were not about to incorporate indirect testing of writing into our placement system, although the All University Writing Committee had supported that method (e.g., to use College-Level Examination Program [CLEP] scores or high school grades along with an impromptu essay). Although more than a third of the nation's colleges still used SAT scores as the sole means of writing placement, repeated study suggests that such indirect test scores can only predict success at similar tests. The same is true of high-school grades, which predict college grades better than they do college writing performance. Indirect testing also disadvantages minority writers (White & Polin, 1984). Here the literature gave us ammunition to defend a position we already held.

The literature also clarified—materialized, so to speak—our intuitions about rating methods. Our first-hand experience with holistic rating had aroused a somewhat unreasoned dislike. So we were pleased to discover in the most current literature a growing indictment of the holistic as a valid placement procedure. A number of scattered points in the literature came together in a subterranean way, where it is hard now to distinguish spark from fuel. We began formulating a more open method of assessment, closest perhaps to the one described at Michigan State (Barritt et al., 1986). Instead of holistic norm-referencing, we would strive for diagnosis of future writing potential. While the holistic forces a comparison of an actual student piece with an ideal and, therefore, highlights the negative, our diagnostic reading would force a prediction of a student writer's success given several different future paths of instruction. Although there was no precedent in the literature for the two-tiered rating system that we eventually used, where obvious placements are made quickly with only one reading (see Chapter 4), and although the theory backing the system would be found only years later and found in a scholarly discipline other than composition (see Chapter 5), the literature of writing assessment must have played a part in our solution to the rating of our initial essays.

The literature also helped us negotiate two basic dilemmas well known in test construction. First, in direct tests of essay writing, a sample of just one mode of writing is less valid than a sample of two or more, and indeed one sample taken at one sitting (with several modes or without) is less valid than two or more taken at different times. For us the dilemma was that a multimode, multisample assessment would not fit the pragmatic constraints of our entry exam. Students arriving on campus in summer for a two-day orientation or in fall for residual registration were too rushed and distracted for arduous testing, and we thought that our brief turnaround time for reporting results forbade complex samples (a thought modified later). With the freshman exams, we had to go with an impromptu, single-mode essay of less than two hours duration, trusting that we could train our raters to diagnose through such effects as unfinished or hastily finished essays, misinterpreted topics, and ragged surface features. Later our yearnings for a more valid portfolio system of testing would be directed at the junior exam.

The second dilemma with the entry exam had to do with constructing the kind of essay prompts that would suit our aims and our students. As we have said, it would have to be complex enough to serve later for upper-division testing, to fit the first-year curricular emphasis on academic writing, and to distinguish between basic, intermediate, and exemptable competency levels. On the other hand, it would have to be simple enough to keep many kinds of students—not only basic writers (and soon English as a second language [ESL] writers) but certain personality types—from suffering the worst effects of pressured, impromptu writing assignments. If the assessment literature taught us any foolproof lesson, it was to give up hope of escaping this dilemma with one radical flourish, overturning decades of trial in higher education. Instead, the message was to rely on an ensemble of partial adjustments to the conventional format. We decided to write rhetorical tasks that were fairly sophisticated, trusting the counterintuitive research finding that simpler prompts, or prompts best liked by students, are not necessarily the more diagnostic. We would, however, make students study the prompt before they began writing by handing out the prompt sheet first and then distributing bluebooks 15 minutes later. Instead of jumping into their essay within a few minutes of reading the assignment, students would be almost forced to compose themselves and comprehend the task. Because ambivalence in audience specification often distracts exam-writers, we decided to explain outright that they should address not some hypothetical readers, such as the editors of a student newspaper, but indeed their actual readers, college teachers using the essay to decide placement. Finally, all students who placed in the basic course would be allowed a retest. In our reading we had noticed that the issue of retesting emerges in a highly contradictory fashion. Our profession has documented the psychological damage sometimes done to students who fail impromptu exams, yet the rare placement procedures that have allowed a retest usually have done so begrudgingly. We decided to honor the assessment truth that certain individuals need more than one trial to show their true capabilities. We would not sit back and wait for the few action-minded and disgruntled students to plead their case but would actively encourage all English 100 placers to try again.

In such ways we mapped out our particular exam from the Baedeker of assessment literature—from experimental studies, theoretical position papers, statistical analyses, historical accounts of failures, and reproductions of actual exams. The literature also provided something less concrete but perhaps more influential. The temptation is to call it a philosophy, but it was more a pervasive sense of land acquired through experience—a kind of old-timer's advice. For us it is summed up in Bizzell's caution that writing examinations can easily become a "counter-agenda for teaching" (1986, p. 67). Over and over the literature reminded us that as teachers of the courses most affected, we should make sure our exam did not belie our best hopes for them. If, as Stock and Robinson put it so forthrightly, testing simply makes "explicit the values inherent in the set of expectations that assessors bring to the act of evaluation" (1987, p. 100), then we would try to manifest values held by teachers. If administrators, institution overseers, and indeed the general public liked the test and its results, so much the better, but we would not put their particular values first.

In retrospect, our picaresque trek through the land of assessment (there is no official tour) was characterized almost entirely by our freedom to react and act as we pleased, and hardly at all by our ceding to foreign laws and customs. We found our options increased, our sensitivity to salient issues shifted, our inklings explained, our direction unchanged but our route shortened, our awareness of dangers expanded and sharpened, our convictions strengthened. Over all, our experience with the literature bore out the encouraging truth for the second generation, that there are advantages to arriving late.

OTHER PARTS OF THE ASSESSMENT PACKAGE

There also is the advantage of doing it all at once. At first it seemed a constraint, or at least a major headache, to have to shape the junior exam at the same time we were refining and installing the first-year exam and both in the middle of the implementation of the university general-education reform. As it turned out, simultaneously working on different parts of the assessment program gave synergistic boosts, often where we least expected it. We are not speaking here of the advantages, real enough, in integrating a complex program, for instance in devising rhetorical tasks that can be used with both lower and upper division tests, or exploring the feasibility of a third-year portfolio of course papers because extended writing was required in first and second year general-education courses. We are speaking of the way that work on one part of the program often sparked creative ideas for another part. This effect is not discussed in the literature of writing-assessment program development and deserves some comment (which will serve as a preview of Chapters 7 to 10).

An illustration. With the first-year exam, we devised a frame-and-slot design (task and paragraph) for the writing prompts because for security reasons we needed prompts that could be permuted during the many separate examination sittings (see Appendix B). That design, we saw, would also allow us to give the junior exam many times during the year instead of once or twice (a schedule that at other schools has caused difficulties). We saw then that with enough rotating of paragraphs, the same three or four rhetorical tasks could be used for both exams, because a student would be unlikely to receive the same one as a freshman and a junior. At that point, the feasibility of setting up value-added studies became apparent, from which followed the idea of creating rhetorical tasks that would be developmentally diagnostic across the undergraduate years (see Chapter 9).

Another illustration is the junior exam, designed later in the spring of 1991 after a portfolio model. The junior exam was more of a communal creation than the first-year exam, and our own leanings toward the portfolio format were furthered and supported especially by the director of Composition (who had earlier installed mid-semester and end-of-the-semester portfolio readings in English 101), the director of the Writing Center, the vice provost for Instruction, and the director of the General Education Office. Our portfolio scheme strove toward construct validity by allowing students to submit a sample of different modes of their writing. Because three of the pieces in the portfolio would be course writings, there was the need for a legitimizing impromptu piece, and we decided that unrehearsed writing should consist of two different modes, argumentative and self-reflective. That in turn prompted us to change, a year later, the first-year placement test from a one-piece to a two-piece impromptu. Similarly, with the first-year exam we had decided to have ESL essays read first by readers who were not ESL faculty—a way of avoiding oversubscription of ESL writers into the ESL writing sequence. That solution was adapted for the junior portfolio, in which we gave ESL writers a first chance to pass anonymously on an reading of their impromptu essays by regular faculty and then on a reading of their entire portfolio with their ESL status known.

All this swapping and mixing of ideas took place during the first formative year, and it did not stop. The two exams, indeed the entire assessment/general education program, kept cooking and self-generating. In an ecological evaluation (Lucas, 1988), it makes sense that innovators not only adventure into assessment but keep adventuring along with it as the whole system—program, students, institution, and faculty—grows (see Chapter 4).

THE PEOPLE

As the creation of the junior portfolio shows especially well, perhaps the luckiest decision we made early on was to involve in our discussions those colleagues who would provide support for the examination. Looking back, we see this was effective for two reasons: a task of this magnitude cannot be done by just one or two people, and once implemented, it becomes a permanent responsibility that needs to be handed over to others periodically. Before we became involved in 1990, the people responsible for design and implementation, the All University Writing Committee, seemed distant from those who would ultimately maintain the exam and be most affected by it. We wanted to take a different approach, though at first this was less a conscious strategy than a desperate lurch to organize the exam. We called together our colleagues—the director of the Writing Center, the administrators of the undergraduate composition program, the leader of the Writing Across the Curriculum (WAC) program, and several writing teachers—for a series of conversations about our courses, our students, our past problems with placement, and our doubts about the earlier pilot tests. From these first discussions, we started piecing together a fuller picture of both our program and the students who inhabited it—a picture that better represented the perspectives we shared as a community.

We also began to identify those students who found their way to the margins: nontraditional students who chose the "bottom rung" of English 100 because they were unrealistically anxious about their writing skills; students who failed English 101 because they needed more assistance than their teachers could provide; students whose high school grades were better than the preparation they had received; and students whose ESL background landed them in inappropriate courses. We discussed individual cases and explored ways that an exam could guide us toward the best possible placements. Our teachers, because of their familiarity with such students, played a crucial role in this process. The discussions, along with the professional literature, began to give our examination its agenda and its final shape.

In the spring of 1991, we entered the second round of discussions with the piloting of the examination in sections of our writing courses,. We wanted to know what characterized the responses of students in English 100 and 101 and, especially, wanted to identify the kinds of problems that marked students whom the pilot placed in the new tutorial course. Once again, the collective experience of participating teachers helped us refine our ideas. By the end of that semester, we had a diagnostic description of our courses, sample essays from students at various levels, and an outline of our analyses of these essays—all distilled into a handbook to be used and modified for training future raters. Though these discussions among colleagues took time, they resulted in tough decisions being made together, generated language for prompts and for the rater's handbook, and gave us a core of supporters. This last point is especially important. Not just one or two but a number of people would be able to answer questions in the rush of implementing the new program. Several people were also qualified to administer the exam and the rating sessions and, later, as team members called in sick or went on sabbatical, could step into leading roles. Similarly, our rating procedure, with its two tiers of readers, provided a system of advancement and rotation to train new readers each year while maintaining a pool of more experienced readers as guides. Because the format we chose for the ratings depends on dialogue, the conversations needed to keep the program running smoothly, or at least running, would continue as part of its normal administration.

DOWN THE ROAD

If honest, travelers' tales are also cautionary tales. Writing teachers willing to take assessment into their own hands should be aware of two inevitable consequences. First, authoring an examination obligates subsequent examination of the exam. To the degree that the test is innovative, and especially at the points of originality, follow-up studies are essential (see Chapter 9). The second consequence is more pleasant. It especially pertains to teachers who have kept their distance from assessment for fear it will take time away from their true work, teaching. In reality, involvement in original assessment projects expands participation in teaching. At WSU, for instance, the people involved had access to conversations from which they otherwise would have been excluded; conversations about general education, upper-division writing courses across the curriculum, and the articulation between our institution, its branch campuses, and regional high schools and community colleges. Even those who tend to detest tests did not entirely regret the time devoted to designing, implementing, and modifying one they detested a little less strenuously.

Not that the view down the road should have pictured a smooth ride. The interface among assessment, instruction, and academic unit would not prove as rosy for other people as we had imagined (Chapter 3); the assessment system would need constant changing (Chapter 4); the innovative parts needed theoretical backing (Chapter 5); worrisome points would not be soon solved, and perhaps never solved (Chapter 6); the very courses that helped shape the assessment would be changed by it (Chapter 7); some courses would change in ways that remained stubbornly problematical (Chapter 8); positive effect of the assessment package would need to be supported publicly (Chapter 9); the entire assessment program would need periodical validation (Chapter 10); the effect on the people most involved, both students (Chapter 11) and faculty (Chapter 12), would need to be investigated; and conversation with administrators would need to be improved and maintained (Chapter 13). The adventure would carry on (Chapter 14), but carry on always, we hoped even then, with the main goal of improving the writing and the education of students. That would mean hard but rewarding work for faculty. It would also mean a second and unforeseen reward, the best adventure of all: increased opportunities to talk and work profitably with others who are committed to teaching.

3

An Assessment Office within a Writing Center: The Butterfly Effect

Lisa Johnson-Shull and Susan Wyche

Washington State University's (WSU) Writing Program is built in large part on a combination of ingenuity, perseverance, and the willingness to improvise when things turn out a little differently from what was originally intended. This chapter is a chronicle of one piece of the writing program, the addition of an Assessment Office to a Writing Center. It is a story that begins and ends with collaboration but reveals the confusion and chaos that often accompany change.

We tell our story for the benefit of other institutions that may be considering similar solutions to state or university mandates. Writing assessment programs are developing as fast as storm clouds in the Midwest and serve institutional or legislative mandates beyond the mission of traditional English departments. Writing centers are well and centrally established at many campuses, provide their services efficiently, and offer expertise on a broad range of writing issues; a match may prove appealing to others for the same reasons that swayed us (Kail & Trimbur, 1987; North, 1984). We benefited greatly from the tales of other institutions whose programs faltered or failed along the way, and we trust that our tale of chaos and (we hope) emerging order proves equally instructive to those who hold a "butterfly" in their hands.

HOUSING THE INNOVATION

In the summer of 1991, matriculating students began taking the new placement examination. In two years they, along with large numbers of transfer students, would be submitting their junior portfolios, a much more complicated and radical procedure. Fairly quickly, the entire undergraduate population of WSU, comprising nearly 15,000 students, would be processed through the testing mill, half of them twice. Who would be in charge of the apparatus? The decision in 1991 was to administer the program through the small campus writing center. It would maintain student records, train faculty readers, and develop tutorial support for students whose portfolio results required additional writing instruction.

The decision to house the testing program in the Writing Center was made for several reasons: the Center had a history of service to the entire university community; it could emphasize instructional rather than evaluative features of the portfolio better than a more bureaucratic Testing Office; it had a record of substantive accomplishments on a lean budget; and the new responsibilities would make it eligible for permanent funding status, which was long overdue. Everyone involved—faculty who designed the assessment, administrators, the director of the Writing Center, various administrative staff—believed the decision was a good one. Though much work lay ahead, the challenges of implementation seemed far less intimidating than getting the program approved initially (described in Chapter 2). No one anticipated the problems that arose or that in less than two years the assessment program would have to be separated from the Writing Center to save both.

Though professional literature often speaks of programs as abstract entities, they have faces and particular locations in space and time that give them shape and purpose. At WSU, the Writing Center was located on the fourth floor of a brick building that housed the English department and classrooms and offices, the Humanities Research Center, and, for reasons no one understood, the Army ROTC headquarters. The central space was furnished in "early Goodwill" and decorated with the art work of children whose parents were busy either tutoring or being tutored.

Until its acceptance of the Writing Portfolio project, the Writing Center had operated as an autonomous, fairly insulated program. The director, who had created the original Center and brought it out from under the "remedial" reputation that writing centers had in the early 1980s, seemed a likely candidate to administer the new assessment. His record as the administrator of a shoe-string-budget student service and his reputation as a skilled and caring teacher suggested that he could handle the challenge of an assessment program demanding frugality, innovation, and

attention to detail. The Center was staffed with a handful of former graduate students who had become temporary faculty, graduate student
interns, and various undergraduate and graduate volunteers. Only a few
of the tutors were paid. Most were there as part of a program, because of
their commitment to the cause, and because the Center had become their
on-campus home.

The Writing Center existed—as many do elsewhere—on the financial
and political fringes of the university, and its history and mission had
produced an internal management structure that was unique within the
context of a traditional research university. It was designed as a series of
concentric circles, with each circle representing levels of function and
expertise. In the middle of the circle was the director, an individual dedicated to a model of shared governance that involved the entire staff. The
first circle out was the managerial team—five to six tutorial staff members
who grew into managerial positions after a year or more of experience as
tutors. The managerial team arranged tutor training, supervised the
tutors, dispatched tutors to give presentations across campus, arranged
writing workshops, brainstormed ideas for tutor recruitment, and created
and maintained the semester schedule. The second circle comprised lead
tutors who had at least one semester of experience and wanted to work
closely with the managerial team as primary liaisons to the third circle,
the general tutoring staff. Responsibilities overlapped between individuals occupying each circle. Such a configuration both represented the
Center's collaborative approach to learning and maintained continuity
when key players graduated or moved on.

PROBLEMS

This structure, although essentially a hierarchy, didn't feel like one,
largely because everybody tutored regardless of the circle occupied.
Information flowed smoothly from one level to the next because all
shared the same physical space, everyone knew to whom to turn when
they had a concern, and all agreed not to value rank as a criterion for
information access. Competence, confidence, and desire—not degree status or university pedigree—determined what a tutor knew and did in the
Writing Center. The mission for everyone was the same: to keep students
coming in and coming back. The testing administration, however, soon
shook this carefully balanced culture of autonomy and shared governance. Overnight the Center became a storehouse of information that had
to be communicated to other university offices—Accounting, the
Registrar, General Education—each with its own systems for administrative communications and record keeping. Administrators in these other
offices were made uncomfortable by a structure in which anyone might
answer the phone and take a message or respond to a request for information. The director, who often worked with students himself, made oth-

ers—even the most high-ranking officials—wait their turn. Faculty and administrators involved with the portfolio became concerned about confidentiality of student records, accuracy of information, and whether a tutor could be trusted with sensitive materials meant only for the director.

Equally disruptive was the amount of information flowing into the Center. Much of it seemed irrelevant to tutors whose sole interest was tutoring. It came not through the internal channels but various external sources with whom tutors were not familiar. It was not only new and cumbrous but also constantly in flux. Unanticipated problems required changes—some minor, some major—in policies and procedures, and these were usually made by the faculty designers, who maintained a proprietary interest as the project unfolded. Though Center staff acquired greater responsibility with the advent of the Portfolio submissions in 1993, many felt an increasing sense of powerlessness as "outsiders" dictated internal practices. Many tutors learned everything there was to know about placement and Portfolio issues so that they could answer student questions, but others were more cavalier. To halt the dispensing of obsolete or erroneous information, tutors were eventually asked not to answer questions about the assessment. When only a few "designated" people were allowed to answer student inquiries, the circles of shared information that the director and his staff had worked so hard to cultivate eroded. Resentment grew internally and was met with frustration by those on the outside. Conversations assumed an "us against them" quality, and miscommunications abounded. At one point, rumors circulated that some people would be fired and the Center might be shut down— rumors that baffled faculty and administrators, given the Center's growing tutorial services and responsibility for a new program.

Then there were space problems. The Assessment Office started as a desk tucked in one of the back rooms of the Writing Center. Students had to follow an intricate set of signs to find it, trooping past or through the Writing Center. Seeing friendly faces milling around waiting to help drop-in writers, the Portfolio-bound students usually stopped to ask directions or questions. As the lines lengthened at the Portfolio desk, however, the frequency of interruptions increased. Growing numbers of tutees awaiting tutors and students waiting their turn at the Portfolio desk spilled out into the hallways around the Writing Center, blocking faculty access to offices. Tempers grew shorter on all sides.

The program was in only its second semester and the number of students was still relatively small. Within a year, however, implementation was expected to be complete and over two thousand students would crowd the hallways. Space had become critical. Center staff and faculty wrote memos and complained at every opportunity, but no one seemed to pay attention. Strangely enough, the lack of support from administrators was not totally unexpected. The Portfolio had, from its very inception, been designed to support itself on student fees. The student fees, however, could not buy more space. At first, because the assessment had been state-mandated and approved by top administrators, everyone believed the necessary space and resources would be forthcoming once the magnitude of the problem was understood. The silence in response to repeated pleas began to take its toll. Even energetic outings to scare up funds from private donors were of limited success. The director of composition and the assistant Writing Center director donned suits and knocked on doors of the University Development Office, the Board of Trustees, the Board of Regents, even the Washington State Legislature.

Whether it was their campaign or the report that the fire department filed on fire code violations (after an anonymous tip about students blocking access to emergency exits), the administration finally generated enough funds to employ—for the first time in Writing Center history—a secretary. She needed an office, however, and all that could be found was a small room with no windows, no shelves, and barely enough space for a desk, file cabinet, computer, and table-top copy machine. The more optimistic faculty saw this as a sign that the administration was finally paying attention, but Center staff felt that it was more likely an attempt to make the larger problem go away. Equipment and personnel needs for implementing the program clearly had been underestimated, especially during the labor-intensive startup; however, "too much work, too little space" did not fully explain the emotional turmoil. In fact, many of the feelings expressed by Center staff contradicted the obvious reality. The Center was finally emerging from the underfunded fringes to a place of higher visibility and increased institutional respect. Faculty coordinating assessment with the Center understood the pressures that the Center staff were under as they labored side by side on the project. Yet no one had the clout to secure needed resources from an administration that was itself occupied with major cutbacks in state funding. The long hours and the additional responsibilities were taking their toll. By the end of the first year, everyone feared not only that an exciting and innovative program would self-destruct, but that friendships and good professional relationships would be destroyed as well.

Then two events occurred that sealed the fate of this increasingly uncomfortable arrangement. In the second semester of portfolio implementation, the budget for the Writing Center was cut by 65 percent because of an administrative error. The Writing Center director, not realizing it was unintentional, accepted the financial oversight as one more piece of evidence that University administrators were not paying close enough attention to the really important business of the academy: the education of students. His reaction was to refuse to proceed with business as usual. He threatened to close the Center, stage a public walkout, and hold a bake sale on the sidewalk for funds to reopen the service.

Fortunately, the mistake was discovered and the Center was given the go-ahead for deficit spending until the error could be rectified (which it was the following semester). The blow to staff morale, however, had already occurred. The director feared that the university would never stand behind the assessment program with the needed funds to ensure its success. He worried that expenditures required to get the assessment program running would be taken from the limited funds for tutor wages and that the Center would disappear entirely, to be replaced by an assessment office. Repeated assurances that the College of Liberal Arts and the Office of General Education would back up costs until the assessment was on its feet did not ease his anxiety over managing a debt-based program.

As a result of these complications, the director slowly withdrew. He continued to engage students and tutors in Center business but avoided the meetings and communications required of a complex, growing program. Without his leadership, relationships between administrators, portfolio designers, and Writing Center staff began to deteriorate, developing first into a distant wariness and finally an abyss of mistrust. The final misunderstanding was also the most ironic. Though the director no longer participated in universitywide discussions concerning the assessment design, the Center was still directing day-to-day implementation of the project as the first few portfolios trickled in. Then a student complaint about inconsistent requirements landed on the desk of a campus administrator, and faculty learned that the director had been meeting individually with students to develop "personalized" requirements—including exempting some students whom he felt should not be required to complete further coursework.

From a Writing Center perspective, of course, this made sense. The mission of the Center was to provide students a haven where they were given individualized attention. From an administrative vantage point, however, not only were these one-to-one conferences costly and time-consuming, but also they set a precedent that could not be sustained once the trickle became a flood. A less labor-intensive way of guiding students through their options was needed. The director was asked to follow set requirements and cease the individual interviews. Convinced that too much standardization in the assessment would result in one more bureaucratic structure, the director dumped his responsibility in the laps of faculty—individuals who had not time, staff, or resources to cope with it. The once ambitious program was adrift.

INFORMATION FLOW IN AN "EGOCENTRIC ORGANIZATION"

We pause here, as we did then, to reflect on what went wrong. Why, equipped with dedicated faculty and staff, did the attempt to make the Writing Center a compatible place for an instructional assessment fail? What made the project so complex that Center staff and portfolio designers reached a communication impasse only a few months after the first portfolios trickled in?

Margaret Wheatley's *Leadership and the New Science* (1992), a work exploring applications of chaos theory to organizational management, offers a possible explanation: "Information is an organization's primary source of nourishment; it is so vital to survival that its absence creates a strong vacuum. If information is not available, people make it up. Rumors proliferate, things get out of hand—all because people lack the real thing" (107). Wheatley suggests that poor communication is not so much a symptom of underlying problems but is, typically, *the* problem. People can tolerate growing complexity, long hours, even personal sacrifice, she notes, provided they feel that they know what is going on. When they have to ask, "Why are we doing this?" "Do they know what we are dealing with?" or "Do they recognize our needs?" then the necessary flow of information—and the trust it represents—is lacking.

Wheatley's observations certainly fit our case. Writing Center staff had been given responsibilities for the portfolio but were not included in many of the discussions taking place elsewhere in the University concerning its implementation. Though this is not unusual within the University (budget and space planning rarely involve regular communication with the units involved), the Center staff had no experience with which to compare their new situation—they had always functioned as a relatively autonomous consensus-based, information-open organization with a clearly defined budget and set of expectations.

Because the portfolio assessment was added on top of full-time workloads for everyone involved—Center staff, faculty and university administrators—meetings were scheduled only when serious problems arose. Without the steady supply of accurate information flowing in, however, Center staff generated interpretations out of the bits and pieces to which they were made privy. With little information flowing out, attempts by faculty and administrators to rectify problems after they had developed were awkward, even threatening. Policies and procedures—the focus of most official communications—did not address the Center's growing anxiety concerning issues of direction, control, and support. New phones, computers, filing cabinets, and a secretary symbolized the University's commitment to the Center and its understanding that the Center's information needs would increase, but—for reasons having to do both with the Center's history of independence and the additional workload that everyone shouldered to get the program running—the human network that those tools represented was taken for granted.

In retrospect, much of the conflict we chronicle seems unnecessary. Faculty and administrators tried to communicate both the progress of requests for additional support and personal empathy for the emergency measures required. The director, however, for reasons we may never fully understand, rarely communicated these contacts to his staff and on more than one occasion refused to attend strategy meetings called to respond to the Center's difficulties. When he failed to serve as the official link, informal links developed in his place. The director of Composition and the assistant Writing Center director lived on neighboring farms, so it was natural—as they picked raspberries, harvested tomatoes, pressed cider, and poured over seed catalogs together—that they talked about the problems in the Center. Eventually their friendship became the primary channel for communications—a solution they both disliked but used because they didn't know how to reengage the director or get administrators to share the decision-making process more directly. However, the same message "feels" different when delivered through informal, personal connections than through official channels. When faculty responded to the Center staff's need for direct information, their reports became suspect. The more faculty reassured, the more convinced staff became that something else must be the case—or why wouldn't the director tell them himself?

This series of incidents brought home to everyone, faculty and Center staff alike, that the portfolio program involved the University community in a way that tutorial instruction never had. Central to the problems the assessment created in the Writing Center were both the ambiguous channels of communication and the tendency for Center staff to cling to what Gareth Morgan calls "egocentric organization." According to Morgan, "Egocentric organizations see survival as hinging on the preservation of their own fixed and narrowly defined identity rather than on the evolution of the more fluid and open identity of the system to which they belong" (1986, p. 245). Had staff been dealt with through proper administrative channels or advised by a professional mediator, perhaps the damage to relationships, both personal and professional, might have been avoided. However, no one facilitated a forum that would clarify, for all involved, the confusion that had resulted in conflict.

Herein lies the crux of confusions: the lines of professional and personal authority were dangerously blurred because no one at the grassroots level of the Portfolio project had the administrative authority to take rehabilitative action. Portfolio designers and implementers were essentially all volunteering time outside their compensated academic commitments to put into place an assessment that would mean something for the students who took it and the teachers who evaluated it. The implementation of the assessment was a test in and of itself: the teachers who had invented (and were trying to implement) the assessment had sold it to the administration and the faculty senate with the promise that it would be not only a valid and reliable way to measure outcomes but also would be cost efficient and require next to nothing in contributions from central administration. The unspoken term of the cost-efficiency was that the necessary work be done quickly and quietly without rocking too many boats, depleting too many resources, or involving anyone too busy to be bothered.

THE BUTTERFLY EFFECT

The fact that the assessment was created and implemented by people who had no clear reporting lines among one another brings up interesting issues with regard to institutional structures. Unless the power relationships within a system are clearly defined, misunderstandings regarding who is responsible for doing what will be common. Power relationships can be established autocratically, bureaucratically, technocratically, or democratically, but they must be established (Morgan, 1986, p. 148). Even though the Center staff had worked out efficient, mutually agreed upon communication networks internally, such was not the case in relationships external to the Center. The Writing Center had a sophisticated sense of mentoring students into positions of responsibility but no system for inviting in faculty peers who had other more complex agendas.

In a traditional hierarchy, such as the military, those at the top tell those at the bottom what to do and those at the bottom do it. Although there is the potential for abuse with this system, it provides a communication structure that is collectively understood. The problems that arose as the Writing Center joined forces with an organizational structure demanding qualitative and quantitative accountability resulted in large part from a hierarchy unwilling to admit to its own authority. Theoretically, administrators supervising the implementation of the Writing Portfolio could have pulled rank and insisted that the Writing Center respect established protocols; they were equally empowered to have insisted on forums that facilitated group-generated consensus. Yet neither approach was employed. Instead, a lateral communication occurred, that is, everyone within a certain level of the structure knew what was happening, but communication between levels took place informally. A vague respect existed for the Writing Center as an autonomous unit, but covert challenge abounded, leaving Writing Center staff feeling manipulated and betrayed. The faculty awkwardly straddled the boundaries of both internal Center politics and broader institutional machinations, and no one felt comfortable stating the obvious: we had initiated a project that was more than we could handle.

When designing the junior-level portfolio, we had joked about creating the "butterfly effect" at our institution. The butterfly effect, a concept originally developed by chaos theorists to express the butterfly-like pattern generated by computer predictions of the weather, charts how small changes to a system can eventually lead to dramatic results (Gleick, 1987, p. 20). We believed that if we could implement a small change in the system—in this case, replacing the traditional single-shot impromptu exam with a portfolio assessment—widespread and substantive changes would follow slowly. It is well known, for instance, that if an assessment has real meaning within a system, in terms of penalties and rewards, teachers will teach to the test. So we designed a test to which we hoped teachers would teach. To the extent that we could predict the effects of the Portfolio on instruction within the university, our intuitions proved correct.

Unfortunately, the butterfly metaphor predicted an interim chaos that we ignored: we had given less thought to the impact the portfolio might have on the daily workings of the Center and more to the faculty, administrative, and student resistance to the curricular "disturbances" set into motion. We did not anticipate the strong tendency of all human systems to resist change when not adequately prepared. Faculty failed to share much of the theoretical thinking behind the project with the people who would have responsibility for it. Once the situation deteriorated, theoretical explanations did not seem particularly welcome, in part because belated attempts to explain or solve problems fit the top-down hierarchical model that so rankled Center staff.

DIVORCE AND RECONCILIATION

When the administration finally provided support—in the form of release time for faculty to work more closely with Center staff on implementation policies and procedures and additional support staff to handle data entry and phones—the Writing Center director had already decided that the assessment program would have to be removed from the Center and placed under separate management. And that happened. An autonomous Office of Writing Assessment was created, and it moved to a separate floor with a coordinator of its own. At least temporarily, the separation was a wise move, restoring peace to the Center, routing traffic to another part of the building, and giving us a chance to rethink the original plan.

Then, two years later, the Assessment Office moved back to space inside the Writing Center. The main need was close coordination of the English 102 placement and the tutorial, run out of the Writing Center, that satisfied it (see Chapter 7). Today the Writing Center and the Assessment Office coexist as amicable neighbors. Staff and faculty from both programs meet weekly to discuss common intersections and devise new ways in which writing assessment, instruction, and support can be integrated to ensure students a high-quality undergraduate experience. Program administrators, who remain involved in the portfolio project and in the cooperative effort to combine assessment, instruction, and support, continue to negotiate the delicate balance of the two adjacent programs. Structural problems have been mitigated, if not eliminated, by the creation of a new administrative position, Campus Writing Program director. He facilitates the cooperation between the Writing Center and the Assessment Office and offers supportive counsel and leadership when the programs find themselves at odds.

SOME LESSONS LEARNED

Although it is difficult to predict what lessons other institutions may take from our strange tale, we have a few that we would like to proffer. We still believe that writing centers hold strong advantages over testing offices or other institutional structures for housing writing assessment programs. We still believe that the subversive possibilities of faculty-designed assessments fit the instructional mission of writing centers. We still believe that taking responsibility for assessment can provide funding opportunities that otherwise may be unavailable to writing centers. And, most important, we still believe that practitioners in writing centers have valuable contributions to make to assessment programs.

We would like, however, to add several cautions: writing centers are often perceived, from both inside and out, as marginal structures, designed primarily to support the curriculum. Institution-wide assessment, on the other hand, exerts central influence over the curriculum—at least potentially—and faculty and administrators take a far greater interest in assessment issues than writing center personnel are accustomed to. Student responses to assessment, however student-centered those assessments might be in theory, differ remarkably from responses to tutorial support. A writing center needs to be prepared for the change that dual responsibilities will make in both its clientele and their attitudes. Assessment brings with it increased administrative, budgetary, and communication needs—needs not necessarily required for the training and supervising of tutorial staff. A careful inventory of the interests and skills of the existing personnel should be made, and where new skills are required, a system that provides training and support should be put in place in advance of changes. Above all, a forum for open communication, facilitated by an impartial mediator, should be provided on a regularly scheduled basis to allow faculty and staff to voice concerns and gather information as they adapt to the changing circumstances.

Had we better anticipated the needs of our Writing Center in response to the demands an institution-wide assessment program would make, the cost—both personally and professionally—might not have been so high. But forecasting the future of a program is much like forecasting the weather; one can make predictions based on previous patterns, but the process remains an imperfect science. Like preparing for uncertain weather, however, administrators should consider basic contingency plans for protecting the people and the programs for which they are responsible should the winds of change blow a little harder than expected.

Part II

Toward Outcomes

It's only nine thirty in the morning and the faculty rater is still fresh. She opens up the next examination booklet on her stack. She starts reading the first paragraph of a student essay on California freeway construction and its destruction of old neighborhoods. She reads very slowly, noting every punctuation mark, weighing the choice of transitional phrases, grimacing when she sees the word "existance." She speeds up a bit, however, with the next two paragraphs, nodding her head. She skips to the last paragraph, notes the sentence "Unfortunately, I don't have time to discuss issue of pollution," hesitates, then writes "101" on the back of the bluebook along with her initials, tosses the exam on one of two piles at her feet, and opens up another bluebook. Four minutes have passed. She doesn't think about it in these terms, but she has achieved an outcome.

Not much of an outcome, some would say. The next day the rater will be able to remember this particular placement essay only in bits and pieces, and the writer of the essay will hear from his advisor that he is placed into regular composition and not be surprised. Several weeks later his parents will note that the university has charged their son a nine dollar writing-placement examination fee and not be surprised. A year later this particular placement, now a datum, will be buried in a memo from the Writing Assessment Office to the director of General Education, subsumed in figures reporting the distribution of entry placements by academic course. Critics could use this particular outcome to boost their argument that large-scale writing assessment, for the most part, is much ado about little.

Obviously, the authors of this book disagree. Later chapters, comprising Parts III and IV, will show how a university's writing-assessment outcomes extend much farther and much deeper than this, extend to methods of instruction, notions of curriculum, extracurricular assistance, assumptions about learning, and attitude toward students, extend to the very core of the way a university—students, faculty, administrators—conceives of itself and the way outsiders conceive of it. For just one small instance, it is no trivial matter that this particular rater's decision will put this particular student, whose first language is Chinese and who happens to have lived all his life in Hong Kong, in a writing course where 20 or so American teenagers might hear his thoughts about material progress.

The chapters in this segment of the book, Part II, argue that what leads up to an assessment outcome is just as important as where it leads. It is also no small matter that this particular rater teaches the English 101 course, or that she does not know the second-language status of the writer, or that she is following no preset scoring guide. The three chapters of this part focus on a method of scoring placement writing samples, the "two-tier method," devised at Washington State University (WSU) and still under evolution there (and now elsewhere). Chapter 4 explains the method and shows how its influence on instruction and instruction's influence on it depends on a willingness to keep changing it. Chapter 5 advances a theory defending the method and argues that the theory explains its versatility and its role in expressing and furthering the central philosophical positions of WSU's writing program. Chapter 6 explores problems that the method has in placing certain kinds of students and argues that such honest appraisal advances the program, in part because it shows the program's central desire to improve student writing.

Part II carries on one of this book's major arguments, that a narrow focus on assessment or educational outcomes, as if they were an end in themselves, trivializes both the outcomes and the endeavor of improving student writing, in which complex outcomes (narrowly conceived) play only one part.

4

The Two-Tier Rating System:
The Need for Ongoing Change

Richard H. Haswell

Part I recommends that colleges and universities create, whenever they can, their own writing-assessment programs. The start-up, we acknowledge, may prove sticky or stickery—or adventurous if you want to put our proactive spin on it. In any institution, retroactive forces will be there to resist, and personnel daring to resist the resistance will be scarce. Everywhere people will prefer known brands to locally grown assessments (Huot, 1994). We argue, however, that the situation may prove more amenable to innovation than it looks. For faculty willing to create their own writing assessment, the advice from Chapters 1 and 2 can be reduced to a short list of guidelines for implementation: establish institutional governing principles early, foster innovation not through individuals or departments but through university committees, embed the assessment program in academic programs and university culture, take advantage of faculty expertise, let grassroots concerns and local context shape the program, interbreed the traditional with the new, be informed and inspired by the literature on assessment but not driven by it, and recruit people to start the program who will initially maintain it.

As Chapter 3 illustrates, however, the word *maintain* changes the venue. Contained in these guidelines, like seeds in a burr, lie new problems requiring, with time, new analysis and perhaps a revised set of recommendations. How do you maintain a writing-assessment program that is home tailored and innovative? Chapter 3 argues that you must support and develop the academic units that will administer the exams. But what about the exam system itself? How is that to be maintained? The answers may look quite different if the system is not *prêt à porter*.

One of the appeals of store-bought packages is that they maintain themselves. If a college buys into College-Level Examination Program (CLEP) or Scholastic Aptitude Test (SAT) verbal scores to place students into first-year writing courses, it can let the Educational Testing Service (ETS) service the instrument, let the ETS adjust items in the interest of gender equivalency, or recalibrate scores in the interest of public image. All the college need do is fine-tune on occasion, perhaps revise the way the test is presented in admissions brochures, or alter cutoff scores to accommodate enrollment pressures in the basic course. Otherwise, the testing situation accommodates to a simple one-way cause-to-effect understanding. The test is manufactured elsewhere and administered locally, the student exams are rated elsewhere and the outcomes are applied locally. The results of the administration or the application rarely loop back to affect the manufacturing or the rating.

Indeed, often the manufacturers systematically erect barriers between the local testing application and the central testing process. For instance, when students prepare to take the state-mandated Texas Academic Skills Program (TASP) writing test, the outcomes of which can result in students being summarily placed into a first-year college basic writing course, they must sign an agreement with the testing firm that legally binds them from even talking about the test for 20 years. Personnel administering the test locally are forbidden to copy any part of it, and writing teachers cannot see the test in advance or their students' response afterward. The test makers interpret such restrictions as safeguarding test security, but the restrictions also block feedback from the test takers that might encourage modification of the test. This is barring with a vengeance any attempt to move beyond outcomes.

HOMEGROWN TESTS AND MUTABILITY

It is a different matter with home-tended assessment. Maintaining the spirit of locally constructed programs over time requires the same creative elasticity that went into constructing the programs to begin with. Just as the test arose out of mutable local conditions and was shaped by them, it should continue to be shaped as those conditions change. Test makers who were responsible for the original test will be around, session after session, and will not lose their sense of ownership and responsibility. Test takers will interact directly with personnel, who can change the test or the test apparatus with little trouble. Information about the test will pass by word of mouth to all nooks and crannies of the campus, and beyond the campus to students preparing to go there. A one-directional cause-and-effect understanding of this complex field won't hold water.

Not surprisingly, advice for upkeep of local assessment systems is hard to come by. Even with local exams, much past advice assumes the ideal of an exam that, once perfected, can be administered over and over with no further development costs. Testing of prompts, for instance, often implies that bad prompts are to be weeded out with the goal of amassing a file of good prompts that can be rotated forever. Pilot testing of exams also is sometimes described as a process of elimination and modification that ends with a certifiable exam that is safe to give over and over. By contrast, maintenance in the true spirit of local assessment almost assumes that prompts and the rest of the exam apparatus will have to keep changing. Some of the advice, as it will emerge in this chapter, looks similar to the recommendations for start-up in Chapter 2:

- Don't hesitate to modify and recreate whenever local conditions call for change.
- Listen to the people most closely involved with the program and on whom the program has an impact.
- Develop the program in response to developing needs of the curriculum.
- Self-assess first to inform the program, second to persuade others.

Maintenance advice tends to be highly situational, however, and it will be more honest and insightful to see how advice may be derived by looking closely at a series of specific situations. Such, at least, is this general plan of this chapter.

Some guidelines for maintaining a local assessment program have already emerged in Part I of this book, and more will appear in later parts. Indeed, ways to ensure the longevity of assessment-instruction programs may be thought of as one of the book's central preoccupations (see especially Chapter 10). But in this chapter guidelines are derived by focusing on the method of reading placement essays that we call the "two-tiered system." As Chapters 1 and 2 explain, this system arose intimately out of certain instructional, administrative, and political pressures, and, as Chapter 3 narrates, because those pressures continued to change in the years after its first implementation, the system itself kept changing. It kept changing for internal reasons as well. All in all, the rating system offers itself as a useful example of the way that newly born and innovative assessment programs immediately must either start adapting or start dying.

THE TWO-TIER METHOD OF READING PLACEMENT ESSAYS

To describe the changes, it is necessary to have a more complete account of the rating system, as it was first put into place. Originally, the two-tier system of reading placement essays was my intuitive, somewhat extemporaneous, certainly presumptuous maneuver to meet the first influx of freshman placement essays. It might be called, not unfairly, a desperate simplification to satisfy a complex set of demands. The need was to construct a method of reading two-hour essays written by entering students to place them into their required first-year writing course or to exempt them from it. The four possible placements were: basic writing (English 100), regular freshman composition (English 101), a one-hour tutorial taken in conjunction with regular composition (English 102), or advance credit. These placement results had to be made available within six hours to advisors during the summer orientation sessions and within 24 hours during the fall registration-week session. We expected summer-session groups of up to one hundred students and a fall session of around seven hundred. With about 2,500 students to be placed each year when the program reached full steam, it took no budgetary genius to see that the nine-dollar student fee would not cover, along with other expenses, a traditional reading with two independent readers plus a third to resolve discrepant scores (almost 8,000 readings). Raters themselves were supposed to be drawn in part from teaching assistants and adjuncts, a pool with a high turnover. All these contingencies mitigated against use of the standard holistic procedure as a rating system. From experience, I knew that using the holistic method, however reliable it was in ranking written products, presented difficulties in assessing impromptu essays in terms of writing potential, that is, in terms of best placement in a course (for these and other problems with the holistic method, see Chapter 5).

My "two-tier" procedure was first tried during the 1991 summer orientations. It divided readers into two groups. I called them tiers because they represented the two steps that an individual writing sample might undergo for a placement decision. We expected the majority of essays, however, to undergo just the tier-one reading. That reading was very fast because the reader had only one decision to make: did the student obviously belong in regular freshman composition or not? The emphasis was on *obviously*. If the reader found any reason to question placement of the student into that course, wavered in any way, then the sample passed on to the second tier for a different kind of reading. The only other action to complicate this first-tier work was to set aside possible candidates for advanced credit.

The tier-two reading differed from the tier-one reading in major ways. Readers, who knew that they were dealing with problematic placements, read slowly, thoroughly, and thoughtfully. The tier-one decision to send the essay on tier-two was not taken as an argument that the student necessarily needed basic work, and raters were encouraged to use their experiences as teachers of the courses to make decisions. They knew that the tier-one reading had been very fast, and they assigned a good many of their essay writers to the regular course. They were also encouraged to consult with other tier-two raters over knotty cases, especially with the teachers of the basic course, before they placed a student there. As a last step, the pile of essays of candidates for exemption were read and those decisions made (see Haswell & Wyche, 1996 for a full description of the two-tiered system).

BEYOND PLACEMENT OUTCOMES: MOTIVATIONS TO CHANGE THE SYSTEM

How did that rating system, once in place, evolve? We were open to change in part because the rating system was experimental and in part because both the assessment and the instructional programs it served were still in the process of implementation. As we were to discover, the ways each affected the other were complex and not easily generalized. Certainly sources for changes in the two-tier method have proven diverse and none alike, with some coming right out of left field.

The Experience of the Raters with Tier-One Reading

One outcome of the system was so positive that it never prompted any thoughts of change, and that was the experience of tier-one reading. Intuitively, as we watched it happen, we were satisfied, even impressed, by the two-tier procedure (Table 4.1). We never really questioned its

Table 4.1
Basic Features Distinguishing Tier-One and Tier-Two Rating Stages

Feature	Tier one	Tier two
Number of readers	One	As many as it takes
Decision process	Independent reading	Group consultation
Knowledge about writer*	Masked	Known
Reading speed	Quick	Deliberate
Decision point, when reading stops	Obvious placement into the mainstream course	Agreement among rating corps
Placement	The mainstream course	All placement options including exemption the mainstream course

*This feature was added later.

essential functionality, and only some years later was the system theorized (see Chapter 5). It made for a very quick reading of placement essays, because usually more than half the essays were placed with only the tier-one reading, a reading that sometimes took only a minute or two. The first year we calculated that, compared to a well-run holistic reading, in which all essays are initially read by two independent readers and then 15 percent read a third time to resolve discrepant scores, our procedure reduced total readings by 43 percent (Haswell, Wyche-Smith, & Magnuson, 1992). This efficiency allowed us to pay tier-one readers 20 dollars an hour and tier-two readers 40 dollars—all covered by the income from the nine-dollar student fee for the examination.

In this case, there seemed little reason to change the system. The portion of students placed at tier one, with only one quick reading, has ranged from 41 to 66 percent for the first-year placement and from 60 to 64 percent for the junior portfolio placement (Table 4.2), more than we had originally predicted. We did not encourage tier-one readers to increase their rate of obvious placements (where the economic benefits lie), because that might be to compromise the validity of the decision process itself.

We saw that the method also gave us a natural apprenticeship ladder, with new readers first trying their hand at tier one. There the pressure was off because any essay that a new reader had doubts about could be turned

Table 4.2
Percent of Placements at Tier One and Tier Two for the First-Year and the Junior-Year Examination

Placement into First-Year Writing Courses

	Placement	1991 (N=1,602)	1992 (N=2,134)	1993 (N=2,489)	1994 (N=2,577)	1995 (N=2,556)
Tier one	Regular comp	66%	49%	47%	41%	58%
Tier two	Regular comp	11%	12%	10%	22%	12%
Tier two	Other	23%	39%	43%	37%	42%

Placement into First-Year Writing Courses

	Placement	1993 (N=333)	1994 (N=1,336)	1995 (N=1,500)	1996 (N=2,148)
Tier One	Pass	61%	64%	60%	61%
Tier Two	Pass	15%	18%	21%	19%
Tier Two	Distinction	20%	12%	09%	09%
Tier Two	Needs work	04%	06%	10%	11%

over to the more experienced tier-two corps. If a novice reader made a misdiagnosis, it could result only in students placed too high, not too low, throwing the best possible light on their writing and working psychologically in their favor. Readers took to the new system like a seed to potting soil. At tier one, they enjoyed never being second-guessed, never havingto award a placement unwelcome to the student, never undergoing calibration against scoring guides with multiple scale points. They also appreciated setting aside for other readers the kind of uneven writing that gives tension headaches because it fits no preset rubric. The second-tier corps, who at the start of reading sessions help perform first-tier sorting, liked the process of quickly clearing out the nonproblematic cases so they could settle down and focus on the interesting and difficult ones. One rater compared it to sorting a basket of washed socks by first dealing with the easily matched colors so you can take your time puzzling out the whites.

The Distribution of Placements

It may seem shocking, but one of the first motives for modifying the rating system was the placements that it began to produce. People usually assume that a good placement examination simply matches a student with his or her rightful course. This commonsense notion is blatantly misleading. It assumes that the courses exist before the students are placed into them, when in fact the kind of students who end up in courses always help shape the courses. The notion also assumes that a rating system operates with finely calibrated measures that match student to course like nut to bolt. But a rating system always manipulates the categories as it applies them. The notion also assumes that the test is a machine whose output (in the form of placement distributions) is not the fault of the machine and should not affect the machine. In fact, placement tests are constructed, and there is no reason why they shouldn't be changed to produce a better distribution.

These realities were very obvious to us as we watched the outcomes from the first examinations during the summer and fall of 1991, not knowing how they would turn out. The constructed nature of the rating system was most obvious with the English 102 tutorial, which, as a course that had never been taught, provided only the loosest of criteria for raters. As it turned out, 13 percent of students were placed into English 102, which seemed both a reasonable and a doable number in terms of enrollment. Then an unexpected thing happened with registration in the spring of that academic year. Half of the students who enrolled for English 102 were self-enrolled—they had not been placed there. Evidently, the course was succeeding with students better than even the teachers had surmised. This success in turn had an unpredicted effect on the rating of placement essays during the summer of 1992, now performed by a number of teachers who had taught the course. As we tallied up the results at the end of orientation sessions, we saw that more than 40 percent of students were being placed into English 102—a volume that we knew we did not have the staff to handle in the fall.

It seemed raters were having trouble finding reasons why a student couldn't benefit from the tutorial. At the end of one early session, the director of Basic Writing and I actually went through the stack of English 102 placements and culled out nearly half of them. Though we never told the rating corps, during the next rating sessions we had some frank discussions with readers, and the eventual distribution of English 102 placements for summer and fall of 1992 ended up at 23 percent. We installed a more precise description of English 102 placement criteria in the rater's handbook and constructed a checklist of writing problems for first-tier raters to identify in an essay: conception of topic, focus and organization, logic of argument, support and integration, and so forth (see Appendix C). After 1993, the readings went by the general rule that one or two problems would assign the student to the one-hour tutorial (English 102) and that three or more problems would place the student in the basic course. Over the years, with further circulation between course experience and rating experience, the English 102 rate settled at around 28 percent, which seems reasonable, given what teachers know of writing capabilities of Washington State University (WSU) students, and viable, given the capabilities of the WSU writing program.

Validity Studies from English 101

Somewhat the opposite occurred with our first look at the validity of the first-year placement examination. Validity studies do question a rating system, and if their findings are negative (e.g., minorities students score significantly lower than others), the studies recommend changing the system. Yet our early validity studies ended up changing the two-tiered method very little. At the end of the first year, we looked at the midsemester writing of placed students, and we found that students required to take English 102 suffered one and one-half times the rate of problems experienced by students placed only in English 101; students placed in English 100 suffered nearly four times that rate; and students who had avoided the exam and had placed themselves in English 101 experienced two times that rate. We also asked teachers at the end of the semester to judge whether students had been placed correctly into their course. Only 7 of 832 English 101 students were judged by their teacher as better placed in the basic course (English 100). Only 3 of 96 students in English 100 were judged by their teacher as better placed in the regular course. We also asked students, at about the third week of the semester, if they thought the examination had been accurate in their case: 91 percent of the English 101 students said yes, 61 percent of the English 102 students

said yes, and 59 percent of the English 100 students said yes. This information did not change the examination system. The reason was that the
information stood too much by itself. It needed more context for us to act.
From the viewpoint of teachers, the correct placement rate looked very
good (a 1989 survey of the eight California community colleges found
teachers judging about 20 percent of their students as misplaced; see
Cohen, 1989). Yet the students did not think so. Who was right? How could
the validation be validated? As we will see in Chapter 10, an ecological
understanding of test validation requires triangulation of findings and
other interpretive methods assuming a complex, interdependent situation.

The Examination Prompts

One may too easily assume that essay prompts will not affect a good
rating system. A well-trained holistic team can absorb, without change in
method, new prompts every year. But we found a symbiotic relationship
between rating and prompt. We began running tests for equivalency of
the prompts as soon as we had enough cases to make statistical runs
meaningful. A number of paragraph topics were eliminated on evidence
that they showed significant sex or ESL bias. In this case, we elected to
change the prompt rather than the rating procedure. On the other hand,
when one of the four rhetorical tasks proved slightly but significantly
harder for first-year students (but not for upper-class students), we kept
it because we felt it provided useful developmental information. Orally
before reading sessions and in the rater's handbook, raters were asked to
adjust for the relative difficulty of the task. Some perfectly good prompts
were mothballed because raters got tired of them. The responses to a
prompt on the environment began so to irritate one ecologically minded
second-tier reader that she turned those essays over to another reader—a
temporary adjustment to the scoring system that conforms to its spirit.

Studies of Rater Reliability

What kind of information will change an examination is not predictable. Early on, nervous attention was paid to the tier-one placements,
because these single-reader decisions are the most suspect by traditional
testing conventions, and such a system had no validation record elsewhere. But there was little to be nervous about. Our first study recirculated 29 essays that had been placed in English 101 with only one reading,
and only one was placed differently (Haswell, Wyche-Smith, &
Magnuson, 1992). In a second study, we randomly selected one hundred
students who had been placed in English 101 with only one reading. Of
these, 95 percent received credit for the course, compared to 93 percent for
students as a whole. (Of the five students who did not earn credit, one
never attended and three dropped before the seventh week with no indi-

cation that they were unable to perform at passing levels; Haswell, Wyche-Smith, & Magnuson, 1992.) Later, we recirculated junior portfolios, and the original tier-one obvious-pass decision was repeated in 38 of 40 samples (Haswell, 1995). All in all, the controversial one-reader obvious decision didn't look very controversial, and over the years we have made few changes in it.

In fact, it was on the rating step that seemed most natural and most traditional, the tier-two decisions made by teachers, that validation studies threw a questioning light. Recirculation found English 100 placements often replaced in English 102, and English 102 placements often replaced in English 101. Later with the junior portfolio, we found the same unreliability with "needs-work" placements, where think-aloud protocols showed raters following the rating guidelines eccentrically (Haswell, 1995). Over the years adjustments in tier-two procedures and guidelines have been frequent, including the forming of stable specialized consulting groups. Rating reliability still remains a problem, however. Chapter 6 explores further studies of tier-two decisions and further changes.

Change in Clientele: ESL Students

Only a scattering of ESL writers took the 1991 freshman placement exams. The next year and in following years, all did, just as all took the junior portfolio when it started up in 1993. This special group put new pressure on the freshman-exam rating system, pressure resulting in a modification with major influence on the rating of the junior portfolios.

At issue was, on the one hand, the right of raters with no ESL expertise to put non-native writers in the regular writing class at tier one, and, on the other hand, the tendency of ESL teachers to oversubscribe their own courses when they knew the second-language status of writers. Placing international students is something of a dilemma. They may not always benefit when their second-language status is known and when they are placed by experts, who tend to put writers with only minor second-language problems in ESL course sequences. Yet when their second-language status is kept masked or when they are evaluated by readers not expert in second-language writing, then their specialized second-language problems are sometimes misinterpreted or not recognized. Our solution was to funnel all ESL essays through tier one, anonymously as with all other essays, but then to turn over the ESL writers who had been judged as problematic, ESL status revealed, to a group of second-tier readers who taught the ESL sequence and were trained in the interpretation of second-language writing. The result was an increase in mainstreaming of ESL students. Clearly readers at tier one could not always prejudge an essay as second-language work. Before 1992, when international students were placed by ESL faculty from the start, only 20 percent had been mainstreamed. With the two-tiered system (1992–1996), that rate was doubled:

17 percent were placed in English 101 by first-tier readers, 23 percent by the specialized second-tier group, for a total of 40 percent mainstreamed. Whether or not it was finally a benefit for the students, the tier-two system put more ESL writers directly into English 101.

The lesson learned was that, with expert readers, more rather than less knowledge about the writer benefits students. Some knowledge about the writer, such as sex or chosen academic major or national origin, may tempt biased response from readers, but well-trained readers can control such biases and use the knowledge to interpret the writing and make better, more diagnostically sound placement decisions (this issue is explored in depth in Haswell, 1998d). When the rating system took on junior portfolios the following year, in 1993, much more information about the writer was available. This was because when students submitted their course papers for the portfolio examination, they filled out a data sheet that included information such as name, transfer status, sex, second-language status, major, and reaction to course writings from teachers (see Appendix C). So we adapted the first-year placement reading system for ESL writers to all readings for the junior examination. Tier-one readers read without knowledge about the student, not even name; tier-two readers have all the information on the data sheet. The expert consulting groups at tier two—ESL, pass-with-honors, technical writing, and needs-work groups—make good use of the information, not only to interpret the writings, which include papers written for particular courses, but also to make placement decisions, which involve upper-division courses in the student's major.

Change in Exam Format: Addition of the Reflective Piece

In the summer of 1993, under the influence of the new junior-portfolio format, the freshman placement examination added a 30-minute reflective essay. In the research literature, there is a fairly widespread finding that when students write two essays, the second in a different mode, rater evaluations are more valid than when students write only one essay (summarized in White, 1985). But now with two essays from each student, we had to devise a new procedure for our rating system. In what order should the readers take up the pieces, and what emphasis should they give them? Eventually, with feedback from the reading corps, the standard procedure at tier one became to rely mainly on the analytic piece. Tier-two readers consider the reflective piece to see if it throws new light on problems that the tier-one reader found in the analytic essay. Frequently, for instance, text-anxious students often relax with the second piece and show their writing skills much better (this is especially true of ESL writers). This system was expanded with the more complex portfolio sample. Tier-one readers read only the impromptu essay, and if there are problems, tier-two readers scrutinize the course papers to see if the problems were restricted to the pressured, unrehearsed writing.

The Junior Portfolio

Modifications to allow the reading of a multiple-piece or portfolio sample were not the only changes in the rating system forced by the junior examination. As we've seen, the information about writers available to tier-two readers was much broader and more detailed and jeopardized the rating process with possible biases. Science department members were judging course papers known to be written by humanities students, long-time WSU teachers were appraising students known to be transfers, and teachers were reading course papers assigned and commented on by colleagues in their own department. We encouraged more consultation at tier two and more self-awareness of personal biases. As has already been mentioned, the complexity of the portfolio sample encouraged the formation of specialized groups of readers at tier two: ESL teachers, technical writing teachers, etc. Finally, the awarding of "pass with honors" performance and, later, the selection of best portfolios for cash awards required a new system of identifying exceptional work. For the pass-with-honors certification, eventually we began double checking students with three "exceptional" courses papers because sometimes their impromptu writing received only a simple pass at tier one.

Changes in Raters: The Rating Cadre

Much more so than national examinations, a local testing system develops a cadre of readers whose growth cannot help but affect the test. Over the years, the corps changed in three basic ways:

• It began with a small group of teachers and administrators possessing formal training in composition but expanded more and more outside the department because the junior portfolio specified a cross-disciplinary set of readers.

• The two-tiered nature of the rating process created a natural apprenticeship structure. Over time, tier-one readers are promoted to tier two if their placements are consistent and accurate and if their analysis of samples during rater training seems especially keen.

• Many of the raters return year after year; therefore, the cadre as a whole develops, in experience and in sense of cohesion and purpose.

All these changes in the rating corps must affect the rating itself, in ways both large and subtle. The establishment of a checklist of problems at tier one, for instance, was developed by raters at tier two who could remember their experience at tier one and who could now articulate the problems that most affected their evaluations. The more the members of the interdisciplinary cadre got to know each other, the more they consulted with each other at tier two.

EFFECT ON TEACHERS AND TEACHING

As I have said, reasons to modify the rating system at WSU have been multifarious and are hard to codify. They range from demands on enrollment, to problems in exam format, to disclosure of poor prompt validity, to natural evolution of raters. All along, human choices had to be made, but changes were rarely preemptive; a bad prompt could be dropped or the raters could adapt to it. The founding reason for constant modification, however, remains the same. An institution is complex and itself under complex change, and if an examination is an integral part of the institution, the exam should change with the institution, all the way down to the rating system. Just as it is wrong to imagine that a rating system is to an examination as an operating system is to a computer, so is it wrong to imagine that a testing program is the operating system of a curriculum. Neither testing systems nor rating systems are inevitable or inviolable but ecological and constructed, just as is the curricular program of which they form not really a "system" of their own but just another part. When one part changes, the others should change.

The negative effects of not changing are many: petrifaction, inattention, boredom, carelessness, and dulled edges all around. These "outcomes" are well known in local writing assessment programs, which traditionally have sought stasis and often achieved it, and help account for the common history of programs lasting only from about 5 to 10 years. The virtues of change—of a program that is sensitive, resourceful, resilient, and evolving—have not been much celebrated. "Keep changing" is hard advice for schools attempting innovative assessment, but it is essential advice.

I end this chapter by stressing one unexpected benefit of a changing rating system, and that is the effect it has on teachers. When raters are local teachers, and when they feel they have enough control over the rating method to make changes in it, then positive effects happen beyond test outcomes, circular effects involving teaching and examining. These effects go beyond the experience of regularly reading the sample writings of incoming first-year students and ongoing upper-division students, an experience that gives teachers insights into the persons who sit in their classes and encourages changes in their teaching. It involves a circularity in which control over both rating and teaching improves morale and commitment.

At WSU the stamp of approval from the reading corps was no minor matter. The corps comprised interested faculty from many departments along with English, very astute and knowledgeable. They readily understood the heterodoxy of making some assessment decisions with only one reading, but their recognition of this process as an experiment in which they were participating generated a Hawthorne-effect boost of energy. One member of the economics department, a statistician, surprised us when he said that he wanted to help improve the system because he was aware of standard ways in which interrater reliabilities were calculated in writing assessments and he thought they were "a crock." When positive validation for the single-reader decisions came, in the form of meaningful outcomes, essay recirculation, tracking of placed students in courses, and cost-efficiency studies, this information was passed on to readers during subsequent training sessions and further raised their trust in the method, their interest in bettering it, and their esprit du corps.

The trust, interest, and spirit arose from readers who had a sense that their teacher expertise as well as their responsibility was being called on. Not only were they participating in the development and the mainte-nance of the system, they also were assuming control over placement of students, sometimes into their own courses, and looking for better ways to deal with the complex and singular cases discussed in Chapter 6. Because the rating of the junior portfolios was spread across campus among hundreds of teachers, this sense was not confined to the reading corps. In most departments teachers were aware—some less than others, of course, as Chapter 12 will show—that the school was taking curricular responsibility for student writing, not turning it over to outside testing agencies or administrative manipulators of student records. Workshops of teachers signing off on course papers for the portfolio found them eager to recommend changes in the protocols (see Chapter 10). Even the central administration was aware that serious and maybe "cutting-edge" atten-tion was continually being paid to the rating of essays, through internal reports passed on through the vice provost of Instruction or later, when that position was eliminated, through the director of General Education.

Perhaps it would be reading too much into the situation, but we had the feeling that as a whole the university was not so prone to fall into the common testing fallacy of assuming that the construction that a rating system puts on student performance is not constructed but real. It is too easy to assume that if an assessment procedure places 40 percent of incoming students into basic writing, then 40 percent of the freshman class are "remedial instruction." At WSU enough teachers had participat-ed in junior-exam needs-work ratings to recognize the placement as just that, a *placement*, a best guess to place a student in a next course, a human choice and therefore open to critique and betterment. A rating procedure may rank low among factors affecting a "campus climate toward writing" (White & Polin, 1986, p. 324). Certainly few students were aware of the rating procedure at WSU. However, it has had its subtle but pervasive influence.

5

The Obvious Placement: The Addition of Theory

Richard H. Haswell

As an integral part of U.S. colleges and universities, large-scale assessment of the writing ability of students boasts one of the longest traditions, yet it has also been one of the most uneasy. In 1874 Harvard started requiring an impromptu essay of new students, giving them an hour "to write offhand a respectable little theme." The pieces were judged by teachers. They were not satisfied with the form of the exam, however. In 1882 they added a specimen of "bad English" for students to correct and a half-hour to the examination. In 1896 they extended the exam to two hours. Eventually the faculty got weary of the pressure of reading the essays "under the lash." They also had reservations about the method of assessing writing competence. Some thought it would be fairer to study the writing that students did in all their entrance examinations. Some wanted an examination in English history, judged once for knowledge of history and once for skill in writing. Some wanted to get rid of the correction of improper prose. Others wanted to get rid of the writing exam entirely—which is what Harvard did eventually, only even later to switch back to a direct sample (Brereton, 1995, pp. 57–58).

From the start, assessment by writing sample proved itself an edgy chameleon.

This founding historical vignette displays the two lasting issues: efficiency and legitimacy. Reading a writing sample takes time. Reading even an hour impromptu essay takes time. And when placement decisions have to be made, usually in the weeks or sometimes days before fall registration, there is little time. Evaluators still work "under the lash." In 1874, fewer than 250 students sat for Harvard's entrance writing examination; today, postsecondary first-year enrollments range up to 10, 30, or 50 times that size. Reading a writing sample is also an interpretive process. There is the obvious problem of unchecked tyranny in allowing one person to read, sort, and teach, as the instructors on Harvard's panel of evaluators often did. Yet obvious remedies do not always reduce the problems and usually add to the cost. The use of multiple independent readers legitimizes individual decisions but raises the issue of how to resolve discrepant decisions without resorting back to a single, unchecked voice (e.g., a "table leader"). Further, methods that are meant to avoid multiple interpretations from the start, for example to reduce the student's task to correction of a sample of "bad English," usually run head-on into problems with validity. The history of writing placement in U.S. colleges since Harvard's first sally has been one of short-termed trials or longer-termed trends or—the system with the greatest longevity—resort to the most convenient and cost-effective method combined with an eye fixed anywhere except on the object.

I want to argue in this chapter that these problems of efficiency and legitimacy will be solved not only with a knowledge of past experiences, not only with the nerve to experiment on your own, and not only with a savoir-faire of practical application, but also with a theory of writing assessment as a human act. This ought to come as a surprise. When humans do act to assess writing students, rarely do they invoke theory. How many times a month across the nation are individual pieces of college student writing subjected to formal evaluation by teachers, administrators, computers, and testing-firm workers? Of these thousands of times, how often do these evaluators think of the theoretical implications of what they are doing? Yet theoretical understanding of an assessment practice conveys its own efficiency and legitimacy. Take WSU's two-tiered system of making placement decisions from a direct sample of writing. Its *history* argues that new, serviceable methods of writing placement are still to be found, methods not necessarily better than other good methods but probably better than unscrutinized methods and certainly better than no method at all. But its *theory*—were there one—could go further. It could shape comparisons with other methods, it could defend the system from unsympathetic critique, and—the focus of this chapter—it could assist the transportation and adaptation of the system to other educational locales.

As in Chapter 4, this chapter centers on the first tier of the two-tier system, because it is there that the procedure finesses the double-pronged threat of cost-efficiency and legitimacy that historically has proved the main undoing of other systems. I argue that one particular theoretical underpinning supports tier-one readings especially well. The theory, which is rather new to writing-assessment studies, also helps clarify other placement-reading protocols. At the end of the chapter I offer the tier-one step as a placement maneuver that can be adapted to other educational sites with ease, and one last time I resort to the theory to explain why the maneuver should be so transportable.

ALTERNATIVE SYSTEMS OF WRITING ASSESSMENT

The two-tier procedure admits a large number of variations, but Table 4.1 lists the distinguishing features. A writing sample is read quickly with the name of the author masked by a single reader who decides if it *obviously*, with no doubt, fits the mainstream placement (e.g., English 101); if there is any doubt, the sample is read by a second tier of readers, who have access to knowledge about the writer and who make the placement decision in consultation. The contrast with the other writing-placement systems should be evident.

- *Indirect measurement.* Measurement of a student's "writing competence" or "verbal ability," provided by nationally normed tests such as the Scholastic Aptitude Test (SAT) or Advanced Placement (AP) or Test of English as a Foreign Language (TOEFL), is still the most common way by which first-year students find themselves placed into a particular writing course. This occurs despite years of protest from assessment experts concerning the validity of the method and despite the explicit avowal by purveyors of the examinations themselves that they have not designed their tests to determine placement. In contrast to the two-tier system, indirect testing provides a standardized aggregate mark of past performance on discrete verbal-skill items, machine scored.

- *Holistic rating.* The holistic method is the current, traditional system for deriving placement from direct samples of writing, whether administrators rely on numbers from national essay-scoring firms such as the Educational Testing Service or whether they conduct their own local rating sessions. In contrast to the two-tiered system, the holistic method subjects every essay to at least two independent readings based on a rubric of preset criteria. When numerical ratings or course placement decisions of the two readers differ sufficiently, the decision is usually rendered by a third reader, although sometimes all three rates are averaged. The speed of reading is quick, and information about the writer is withheld from readers. Open negotiation among readers relying on biographical information about the author is alien to the holistic rater's sense of "objectivity" and "performance."

- *Teacher option.* At a few schools the holistic system has been preempted, replaced, or modified with methods wherein teachers read the sample and intuitively decide the placement. Often reading at their own pace and independently, teachers of the target courses decide placements only into their own courses, sometimes only into sections of the course that they will teach (Calpas & Smith, 1995).

- *Directed self-placement.* Periodically revived, directed self-placement provides students with information about the target courses, including descriptive statistics such as mean SAT verbal score or mean high school grade point average (GPA) correlated with past grade distributions in the courses, and then let the students place themselves (Hackman & Johnson, 1981; Royer & Gilles, 1998).

The two-tier system deliberately avoids some of the major problems associated with these alternative systems. Indirect measures, even when combined with other indicators such as high school GPA, predict performance in writing classes erratically. Such indicators are designed to measure past achievement—sometimes years past, as when colleges use a student's junior high school SAT scores—whereas valid placement needs to appraise current performance to estimate future course performance on similar tasks. Directed self-placement relies on the same indirect measures, but turns them over to the student to apply, whose knowledge and self-interests may not be the best judge of either the measures or of their applicability (see Chapter 14 for further discussion of directed self-placement). Instead, the two-tiered system relies on expert readers, and has them read judiciously and, if need be, slowly and in consultation. To that extent the two-tier system buys into teacher-option systems. Both eschew indirect measures, relying on actual essays recently composed, and both look to expert judges to diagnose the work. But just as student self-interests may not be the best judge of a teacher's future instruction, teacher self-interest may not be the best judge of a student's current needs. Studies have shown, for instance, that teachers tend to place problematic or marginal essays elsewhere than in their own classes, perhaps because subconsciously they do not want to teach these students (Smith, 1992, 1993). The two-tiered method deals with problematic cases only through consultation.

The two-tier method also solves several problems of holistic rating when it is used for placement (see Haswell, 1998, and Elbow, 1999, for synopses of the problems). Scoring rubrics strive to render a composite (holistic) judgment, giving equal weight to all features of an essay. But rubrics idealize the variety found in actual student writing and cover up the human tendency of raters to treat subskills unequally. Holistic reading suffers from halo effects, in which some unconsciously valued trait colors the valuation of other traits, and from primacy effects, in which traits first observed color traits later observed. By contrast, the diagnostic checklists used in the two-tier system (see Appendix C) do not assume equal weighting of subskills, and they focus on evidence of future performance in particular courses. Indeed, the essay of uneven performance in subskills, which befuddles holistic readers (e.g., an essay strong in ideas but weak in organization), often turns out to be the easiest to place with the two-tier system. As a final contrast, as well as historically the initial motive for the two-tier system, the time efficiency of its "obvious" first-step reading cuts the costs of the holistic system, which requires that every essay be read at least twice through a need to derive estimates of interrater reliability and to train and retrain readers to keep the estimates respectable.

CATEGORIZATION THEORY: SUPPORT FOR
THE OBVIOUS PLACEMENT

Assessment can operate without theory. In fact, as I have said, that may be its normal mode. For three or four years at WSU, the two-tier placement system was conceived, used, and modified before any theory was advanced to explain or defend it. Ironically, it is when an assessment strategy proves itself unusually successful that people are encouraged to theorize it. How can the success be explained? Then it is discovered that, despite what skeptics of theory may think, assessment also can operate with theory—and operate, it seems, all the better for it.

Quite appropriately the theory that I extracted from the two-tier system looks radically different from the theories that have been offered in support of older methods of placement. The theory conceives of writing placement as an act of *categorization* (Haswell, 1994; the full presentation is in Haswell, 1998c). Categorization, the basic cognitive procedure of sorting things into conceptual boxes, lies close to the center of what people do when they sort students into writing courses. The kinds of labels, for instance, produced by placement readers (humans or machines) are categories. Certainly "belongs in basic writing," "73rd percentile," or "holistic score of 3" are categorical containers, each presumably with a set of defining features and each containing any number of concrete instances. Intuitively, to think of this labeling as an act of categorization is immediately helpful. For instance, it draws a useful and sharp line between the category of "essays that match the traits described at level three of the rubric" and the category of "essays written by students who will run the risk of having to drop regular composition if we put them in it." Categorization theory also asks what readers do when they put students into categories. Here the answers may be counterintuitive, and therefore all the more useful.

Students of categorization—logicians, psychologists, sociologists, and linguists—roughly identify three main types.

• *Classical categorization* assumes that people sort by matching the properties of a new instance with the unique set of properties that define pre-existing categories. Is this object a chair? It is if it is a piece of furniture designed primarily to enable people to sit. Each category has a fixed set of features. Every feature is necessary, and together they are sufficient for categorical definition. Categories are cleanly separated one from another, and all members of a category have equal validity as members because they share the same set of essential properties.

- *Exemplar categorization* assumes that people sometimes categorize by comparing a new instance with intact memories ("exemplars") of similar instances, perhaps by rummaging through episodic memory ending with a gestaltlike pattern recognition. Largely unconscious, the way features of those old experiences connect with features of the new experience depends greatly on context, including the context of the categorizer's previous encounter, subsequent encounters, and current motivations. An adult may decide not to sit in a beanbag chair because he categorizes it as for children, having most recently seen one for sale in a toy store.

- *Prototype categorization* assumes that people categorize by judging how similar the yet-to-be-categorized instance is to the best example or most representative member of possible categories. The best example (prototype) of a category is not a specific member but an idealized construction. Within prototype categories, members are organized by gradience, each being judged further or closer to the prototype. Gradience is complex, because no particular set of features need be shared by every member. Prototype categories usually have "fuzzy" edges because as members lie farther and farther away from the prototype, they lie closer and closer to the prototype of neighboring categories. Some people may categorize the large beanbag in the corner as a chair, some as a couch, some as a cushion.

This is only a bare-bones synopsis (an excellent extended account is Homa, 1984) but it serves my purpose, which is to show how readily these three models of categorization line up with the three common procedures for placing writing samples. The holistic method relies on a concept of classical categorization, teacher decision relies on exemplar categorization, and the first step of the two two-tier system (the "obvious" placement) relies on prototype categorization. During holistic evaluation, the defining features of placement categories are established by the rubric, category boundaries are clean-cut (usually designated by scale points), every essay belongs to only one category, and members within a category (say, "basic writers") are not further distinguished one from another. During teacher-option placement, readers do not rely on an essential set of features but rather on previous experience. An essay may place a student within the teacher-rater's course because it strikes the teacher as similar to essays (exemplars) of previous students; another essay with quite different features may place its author in the same course for the same reasons. In the two-tier system, the "obvious" placement relies on a sense of prototypicality, on a sense that certain essays lie so close to the central construct of "writing typical of regular first-year composition" that there seems no doubt that the writer falls into that placement or category. Other essays do not have that sense of centrality, are marginal in various ways, and therefore are set aside for closer consideration.

Let me expand on this third method of categorization. Prototype decision may seem unsystematic, but studies show that the act possesses quite regular features that not only defend the "obvious" placement as rational and reliable but also provide a strong defense for some of its most unconventional and useful aspects. Consider the perilous allowance of one reader alone to make a placement decision. One of the most established of findings in prototype studies is that categorizers show the highest agreement with instances that lie closest to the prototype. People disagree over whether a tomato is a fruit, but everyone categorizes an apple or an orange as a fruit. At a certain point on the color spectrum is a hue that nearly everyone categorizes as "blue," at another point a hue that nearly everyone categorizes as "green." Those are the prototype hues for those two color categories, and hues very close to them show almost perfect agreement among raters—an agreement that disintegrates as we move toward the marginal hues, where there are frequencies that half of us will call "blue" and the other half will call "green," and probably be willing to fight over it. It is not surprising that essays receiving a tier-one placement of "obviously regular composition" on recirculation achieve a second placement (independent of the first) of regular composition close to 100 percent of the time.

Or consider the allowance of a rapid, even a partial, reading to make the tier-one "obvious" decision. A second perennial finding of prototype studies is that response time, how long it takes a person to decide on a category, speeds up as we near the prototype. People will decide on "blue" much more rapidly when the hue is close to the prototypical frequency for blue than when it lies in the marginal "blue-green" frequencies. Or consider the use of a checklist of possible problems instead of a rubric of necessary criteria. A third early finding of prototype research, repeatedly confirmed, is the presence of "family resemblances" in categories of even moderate trait complexity (Rosch & Mervis, 1975). Prototypical birds do not share all features. Unlike robins, seagulls do not nest in trees or sing, yet both animals are prototypical for the category of *bird.* In holistic scoring, to fit a rubric category of "4" on a 5-point scale, for example, an essay must "perform" well in all criteria of the scoring guide, and raters struggle when certain criterial features are missing or poorly represented. By contrast, in a tier-one reading, one essay judged as an obvious placement into regular composition may be long, solidly supported, and well structured, although spotted with surface mistakes; another may be mechanically letter perfect with a sophisticated awareness of audience, but structurally and logically rote; another may be robust and frisky in wordplay, although lackadaisical in almost everything else. Only prototypical categorization can handle such family-trait configurations. Finally, consider the use of new readers to make the obvious placement at tier one. Some evidence shows that prototype categorizing is the best place to begin for novices. Inexperienced readers seem more at home working with a single and centralized prototype than with problematic marginal cases; they prefer conservative, either-or decisions ("chair" or "not chair") with a large not-sure category in which to discard the beanbag decisions.

THE TWO-TIER SEQUENCE: FROM THE OBVIOUS TO THE PROBLEMATIC

Although the point encroaches on the next chapter, categorization theory also supports the second step of the two-tier system and its radical change of evaluation method. If the placements at tier one seem to be prototypical categorizations, the placements at tier two are more nearly exemplar categorizations. For instance, it makes theoretical sense to use novices at tier one and old hands at tier two. Novices have less experience and therefore fewer concrete memories available, and so they prefer the confirmatory and normative exercise of prototype choice. At tier two, experienced or specialized readers have the knowledge to support exemplar categorization, which uses experience to solve borderline and otherwise quizzical cases, sometimes arriving at surprising and abnormal solutions (Kahneman & Miller, 1986). At tier one, hiding extenuating and individualizing information about the writer only makes the obvious decision easier. It also helps reduce the main danger of prototype categorization, at least when it deals in human performance, namely stereotyping. This does not mean that prototypical thinking will be completely barred from tier two. No doubt tier-two readers will evolve prototypical structures for courses within their special jurisdiction, such as basic writing or English as a second language (ESL). As experience deepens, exemplars themselves become generalized (Smith & Medin, 1981) and may assume a prototypical shape. In all kinds of expertise, the ability to make tricky distinctions grows with experience. Initially, someone may find it easy only to distinguish between hand-made and machine-made oriental rugs but with experience may be able tell a Tabriz from an Ardabil at a glance.

As a sequence, the two-tier method matches especially well the continuum of person impression formation outlined by Fiske & Neuberg (1990), a continuum of categorization of human performance that proceeds from confirmation to "recategorization" to "piecemeal integration of attributes." A new person or record of performance of a person is encountered; if a standard category satisfies the information, then the first impression serves (confirmation); if not, then other categories are tried using subcategory or exemplar or self-concept strategies (recategorization); if these are not successful, then the attributes are patched together to form an impression of an individual who fits no convenient category (piecemeal integration). In the two-tier placement continuum, tier-one readers first try pro-totypical processes with a sample. If that does not succeed, tier-two read-ers acquire more information, resort to exemplar knowledge, and try to recategorize the sample. In the junior portfolio, an essay judged question-able at tier one may turn out to have been written by a student whose course writings seem quite competent, and who is then at tier two put into the exemplar category of known students who are decent writers but happen to have trouble with impromptu composing. If recategorization does not work, however, then readers resort to a kind of "decategoriza-tion," looking for the best placement of an anomalous person who does not readily fit standard sizes.

ADAPTABILITY

To sustain an assessment procedure within an institution, it may be enough to cultivate a perennial conviction that the method feels right, runs happily, and bears useful and encouraging results. To transplant the method within other campus walls, however, to give it the vitality that will take to alien institutions, requires a theoretical understanding of it. Theory hazards the genetic structure that shows how a method can be engineered to fit new local conditions and still function. And what proto-type theory suggests about the obvious placement is that the strategy seems to have an especially high potential for adaptation. The explanation is fairly simple. If all writing-placement categories have a large prototyp-ical center where high-agreement decisions can be made quickly even by less experienced readers, then whether the reader's decision is a lowest-stakes course (e.g., "regular composition") or a curricular protocol (e.g., "qualified for upper-division work"), a sizable portion of placement deci-sions can be made safely with one reading, with savings of time and money at the beginning to allow careful and multiple readings at the end. In short, the underlying procedure of the two-tiered method taps into a universal cognitive strategy that is broad and versatile. It is a perfectly common mental tactic open enough for any number of variations, adapt-able to differences in time, place, funds, personnel, and curriculum.

Several such adaptations have already occurred at WSU. During the second year of its use, the two-tier method was expanded to place inter-national students into an ESL sequence (Chapter 4). All student essays, with first-language status masked, were given a tier-one reading, and then the ESL essays that had not been identified as obvious English 101 placements (about 80 percent) were culled out and handed over, with the author's identity revealed, to the teachers of the ESL classes for tier-two reading. The two-tier method also proved adjustable when the writing test for all students was expanded from a single two-hour essay to include a 30-minute self-evaluation essay. Tier-one readers focused on the analyt-ical essay to make their "obviously regular composition" decision, and tier-two readers considered both essays. The third year, the procedure was again modified to handle writing portfolios of five pieces for the junior-level placement exam. Tier-one readers made a judgment of "obviously needs no more writing coursework" on just the two impromptu, sit-down pieces; problematic essays were passed on to tier two, where readers considered the entire portfolio.

How might the system work elsewhere, where changes in it could be more severe? Consider a school with a large special population— international students, for example. Their placement writing could be cut from the rest right from the start and passed on to readers with ESL expertise, who would apply the full two-tier sequence. These ESL experts ought to have a prototypical grasp of this special population. Tier-one decisions then might entail obvious placements into the last of a two-course ESL sequence, the one earning regular-composition credit. Consider a different special group, candidates for honors composition as tagged by high school grades. Honors writing teachers could conduct a tier-one reading of placement essays in which students obviously placing in honors composition would be quickly identified; tier-two reading would decide which ones of the remaining—the tough cases—were instead assigned to regular composition. Another scenario: a large university facing huge numbers of entering students in need of placement. It could use a formula composed of national standardized test scores and high school records to automatically place a certain number of incoming students—say, half—in the mainstream course. These would be students in the center of the curve. Only the quarter at each end would write placement essays, which would undergo the usual tier-two process and place students into basic, regular, and exemption categories. Another scenario: a large university that wants to test the writing of students at the junior level but expects only about 15 percent to be assigned further coursework. The university is concerned about making the great majority of its students provide valid evidence of their writing ability when no change in their coursework will result. A solution is to have all students write an impromptu essay—little effort— and a tier-one reading quickly select out around three-quarters as obvious passes. The remaining quarter of students are required, as a second step, to put together a portfolio of writings from previous courses, which undergoes tier-two readings. The constant theme in all these variations is the prototypical shape of the first placement decision, a shape that confers centrality and legitimacy to a large area that can be considered "obvious."

A last point about the two-tier method, the theory, and its adaptability. If placement decisions at both tier one and tier two are essentially categorizations, relying on categories with a prototypical shape, then those decisions can be thought of as rooted in the particular climate and mindset of the local university writing program. Especially at tier one, a rater's reaction of "obvious" emerges directly from the ecology of the individual program: its values, emphases, students, and curricular design. To repeat, prototypical structures are constructed, not given. The decision of "obvious" is not shaped to some abstract idea of "good writing" broadcast across the nation in the form of a universal scoring guide but emerges out of the local needs and expectations of the university. At two different institutions, the particular configuration of the prototypical area "obvious placement" would differ, although the prototypicality of the category itself would not. A configuration, therefore, can be modified to fit the institution and can be changed as the institution changes, and readers new and old can be trained to act in accordance.

The obvious placement is not a procedure entirely new to writing administrators. Burnham (1986) describes a system at New Mexico State University where only first-year writing students who want to compete for a course grade of A or B submit portfolios, to be judged by other teachers—a method in the spirit of two-tier assessment. The "obvious" placement, however, is a procedure too little explored in placement-test construction, and one that ought to be considered before abandoning placement using teacher expertise because it costs too much money or effort. What will aid that exploration is the theory behind it, which provides a general explanatory frame and shows how the method will work consistently in a wide variety of local contexts. Theory undergirds the adaptability. Future placement practices will be developed locally that respect the diagnostic skill of experts yet sidestep—out of practical experience, in light of research evidence and, let's welcome it, on theoretical grounds—the expensive custom of multiple readers for all samples.

College writing assessment may always be a restless animal, but there is one historical consistency of writing placement at the postsecondary level. That is the fact that students who have been categorized as needing remedial work, however that is defined, usually have made up only a minor portion of the student body, say between 10 to 20 percent. Remember Harvard's first multisubject entrance examinations. They were not so much an admissions test, because they barred only a few students from matriculation (17 percent in 1874). They served more as a placement instrument. Students who failed the English portion were required to get a tutor or to take a preparatory course not taught at Harvard. "Conditioned" students, those earning a failing mark, went ahead and took the required freshman composition course (English A, implemented in 1885) with other students, to the dismay of instructors. Outcomes on the examination look surprisingly like those of entrance placement examinations since. In 1892, apparently similar to other years, the distribution was 20 percent failing, 27 percent unsatisfactory pass, 51 percent satisfactory, and 2 percent "credit" (e.g., a mark of "honors" on the student's record). The point is that even a century ago, the great bulk of students, over three-quarters of them, were not deemed basic. The two-tiered system simply recognizes that *this* largest category, the okay students, seems not to be site specific and does not need the cautious and time-consuming scrutiny that the other students need and deserve. Categorization theory—and another theory might serve as well—helps us understand and defend that recognition.

6

Exploring the Difficult Cases:
In the Cracks of Writing Assessment

Galen Leonhardy and William Condon

Over the past 30 years, new assessments have arisen, principally out of the desire for greater validity. Early in the 1970s the California State University system, under Edward M. White's leadership, developed a system for direct testing of writing (timed writings, under controlled conditions, holistically scored) that could replace indirect tests (multiple-choice question tests). Direct tests were viewed as more valid, because they examine an actual sample of the construct (writing ability) being tested (White, 1994b). Later, portfolio-based systems emerged out of the same impulse (Elbow, 1991), increasing validity by bringing the sample closer to the kinds of writing students actually do—in other words, to more extensive samples taken from the work students were producing in their classes. In each evolution, validity has increased at first, at the expense of reliability—and yet, eventually, newer assessments have met the challenge of scoring longer, more complex, more varied samples consistently. In this way, the field of writing assessment has achieved the significant goal of greater validity.

At the same time, a different, perhaps more important reason for developing and maintaining an assessment process has arisen. As assessments become more valid—and *validity* itself is now seen as a more complex concept (Messick, 1995, Moss, 1994; Moss, et al., 1992)—they can generate rich sets of data for evaluation. As the validity of the sample rises, so does the number of potential uses for that sample. The outcomes of an indirect test have extremely limited use. The test is neither explicitly connected to local curricula, nor (in the case of writing) does it measure a sample of the construct being evaluated; therefore, all one gets is a score and, perhaps, a percentile ranking. These outcomes can be used to make only the most limited judgments about writers or writing programs (Hamp-Lyons & Condon, 2000). As the validity of the sample increases, the assessment examines more of the context within which the sample was collected. Typical indirect tests, therefore, are a contextless form of assessment, because they originate outside the instructional context and so can give little information about it. Direct tests, even of tightly controlled timed samples, bring some of the instructional context with them—typically because they are locally developed (as described in Part I) or because, as in the case of Educational Testing Service's Advanced Placement tests, they are designed to test the abilities generated by a specific curriculum. These direct tests, severely constrained by the limitations of time and circumstance, might be described as context-poor. They allow for more varied and more certain judgments about students' performance and about the effectiveness of the teaching and learning experience, but the conclusions one may draw are still extremely limited. The class of assessments known as *authentic* assessments, which includes *performance* assessments, which in turn include portfolio-based assessments, may be called context-rich (Hamp-Lyons & Condon, 1993). These assessments include samples from actual work environments (classrooms in our case, but these assessments are not limited to classroom uses) and samples produced under actual working conditions. These assessments, therefore, are intrusive, in the sense that they are also assessments of the learning environments in which the samples were produced. The actual samples bring with them, in effect, the assignments that elicited the performances on exhibit and the curriculum that produced the assignments, the teaching methodology(ies) that inform that curriculum, and even the administrative conditions within which the teachers function (Condon, 1997).

Because performance assessments are intrusive, they collect data that can be used in far more ways than the mere assessment of writing ability— indeed, perhaps the least interesting and least important use of performance assessments may be the judgment of the learner's writing ability. We can see this realization dawning at WSU in the progression from the All University Writing Committee's seven principles of the writing program in 1988 (Chapter 1) to the first notions of the junior portfolio in 1991 (Chapter 2), to the integration of the portfolio assessment and the Writing Center in subsequent years (Ch. 3). We will also see the progression from a focus on outcomes (Part II) to the uses of outcomes (Part IV). This broader, more complex data set allows for placement, certainly, but it also provides information about the classes the student took, the curriculum within which the classes occurred, the effectiveness of the writing program(s) as a whole, and, in short, the intellectual *ecosystem* within which the student's learning experiences have occurred. This richer data set results from a local assessment, designed by local teachers and administrators in response to local students' needs within the specific curriculum within the specific context of the local institution. If, as the Honorable Tip O'Neill said, "All politics is local," then so, we would argue, is all good assessment. The closer the assessment comes to the local context, the more information it yields for evaluating and improving that context. Improvement, we are all rapidly discovering, is the most important end for assessment. Modern writing assessment may have arisen out of White's maxim, "Assess yourself, or someone else will do it for you," but the field has progressed to the point at which the end is not mainly self-defense but self-improvement. Any assessment must meet the basic requirements of validity and reliability, but the ultimate test for success is whether the assessment promotes improvement, not only in the students who undergo the assessment but also in the very program that requires and conducts it.

Over the past few years, WSU's Writing Assessment Program has routinely gathered a rich set of data in the process of evaluating students' writing (see Appendix C). Those data have provided many opportunities to direct the lens of evaluation onto the Assessment Program itself. This essay provides several examples of that use. We chronicle those self-evaluations here not only to establish that what we have argued earlier is true but, more important, to demonstrate what we see as the primary reason for developing and maintaining a robust assessment program: the ability to improve vital aspects of the program itself and the institution in which it functions. In conducting the studies that produced these examples, we focused on several important questions about what we have identified as the difficult cases. A difficult case occurs when the writing being measured or the act of measuring itself somehow stretches or even violates the context of the assessment, the set of parameters established by the given, or assumed, set of learners. Here are the questions we address:

1. What happens when transfer students present writing from their previous college experience—papers from institutions other than WSU?

2. How fair and consistent are the judgments about writing from non-native speakers of English?

3. What happens when the writing in the portfolio comes from coursework in one discipline, but the rater's background lies in a very different field?

4. What happens to the writing that falls in the gray areas between placement levels? What happens, in effect, to the students who fall into the cracks of the system?

THE ASSESSMENT CONTEXT OF THE JUNIOR PORTFOLIO

WSU's University Writing Portfolio uses a system of shared assessment and a simplified decision tree that, as Chapters 4 and 5 reveal, allows faculty raters to make highly reliable decisions about writing samples that possess a high degree of validity. This new kind of rating system has already been recognized for its potential to change assessment practice in the area of direct tests of writing and performance testing of writing (Huot, 1996, Harrington, 1998). It has also proven, locally, its ability to create and sustain a university-wide faculty investment in and involvement with writing assessment and its inherent support of writing across the curriculum. If, however, this rating system is to be effective in a wide range of assessment contexts—if it is to take its place in the writing assessment toolbox alongside holistic scoring, primary trait and multiple trait scoring, and so forth—then it will have to undergo even greater scrutiny. Overall reliability is an initial and significant test. So is validity, in all its various manifestations. As earlier chapters demonstrate, WSU's portfolio assessment passes those major tests.

WSU's portfolio assessment process is a competency-based program designed to determine which students need additional support as they enter upper-division writing-enriched courses. Our intent is to provide students with knowledge of their own writing abilities when they have accumulated approximately 60 credits of coursework. The process enables us to determine whether a student's writing abilities are acceptable (ac) or exceptional (ex), but the primary objective is to provide assistance to students whose writing abilities might not support the rigors of upper-level writing-enriched coursework: students whose writing receives a needs-work rating (nw). We also attempt to provide students with the resources or bridge that will help them to succeed and learn without falling behind or failing because of low writing ability. Accordingly, our assessment process is not designed to categorize student writing abilities so much as to assist student stakeholders through a collaborative process of shared evaluation and negotiation that involves the entire university.

The two-tier system with the junior-portfolio evaluation is best understood as a cumulative portfolio interaction. Each reading tier provides both students and readers with information about individuals' writing abilities, and each portfolio is read in its entirety at least once (the first time, in parts, by four readers and, if necessary, a second time at tier two by a single reader). The decision to have the portfolio sent to the second tier, however, is dependent on the ratings given by each of the tier one readers and the amount of information needed to assist the student.

The tier one portfolio reading utilizes the experience of four readers from a variety of contexts who share the responsibility for reading three writing samples that the student selects from his or her coursework and two essays from a timed writing process. The instructor who originally created the assignment and graded the writing reads each of the self-selected essays. Each of those instructors then makes a binary decision concerning the student's writing, rating each of the three essays as either acceptable or exceptional. A fourth reader is responsible for reading the two timed essays and rating them collectively as either acceptable (pass), exceptional (pass with distinction), or needs work.

With few exceptions, if a student's timed writing and the three essays selected from coursework are all rated as acceptable at the first tier, the student's portfolio will not be read by second-tier readers. However, if the three essays collected from coursework are rated as exceptional or if the timed writing receives an exceptional or a needs-work rating, the portfolio will be sent to the second tier. If a student's writing warrants an additional reading, the timed writing is combined with the student's three writing samples to form a unified portfolio that is read at the second tier. The portfolio is then rated as either acceptable, exceptional, or needs work. Tier two readers are trained to look for specific patterns that can be used to describe the reasons for their decisions. They are also expected to determine the most beneficial course of future action for each individual whose writing indicates that he or she should receive additional support. The portfolios, therefore have to pass through one of the five sequences in Figure 6.1.

Figure 6.1
Five Scoring Sequences in Tier-One and Tier-Two Readings

---

ac — All three class papers are rated *Acceptable* and the timed-writing received a *Pass* rating (**ac**) for the first portfolio reading, so the portfolio was not read at the second tier (—). Such ratings indicate that each of the five pieces of writing supports the belief that the student has achieved a level of proficiency that will allow him or her to function in a writing enriched course at the junior level. These ratings are recorded as acceptable at the first tier and unmarked at the second.

acac
or
acex   The timed-writing received a pass rating (**ac**) while all three of the first tier submissions were rated as exceptional (**ex**). In such cases, a Tier II rater will evaluate the whole portfolio in order to determine whether it is passing or exceptional. In these cases the first and second tier ratings are combined (first tier/second tier) and recorded as either acceptable/acceptable (**acac**) or acceptable/exceptional (**acex**).

exac
or
exex   The student's timed writing was assessed as exceptional (**ex**). In such cases, second tier evaluators will assess the portfolio as either acceptable (**ac**) or exceptional (**ex**).

nwac
or
nwnw   The student's timed writing received a needs work rating (**nw**). In such cases, the whole portfolio is read at the second tier and rated as either needs work (**nw**) or acceptable (**ac**).

acnw,
acac,
or
acex   Students may receive an acceptable rating (**ac**) for the timed writing, but the portfolio is sent to the second tier because the student was unable to find the original instructor to assess the three class essays. In such cases the student could receive an acceptable rating at Tier I (in most cases resulting in a Pass rating), yet receive an exceptional, acceptable or needs work rating at Tier II.

Despite the existence of gray areas—basically, placements at or near the "cut points" between scoring levels at tier one and tier two—portfolio assessment at WSU has proven to be a fair process in the vast majority of cases. We know that the interactive process of first- and second-tier readings creates the high level of reliability that we currently enjoy. The primary investigation in this area was done by Rich Haswell when he studied reliability by recirculating 40 portfolios that had originally received ratings we have come to call simple passes (ac—) (Haswell, 1995). Simple passes occur when a timed writing sample is deemed acceptable. In such cases the portfolio as a unified whole is not read again at the second tier. Haswell felt that the 40 simple passes were more likely to indicate reliability issues because those portfolios had not been through both tiers of the assessment process. As it turned out, only 2 of the 40 final placement decisions changed, which indicated that the two-tiered process was 95 percent reliable for determining acceptable writing. Despite the fact that our process was functioning effectively, we began asking ourselves critical questions, such as whether the apparent high level of reliability was real. That is, we started wondering whether the consistency of our assessment practices could be the result of uniform but prejudicial discourse expectations.

TRANSFER STUDENTS

One of the basic assumptions our assessment system makes is that it supports students from matriculation to graduation. As the introduction to this book notes, students enter the system by taking the Writing Placement Exam, proceed through English 101 and WSU's writing-rich General Education Program, pass through the junior-level Writing Portfolio assessment to qualify to take two Writing in the Major courses, and, finally, proceed through their home departments' end-of-program assessments (see Figure 0.1). Yet over the years since the Writing Portfolio was established, an increasing percentage of WSU graduates has come to the university as transfer students. In fact, 60 percent of the students who submitted portfolios between June 1997 and May 1999 were transfer students (Norris & Webber, 1999). These students did not take the entry Writing Placement Exam and did not share with "native" students the experience of WSU's General Education Program. Yet the Portfolio is a graduation requirement for all WSU students, native or transfer.

Because all students are subject to the portfolio requirement, we collect data about transfer students' status to compare their performance with that of students who enrolled at WSU as first-year students. Table 6.1 summarizes the data on the performance of native and transfer students. Native students whose first language is English perform almost identically—within one percentage point—with transfer students whose first language is English. The figures for nonnative speakers of English are also quite similar, with the exception of a 9 percent difference in their overall needs-work rate—a topic we discuss in some detail in the next section of this chapter. Our data tell us that transfer students who are native speakers are not disadvantaged by the Writing Portfolio requirement, that their Associate of Arts (AA) degrees (or other higher education experience before enrolling at WSU) are preparing them as well for this midcareer (or, for transfers, entry) assessment.

NONNATIVE SPEAKERS OF ENGLISH

As Table 6.1 reveals, there is some question about whether the portfolio assessment is fair to nonnative speakers of English. In fact, earlier data confirmed that WSU is not meeting these students' needs (Bonnema, Haswell, & Norris, 1997). Table 6.2 shows placement data for the 1995 to 1997 reporting period.

These figures, showing that both native and transfer nonnative speakers of English fare significantly worse than students whose first language is English, caused us to take a hard look at the reasons for the discrepancy.

We found, first, that WSU's curriculum did not address the needs of nonnative speakers at all well. In fact, the only writing course in the curriculum that was available for a nonnative speaking transfer student was English 403, an ESL version of Technical and Professional Writing. Tutors in General Education 302 were not routinely trained in addressing the needs of nonnative speakers, either. So there were no instructional resources to help these students. Second, the English Department's curriculum actually discouraged nonnative speakers from fulfilling their first-year composition requirement at WSU. Students placed into an ESL composition class could be required to take as many as three semesters of

Table 6.1
Placement Outcomes on the Junior Portfolio by
Transfer and Language Status: 1993–1999 (N=12,424)

		Timed Writing			Entire Portfolio		
Status	All Students	Pass with Distinction	Pass	Needs Work	Pass with Distinction	Pass	Needs Work
Non-transfer/ First-language	5367	12%	67%	21%	11%	84%	5%
Transfer/ First-language	5775	13%	65%	22%	11%	83%	6%
Non-transfer/ESL	352	4%	46%	50%	3%	74%	23%
Transfer/ESL	930	3%	33%	64%	3%	65%	32%

Table 6.2
Placement Outcomes on the Junior Portfolio by
Transfer and Language Status: 1995–1997 (N=4161)

		Timed Writing			Entire Portfolio		
Status	All Students	Pass with Distinction (%)	Pass (%)	Needs Work (%)	Pass with Distinction (%)	Pass (%)	Need Work (%)
Nontransfer/ first-language	1712	11	67	22	10	85	5
Transfer/ first-language	1956	13	65	22	11	83	6
Nontransfer/ESL	129	6	37	57	1	70	29
Transfer/ESL	364	1	32	67	2	61	37

ESL = English as a second language.

writing before being able to enroll in English 101, the standard required course. Third, interviews with several nonnative speakers whose portfolios had earned needs-work ratings revealed that they often made poor choices when selecting their three class papers. Many of these students were including only shorter pieces in their portfolios, sometimes out of consideration for our faculty readers and often because they felt that the shorter their selections, the less room there would be for weaknesses to appear. Finally, conversations with faculty raters uncovered significant confusion about how to regard the writing of nonnative speakers. The raters had a hard time distinguishing fossilized errors, for one thing. For another, some raters felt that they should hold nonnative speakers to a different standard from native speakers. Generally, raters relied more heavily on the Timed Writings, in which errors were more likely to appear. This problem was caused, in part, by the brevity of the three class essays; with so little revised writing to evaluate, raters naturally relied more heavily on the Timed Writings, which were often the longest pieces in the portfolio.

Having made these unpleasant discoveries, we proceeded to make a number of changes. First, we revised the advice we give to students. We now stress that the raters want to see a significant amount of writing from classes, and we are careful to inform all students, including nonnative speakers, that the quality of the essays from classes tends to override any problems that may appear in the Timed Writings. These students now know more about how to put together a successful portfolio. Second, we have taken measures to ensure that General Education 302 tutors have some training in addressing the needs of nonnative speakers. Third, the

English Department has completely revamped its ESL offerings in the English 101 program. Now, if a student is placed into English 105, that course fulfills WSU's Composition Requirement. In addition, students who receive a lower placement are required to complete English 104—only one course—before they can enroll in English 105. Both courses have been completely reformed, and a prominent feature of the new curriculum is preparation of the Writing Portfolio. As a result, nonnative speakers are now encouraged to complete their Composition Requirement at WSU, rather than taking it elsewhere and transferring it. Fourth, we have incorporated heavy doses of nonnative speakers' portfolios into our rater norming sessions. The ensuing discussions have helped raters distinguish between serious writing problems and nagging, but relatively harmless, surface errors. Finally, we are currently recruiting raters from our Department of Modern Languages, raters who, together with our lone ESL specialist, can help native English-speaking raters make sounder judgments about the writing of nonnative speakers.

The early results of these efforts appear in the findings for 1997 to 1999, as shown in Table 6.3. Comparing the findings in Table 6.2 with the findings in Table 6.4 reveals improvement across the board for nonnative speakers of English. Those who started at WSU dropped their needs-work rate from 29 percent to 21 percent; transfer students' needs-work rate dropped from 37 percent to 28 percent. In both cases, results for nonnative speakers improved by 8 percent to 9 percent. We expect the rates to improve even more, because most of the remedies discussed earlier were not put into place until the 1998 to 1999 academic year, and our new cadre

Table 6.3
Placement Outcomes on the Junior Portfolio by
Transfer and Language Status: 1997–1999 (N=5778)

Status	All Students	Timed Writing			Entire Portfolio		
		Pass with Distinction (%)	Pass (%)	Needs Work (%)	Pass with Distinction (%)	Pass (%)	Need Work (%)
Nontransfer/ first-language	2230	12	67	21	11	84	5
Transfer/ first-language	2978	14	64	22	12	83	5
Nontransfer/ESL	131	5	46	49	3	76	21
Transfer/ESL	439	4	34	62	3	69	28

ESL = English as a second language.

of Modern Languages' faculty came on board in 2000. We also continue to work on the curricular issues—most prominently by developing a junior-level course devoted to revision and enrolling nonnative speakers exclusively (a separate course will be available for native speakers). In sum, our biennial findings pointed out a significant problem, and they also reveal that the early results of our efforts to correct the problem are positive. We continue to work on solutions, and our next biennial report will help us know to what extent we continue to be successful.

WRITING AND WRITERS THAT FALL IN THE GRAY AREAS

As a result of the practice of tier two shared evaluation, we know that raters with backgrounds in scientific areas evaluate the written products of students who come from both scientific and nonscientific contexts. We also know that evaluators with backgrounds in the humanities assess the writing of students from both scientific and nonscientific contexts. As Haswell's early reliability studies demonstrated (see Chapter 4), the judgments these raters make are extremely consistent in cases in which portfolios were judged pass at tier one (that is, in cases where the three class papers were rated acceptable and the Timed Writing received a rating of pass (ac— in Figure 6.1). The very fact that these evaluators were agreeing with such a high level of reliability caused us to ask whether the reliability was real. As Smith (1993) demonstrates, even though the evidence may indicate that the rate of placement is adequate, deeper probing can expose cracks in the facade. Of the 40 original simple pass (ac—) submissions in Haswell's study, 13 were not rated as simple passes after being recirculated (32.5%). Because four were rated as exceptional (exac) and nine were given a needs-work ratings (nwac) at tier one, 13 of the original simple pass portfolios were read at the second tier. In short, we realized that the tiered rating system tolerated a substantial amount of disagreement—a good thing—but we also wondered about the effects of disagreement on students' outcomes.

This is not to say that the system was failing. Rather, we noticed that disagreement was an aspect of the process, and, quite naturally, we started wondering about that disagreement. Again, we turned to Smith's study. To examine how his students were being matched to their classes, Smith (1993) used what he termed the "gray area hypothesis," which holds that there will be students whose writing will not support a definite placement: "If we assume that the writing abilities (or whatever is being measured) of the students are distributed on a continuum, the probability of having courses which adequately overlay this continuum is small" (155). Following Smith's lead, we speculated that if the writing abilities of our students are distributed on continua of scores and discourse community conventions, the probability of having ratings (placement decisions) that adequately overlay those continua is small.

Knowing that our raters come from various backgrounds or contexts, we hypothesized that those raters would tend to disagree about student writing when that writing was on or near the borderline between two scoring levels and when the writing exhibited the patterns of particular discourse communities. In effect, we asked ourselves the following questions:

1. What happens to reliability when the sample is drawn from the minority of portfolios that are located at or near "cut points" in our rating scale, rather than, as in Haswell's study, from the majority that are located near the prototypical center and receive a pass at tier one?

2. What happens when students achieve the ability to communicate with the discourse expectations of their respective communities before having their writing assessed?

3. What happens when an evaluator with a background in the humanities reads a paper written by a student whose major focus has been in the sciences, or by a student who has written his or her best papers for the conventions of a discourse community quite different from the evaluator's?

To satisfy our curiosity, we organized a test that would provide information about the kinds of choices evaluators make in these situations.

We collected 10 portfolios for each of the 6 assessment categories described earlier (see Figure 6.1). We chose to examine portfolios from the six categories because each of the categories requires that the writing receive two ratings, at tier one and tier two, and that the raters have to make a specific, binary decision about that writing (needs-work or not; pass with distinction or not). For example, an nwnw rating requires that two evaluators determine that the timed writing and the submitted writing from the first tier process are not acceptable. Such choices require that the evaluator must invoke a set of expectations that lead him or her to make such a decision. Additionally, such ratings will fall along a continuum of certainty from what we might call a deep needs work to a borderline performance that falls into the gray area between the needs-work rating and pass. Of our 60 portfolios—10 at each of the 6 score levels—five were submitted by students declaring scientific majors and five by students declaring nonscientific majors. Each portfolio, to be selected, needed to have at least two writing submissions from the first-tier process that matched the student's declared area of study. Believing that the best place to test our hypothesis would be at the extremes of the continua of student writing abilities, we selected portfolios in which the writing was examined at both tier one and tier two, writing that was not easily placed. In effect, we selected portfolios in which the writing might have received gray area ratings and was likely to carry the conventions of particular discourse communities.

After the 60 portfolios were rescored, the humanities and science evaluators had assessed the same written works a total of 31 times. They agreed about the evaluation 11 times (35.5 percent agreement), and they disagreed 20 times (64.5 percent disagreement). This interrater reliability suggests that raters from different contexts have disciplinary and professional standards that carry over into the context of portfolio assessment, that evaluators from different contexts evaluate student writing differently when that writing exhibits discourse conventions common to particular communities. However, on these gray area portfolios, evaluators from the same context disagreed at a high rate also—not as high as the cross-disciplinary ratings but at a rate that confirms the gray area hypothesis we were testing.

We examined what happens when one of the two evaluators and the student did not share the same background (student=humanities/rater=science) and when science students are evaluated by a rater with a humanities background (student=science/rater=humanities). In each case, however, one of the evaluators needed to have the same background as the student so that we could determine if the evaluators agreed or disagreed about the student's rating. In these cases, because they were relatively few, we combined the readings from the first and second tiers, because we were concerned with issues of agreement more than issues that might involve the kinds of differences that exist between timed writings and more polished works.

When the humanities students were evaluated by a rater with a science background and by a rater with a humanities background (Table 6.4), the raters disagreed 9 times out of 14 (64.28 percent disagreement). In cases in which science students were evaluated by a rater with a humanities background and by a rater with a background in the sciences (Table 6.5), the raters disagreed 11 times out of 17 (64.7 percent disagreement). Interestingly, the disagreement between raters produced an increase in the student's rating 13 times out of 20 (65 percent of disagreements result in a higher rating of the student's writing). But, as stated, the raters disagreed 20 times out of 31. Because there were so many occasions in which both science and humanities evaluators evaluated humanities students,

Table 6.4
Recirculation of Junior Portfolios Written by Humanities Students (N=14)
Evaluated by One Science Reader and One Humanities Reader

Evaluators= One Science and One Humanity	Students= Humanities	Change	Up	Down	Agreement
Total	14	9	6	3	5
Percentage	100	64.28			35.72

Table 6.5

Recirculation of Junior Portfolios Written by Science Students (N=17)
Evaluated by One Science Reader and One Humanities Reader

Evaluators= One Science and One Humanity	Students= Humanities	Change	Up	Down	Agreement
Total	17	11	7	4	6
Percentage	100	64.71			35.29

we also examined the kinds of change that occurred when the writing of both science students and humanities students were evaluated by humanities evaluators (Tables 6.6 and 6.7). Unfortunately, there was only one instance when two science evaluators evaluated the writing of either a science student or a humanities student. So we were not able to determine the agreement and disagreement percentages of science evaluators in the same circumstances.

As indicated in Table 6.6, raters with humanities backgrounds agreed about science students' writing 21 times out of 38 (55.26 percent agreement), and they disagreed 17 times out of 38 (44.74 percent disagreement). On the other hand, as illustrated in Table 6.7, humanities evaluators agreed about humanities students' ratings 16 times out of 30 (53.33 percent agreement), and they disagreed 14 times out of 30 (46.67 percent disagreement). In both cases it was more likely that the disagreement would produce a lowering in the assessment rating of a student's writing.

In sum, Tables 6.4 through 6.7 demonstrate that even in a system with high overall reliability (in our portfolio assessment, overall ratings are consistent more than 85 percent of the time, and Haswell's study points out that simple passes are consistent 95 percent of the time), we can locate samples on which reliability will be low. This sample combined two factors that we predicted would result in lower reliability: gray area portfolios and disciplinary dissonance between raters and students.

Table 6.6

Recirculation of Junior Portfolio Examinations Written by Science Students
(N=38) and Read by Faculty Evaluators from the Humanities

Students= Science	Evaluators= Humanities	Change	Up	Down	Agreement
Total	38	17	6	11	21
Percentage	100	44.74			55.26

Table 6.7
**Recirculation of Junior Portfolio Examinations Written by Humanities
Students (N = 30) and Read by Faculty Evaluators from the Humanities**

Students= Humanities	Evaluators= Humanities	Change	Up	Down	Agreement
Total	30	14	5	9	16
Percentage	100%	46.67%			53.33%

Still, even when we know that we have set up a sample to produce low reliability, we are disturbed by the inconsistency of the decisions, so we have taken steps that we hope will improve our record even on these high-risk portfolios. First, the current director of Campus Writing Programs and Writing Assessment coordinator have instituted norming sessions before each reading session. During these sessions, raters typically score one portfolio and discuss the characteristics that resulted in the score. One objective is to produce consensus on the sample portfolio, but the principal objective is for raters to listen to each other, to discuss their standards, and to develop in our community of raters a shared sense of criteria and scoring levels. The coordinator selects the norming portfolios so that raters will explore a variety of factors: nonnative speakers' writing, writing that is heavily marked by the conventions of a particular discourse community, portfolios from students who are appealing their placements, portfolios about which raters have already disagreed, portfolios raters nominate as problematic, and so forth. Finally, as we conduct rating sessions, we encourage raters to confer about the difficult cases, feeling that if they talk with each other, they will be more likely to make a decision that reflects the rating community's standards. Over time, we hope that these conversations will bring greater consistency even to the very difficult set of portfolios we examined in this study.

CONCLUSIONS

James Gleick notes in *Chaos: Making a New Science* that "Those studying chaotic dynamics discovered that the disorderly behavior of simple systems acted as a *creative* process" (1987, p. 43). What we are describing in this chapter are some of the disorderly behaviors in our context, the dynamic or the creative moments in our assessment process that we call gray areas, or what Chapter 5 calls fuzzy edges. Our intent is to show that our constructed system has flaws, writing situations that do not appear to maintain the same level of "fairness" as other writing situations that occur in our system, writing and assessment situations that call our own practices into question. But that is a fundamental aspect of our assessment construct—or any system evaluating direct samples of writing, if it is honestly appraised (Smith, 1992; Harrington, 1998; Haswell, 1998c). We believe that a context-specific system of assessment must maintain contact with the context in which it was created. To maintain that quality in our assessment process, we support reflective evaluations of our own system so that we do not have to fear its problematic aspects. Instead, we attempt to maintain a critical awareness of our own assessment process and its contextual role. We consider the weaknesses in our system to be one of the most creative aspects of our process because the practice of critically examining our own weaknesses requires us to reexamine, reevaluate, and recreate our system of assessment.

We should note that none of the examinations we have detailed are possible in the absence of a robust, local assessment program. If we were not examining actual samples of writing, we could not ask the questions we have asked. Because our assessment exists within our local institutional context, it gives us information that helps us improve the way that context functions. Because the assessment is tied to specific programs' curricula, we can ask questions that help us learn how better to meet students' needs. Finally, because we are gathering a rich set of data, we can, as we do throughout this volume, turn the lens back on ourselves to evaluate the strengths and needs of our own assessment program. The ultimate test of an assessment program is whether and to what extent it promotes improvement. Evidence that the assessment is working well generally supports the assessment, much as Haswell's study of the 40 simple passes did. This kind of evidence is important, because without it the assessment fails to establish itself along the traditional lines of reliability and validity. Once the assessment has established its effectiveness, however, the difficult cases provide the information needed to diagnose and address problems in the assessment. The difficult cases spur the greater improvement.

Part III

The Circle of Assessment and Instruction

In 1989, the State University of New York at Fredonia had entering freshmen and juniors write a 50-minute essay. Analysis found significant improvement from first to third year in every subtest of the writing. Then in 1995 the assessment was repeated, but this time no significant gain was found. There was a certain amount of soul searching. Faculty began to question the test. What was valid about a 50-minute impromptu essay? How many students write anything like that in class? Discouragement set in. "We have begun to lose energy for the commitment to improving student writing" (Hurtgen, 1997, p. 64).

The present book argues that this vignette may project something of a broken circle. As faculty at Fredonia realized, actual experiences of students in the classroom did not enter into the formation of the instrument used to assess the students' writing competence. We would add that movement the other way was also blocked. Once the assessment was finished, the outcomes were not integrated back into instruction. Dubious as the instrument was, should not people have asked in what ways the students showed no gain, how no-gain might be associated with current lower-division writing instruction, and whether gain might not be achieved with changes in that instruction? Validity of assessment methods is one matter, but assessment and instruction must form one synergistic whole or both will "lose energy."

Trudy Banta says, "Assessment requires attention to outcomes but also and equally to experiences that lead to those outcomes" (1997, p. 90). A subsequent segment of this book, Part IV, will expand Banta's statement, focusing on collegiate experiences that lead both from and beyond outcomes. Part III contends that assessment and instruction should lead to each other, should be "esemplastic" in Coleridge's still provocative word, each shaping the other into an evolving whole. Chapter 7 uses theory from Gregory Bateson (1972) and Arnold van Gennep (1960) to show how assessment and instruction can be integrated into a cyclic rite-of-passage, for students, tutors, teachers, and academic units such as writing centers. Chapter 8 looks at the restless history of the basic writing sequence at Washington State University (WSU) (English 100) and narrates graphically how assessment changed the program and subsequently how the program is changing the assessment. Chapter 9 takes a revisionary approach to value-added studies, the kind of educational outcomes approach used at Fredonia, and suggests that whereas new designs may or may not increase the chances of recording gain in writing performance across the undergraduate years, value-added studies will always prove beneficial when they are incorporated into the writing program afterward. Chapter 10 makes the same point, only with program validation, with assessment not of the student's writing but of the entire assessment-instructional system at a school. The chapter contends that Fredonia's problems might have been avoided with a multiple-pronged inquiry into their twice-repeated assessment.

In the recent past, many colleges and universities, forming the widest spectrum, have tried to assess the effect of instruction upon student growth during the undergraduate years, not only SUNY Fredonia but Ball State, Harvard University, Miami-Dade Community College, Ohio University, Trenton State College, University of Tennessee at Knoxville, the Virginia Military Institute, and Western College of Miami University—to give just a taste of the range. WSU's experience argues that the effort will be short lived and of little profit unless testing and teaching are deeply integrated, as they are in three of the longer-lived programs, those at Alverno College (Loacker & Mentkowski, 1993), Truman State University (Magruder, McManis, & Young, 1997), and California State University at San Bernardino (White, 1991).

7

Writes of Passage: Conceptualizing the Relationship of Writing Center and Writing Assessment Practices

Lisa Johnson-Shull and Diane Kelly-Riley

After a rocky start (see Chapter 3), the Writing Center and the office of Writing Assessment at Washington State University (WSU) now work side by side to ensure that students both recognize the institutional importance of good writing and get the instructional support they need to develop their writing to meet academic expectations. The Writing Assessment office creates, distributes, and stores exam materials; recruits, trains, and supervises faculty readers; diagnoses student writing ability; places students in courses deemed appropriate by faculty evaluators; and reports pertinent information to the Office of the Registrar. The Writing Center hires, trains and supervises peer tutors; offers writing tutorials both on a walk-in basis and through credit-based support courses; and offers faculty a place to receive assistance with course design and assignments regarding writing. Together these two organizations formally assess and provide compensatory support for student writing at both the freshman and the junior level. Informally, these two programs provide writing guidance and advice for all students at all levels of their education at Washington State University. Although the division of labor between these two institutional entities is fairly straightforward, the way in which they intersect and interact to sustain and energize the ambitious undertaking of the WSU Writing Programs is less easily explained.

THE FEEDBACK LOOP OF INSTRUCTION AND ASSESSMENT

Theoretically, writing assessment and writing support services are a good match because of what cyberneticists would call a feedback loop: two counter forces working in opposition to each other to establish equilibrium (Capra, 1996, p. 56). Assessment creates and enforces a firm standard, and the Writing Center mitigates the formality by offering a flexible mechanism as a support. Assessment begins the process by introducing students to a particular value system—in this case the importance of good writing. The test initiates a momentum of student energy whereby they are initiated into a world where critical engagement with writing is a goal. The classroom instruction reinforces the goal by providing both opportunities for improving writing proficiency and additional performance assessments. Students who continue to have difficulty steering a course to the goal of proficient writing are supported by Writing Center services to redirect them or provide the "countersteering" incentives to help get them back on a course to face future assessments.

The key elements to this cybernetic system are the communication channels between the combined programs that allow adequate feedback on student need and performance to provide the necessary response to keep the student on a balanced course toward educational success. If assessment is disconnected from instruction and from instructional support, there are no communication channels that ensure programmatic intervention that would allow a response to the findings of an assessment.

This discussion introduces the WSU Writing Programs as a functional cybernetic system constantly involved in the dynamic interplay of both self-balancing modifications and self-reinforcing patterns. Those modifications and patterns begin with institutional Writing Assessment acting as the governor of energy initiation both by "kicking off" the process of writing instruction and by creating and enforcing a firm institutional standard of acceptable writing. The Writing Center acts as the counterbalance by offering tutorial assistance.

Institutional requirements on one end and instructional assistance on the other establish two ends of a spectrum and engender what Neil Postman would call a thermostatic relationship—the "oppositional complimentarity" of the two programs keep each other's contrasting tendencies in check (Postman, 1976, p. 18). For example, if students received only support for their writing without the promise of evaluation to give social meaning to their work, they would have little incentive for critical engagement with academic writing. If students were only evaluated without being offered compensatory support for their identified weaknesses, they would reject the assessment process as static and punitive. Far from canceling each other out, assessment and instructional support generate energy in their polarity and circularity.

According to Gregory Bateson, all evolving systems "consist of complex cybernetic networks, and all such systems share certain formal characteristics. Each system contains subsystems that are potentially regenerative. The regenerative potentialities of such subsystems are typically kept in check by various sorts of governing loops to achieve 'steady state'" (Bateson, 1972, p. 447). Bateson's explanation of cybernetics helps provide a theoretical basis for the ways in which writing programs that are counterbalanced by both assessment and compensatory support offered by the Writing Center develop and sustain themselves over time. Bateson defines two actions within these causal networks that are particularly relevant to an understanding of the ongoing influences between assessment and writing centers: energy transfer and feedback. Simply put, energy transfer depicts the influence of entities on each other, and feedback signifies the energy of the recipient to respond. The Writing Center and the Assessment Program at WSU affect each other because the structure of their relationship allows each program to muster a response to the changes within the other program. Administrators and staff from each program meet weekly to discuss programmatic changes and to collaboratively problem solve. Consequently, few, if any, changes occur in either program without the other program knowing about it or being involved in the decision-making process for the proposed change.

There are numerous relationships between writing assessment and writing support: interactions between students and tutors, readers and writers, administrators and staff, evaluators and evaluated, students and teachers, and administrators and students, and there is the relationship of the program to the university as a whole. The many relationships, however, complicate the pattern of interactions between assessment and instruction. As a result, cybernetics only works to explain the boundaries of the combined programs; it does little to describe the web of movement that occurs within the established structure and does virtually nothing to qualify the substance of the interactions.

LEARNING AND RITES OF PASSAGE

The most important activity that occurs within the dynamic system of the Writing Programs is student and faculty learning. Consequently, the emphasis of the work we do centers on creating opportunities that urge students and faculty into situations that encourage learning. Because dissonance in the comfort levels of individuals has been shown to push them into more sophisticated levels of critical engagement (Perry, 1970), situations that require students and faculty to grapple with uncertainty and ambiguity exist at each stage of the assessment-instruction circuit—be it assessment readers calibrating their standards or students making decisions in responses to a conversation with a writing tutor.

In the context of community formation, the reconciliation of ambiguity is what anthropologist Arnold van Gennep (1960) would call the last aspect of a three-stage process of human transformation in the service of *communitas* (Torrance, 1994). Using the concept of *thresholds* as his driving metaphor, van Gennep introduces three recursive phases (and the thresholds that occur within those phases) as illustrative of the processes of learning: preliminal, liminal, and postliminal stages (p. 21). The preliminal stage recognizes the passage from a previous state into a separation from that state—a doorway through which one steps from a fairly fixed identity into one that may not be so familiar. The liminal stage is the space within these two doorways, a borderland "betwixt and between" an assigned cultural position (Torrance, 1994, p. 10), and the postliminal signifies the completion of a passage. The postliminal stage affords an opportunity for process and reflection of the "arrival," and inevitably reincarnates into the preliminal stage of yet another passage, thereby perpetuating the recursive nature of the process. (These stages are alternatively described as separation, transition, and aggregation: van Gennep, 1960, p. vi.) Originally used to describe the processual transformation that occurs in a rite of passage, van Gennep's stages can also apply to the transitions that occur within the secular space of education. In our writing program, initial assessment separates; subsequent instruction provides a transition; and aggregation occurs when the second assessment closes the transition reuniting the student with community expectations.

In the WSU writing program, the feedback loop of assessment and instruction provides the momentum to initiate students into an educational rite of passage. The points at which assessment, writing center support, and instruction intersect provide the structure for the initiation and completion points of the passage: students pass though the thresholds of assessment into the turbulent processes of learning and back into assessment territory. Assessment informs students about their relationship to the community and the community expectations that they are about to confront. Instruction then feeds back to students an image of who they are as they begin to analyze and synthesize their relationship to the instruction. Assessment acts as a conduit for the instructional experience both ending a process by establishing a secular ritual of closure and beginning a new phase by inviting students into a new instructional dimension. In the WSU Writing Program, a fairly set routine exists for facilitating students' passages through their undergraduate education, a routine that exists as a continuous educational cycle.

Those of us involved in writing support and assessment at WSU see our main task as pushing or encouraging students and faculty into a state of liminality. We do this by facilitating them through what could be viewed as a "reverse" rite of passage. In tribal cultures, a rite of passage sends a person from a communally organized group into isolation for the purpose of returning to the community later with new insights and appreciations. Traditionally, university training does not emphasize collaboration or becoming part of a community; instead the culture encourages the solitary pursuits of student and scholar. Students and faculty engaged in our writing program, however, are required to cooperate with a group of people around the issue of writing. Rather than expect students and faculty to work in academic isolation to arrive at some epiphanies as solitary scholars, small groups build communities in which structures prepare them for future independence and interdependence. The potential transformation that takes place in this communal region is what gives the program the collective strength that maintains it.

When students enter WSU as freshmen, they are required to take a writing examination that will place them in the appropriate first-year composition course. The exam requires students to produce, under timed conditions, an argumentative essay in response to a paragraph prompt that addresses a cultural controversy. Students can be placed into regular freshman composition, be assigned a credit-bearing writing group to accompany their freshman writing course, or can exempt out of the requirement completely. For students, the feat of taking the initial placement test, regardless of the results, separates them from their previous role as high school students and acts as a gateway into their new identity as college writers. The test acts as a preliminary gateway into a phase of ambiguity, and uncertainty prevails.

To assist students in this phase of liminality, WSU implemented a small group tutorial course, English 102, in the fall of 1991 to supplement the instruction students received as a consequence of their placement exam results. Originally conceived as a writing group for at-risk students, the course quickly metamorphasized into something much larger and significant than had originally been envisioned by its founders. In its second year, course enrollments had doubled because of an upsurge in volunteer participants. Despite the stigma that is often associated with remedial courses designed for underprepared students, the writing group experience had proved so helpful and nonthreatening to the students placed in it that they began to recommend it to their peers. As a result of the common needs the course addressed, English 102 course enrollments jumped from one hundred students in 1991 to seven hundred in 1999 (with approximately 60 percent volunteer enrollments).

The communal forum that English 102 uses to prepare students to function as independent writers compels students to face issues of cooperation and negotiation that may be unfamiliar to them in the educational context. The grading for the course is pass or fail and is based solely on student attendance and the production of a two-page evaluation at the course's conclusion. This structure removes the peer tutor from the subjective responsibility of acting as a judge of student performance. To be counted present, students must bring a piece of their own writing to the group to share. Four or five students spend an hour each week giving and receiving feedback on each other's writing with the guidance of a trained Writing Center tutor. The evaluative essay allows the tutors and course coordinators the feedback they need to help students revise continuously and to develop the authority to respond to each other's written words.

The primary goal of the course is to encourage students to accept authority for their own writing. Empowering students to accept this authority means first persuading them that writing is communication, rather than a formulaic, properly cadenced academic exercise. Creating an environment for students to interact as a group helped us to realize how desperately students crave detailed response to their work—rhetorically thoughtful response from interested listeners rather than mistake-focused diatribes from evaluators. The dramatic increase in voluntary enrollments in this course confirmed students' desires to interact in an institutional forum where what they said was the central focus of the enterprise. The Burkean parlor atmosphere described by Andrea Lunsford (1991) combined with Bruffee's model of communal information generation (1984) allowed the students a creative arena in which to carve out their academic identities.

Once students have successfully completed their freshman composition course and have completed 60 hours of lower-division coursework, they are required to complete a second diagnostic exam: the rising-junior Writing Portfolio. This system has a threefold agenda: to predict student readiness for upper-division writing-intensive coursework, to assess the effectiveness of the writing instruction students have received at the lower-division level, and to offer appropriate support for writers who may need it. The exam, which is postliminal in that it marks a phase of completion in a recursive cycle of instruction and assessment, also represents initiation. It labels student writing as acceptable, exceptional, or needing work and then responds to the assigned label by ushering students through to an appropriate instructional avenue. In most cases the instructional response is simply the normal coursework in the student's major. For students identified as needing work, the instructional requirement is a one-credit course (General Education 302), similar to the English 102 model, that focuses primarily on helping students meet the writing challenges in their upper-division coursework. In cases in which the writing problems are severe, students are assigned three-credits worth of writing instruction. Once they have completed the instructional requirement, the University assessment process leaves the student free to navigate instructional waters independently if they so choose. Students who desire continued support with their writing have unlimited access to the walk-in tutorial service offered by the Writing Center.

TEACHERS AND RITES OF PASSAGE

The assessment process is sustained by a collaboration of classroom teachers working in various venues to ensure that students receive the education and educational support that they need. The evaluation of the Writing Placement exam, for example, is done by the teachers of the courses into which the students are placed. These teachers have experience working with a variety of writing but learn to identify problematic writing in short, timed writing samples. This "two-tiered expert reader system," explained in Chapters 3 and 4, assumes that the teachers who direct the instructional contexts are the best ones to distinguish acceptable writing from that which demonstrates a need for additional support. In this relationship, students can expect to encounter teachers who have collectively determined the entry criteria for the offered courses and are consequently personally invested in the students who arrive in their classrooms. Teachers can expect to see a certain caliber of writer in their courses because they have participated in deciding what level of writer belongs in their courses. Further, the teachers who participate in the Writing Placement exam evaluation gain experience in reading and responding to student writing and in collaborating with their instructional peers.

Similarly, the evaluation of the rising-junior Writing Portfolio employs the same strategies. Evaluators are recruited from among the ranks of faculty from across the disciplines who have signed off on student course paper submissions. By 1997, over a thousand different teachers at WSU had signed off on Portfolio submissions. Currently, two or more papers have been submitted from over two thousand different courses at WSU campuses from 89 different departments (Norris & Webber, 1999). Evaluators, who may also teach the upper-division Writing-in-the-Major courses, are trained to make the final distinctions between acceptable, outstanding, and needs-work writing. To date, the Assessment Office has hired 150 faculty members as Portfolio readers.

The appointment of faculty (tenured, adjunct, and graduate students) to this position represents the preliminary threshold into the liminal ambiguity of learning to be a collaborative reader. The reader negotiation creates a dimension of unpredictability that may be uncomfortable for some who function in very specialized domains. Furthermore, the two tiers that differentiate readers only by their experience destroys the safety net of prestigious labels and allows the readers to participate with equivalent status. The criteria for becoming a successful portfolio reader is the willingness to set aside individual and discipline-based definitions of acceptable writing and embrace a standard that is in continuous revision based on evolving discussions with other faculty readers. Although original standards were established by composition faculty Portfolio administrators, faculty participation in the ongoing conversation maintains the standards for undergraduate writing at WSU.

Based on their experience as first-level readers and from teaching the upper-division Writing-in-the-Major courses, readers advance from the first tier to the second of Portfolio evaluation. The shift from tier-one reader to tier-two reader forces the evaluator to view the Portfolio submissions in a different way and to employ a different strategy of thinking. Chapter 5 describes these processes as prototypical categorization at tier one, and exemplar categorization at tier two. At tier one, the evaluator "categorizes by judging how similar the yet-to-be categorized instance is to abstract schemas they have of the best example or most representative member of possible categories" (Haswell, 1998c, p. 246). At tier two, categorization is accomplished by comparing a new instance with intact memories of similar instances. Essentially, tier one readers sort obviously competent upper-division writing from questionable writing (either strong or weak) and tier-two readers must compare the writing that they have previously read to make an appropriate judgement.

The participation in a conversation that continually articulates the qualities that make up good writing not only helps faculty develop as evaluators within the context of the Writing Assessment Program but also extends into their own work in the classroom. This is perhaps the trickiest arena to measurably claim a difference. A professor of accounting states that the influences of the Portfolio evaluation have dramatically influenced her teaching:

> Prior to being a portfolio reader I graded almost entirely on content. I now split the grade about fifty-fifty between content and writing. Having read numerous "needs work" portfolios where students submitted "A" papers in which spelling and grammar were atrocious, logic was non-existent and/or punctuation consisted of random dots on paper, I can see the unintended consequences of content-only grading. I also have begun including in my course syllabus the specific grade needed in order for me to consider a paper "acceptable" for writing portfolio submission (students are allowed to revise unacceptable papers if they choose). Finally, having read some truly excellent portfolio submissions I am more critical in terms of my assessment of acceptable versus exceptional writing when signing off on student's papers.

A professor of engineering describes the outcomes of his Portfolio evaluation experiences as "[helping] me in evaluating how students write in the freshmen engineering course (Engineering 120). Being a Writing-Portfolio evaluator has helped me to look beyond the technical content of a report to how a student is able to communicate on paper. This experience has helped me distinguish between excellent, good, and poor written communicative skills."

Unlike students who eventually end their immersion in the Writing Program and reach the postliminal phase to their undergraduate education, faculty who work for the Assessment program are afforded the unique opportunity to continually shift from the liminal to postliminal phases as they move from classroom instructor-scholar to Portfolio evaluator and back to the classroom. This movement shapes and transforms the faculty involved in the process, and students benefit from having better prepared teachers in the classroom.

CAUTIONS AND RECOMMENDATIONS

As Chapter 3 should make clear, combining an assessment office and a writing center is not clear sailing. Our Writing Program has had to adapt and modify our philosophies and structures to work better with each other. Our attempt to enact the hybrid of traditional writing center administrative practices with traditional hierarchical and linear assessment practices has led us to adopt both a cybernetic metaphor to explain the relationship of the programs and a sociological theory to articulate what we do together. Consequently, we have learned to "practice what we preach," and use the same negotiation strategies in our administration that faculty and students involved in the Writing Program use.

The metaphors of feedback loops and energy transfer play central roles in how we understand and structure our program, and we recommend the metaphors for people elsewhere who want to understand better the problems they may be experiencing in hybrid academic units. We may even recommend the marriage of units that are now separate and need rejuvenation. Organizational hybridization is always risky. At WSU the Writing Program may be pedagogically responsive, dynamic, and recursive, but it also has elements of unpredictability. We believe, however, that that unpredictability can be good for student learning, faculty development, and program evolution. Van Gennep's concept of liminality demonstrates the cultural-instructional value of existing in ambiguous space. Without liminal experience, individuals cannot progress into spaces of more defined identity. This is true of programs and individuals.

Edward White (1985), among others, argues that good assessment should be tied to instruction. The combination and close relationship of assessment, instruction, and instructional support completes a processual loop that provides the instructional momentum to all parties and programs involved. Because assessment has a traditional tendency to be a static enterprise, that is it provides a label, fixed and measurable, it is a system that challenges the tendency to ensure an assessment that is always changing and responsive. This type of dynamic assessment places students' needs over the conventional desire for measurable outcomes that tend to overlook the active nature of the humans involved in the system. Although cybernetics and rites of passage describe for us the motion of our program, the possibilities for other organic metaphors as models for other programs are perhaps endless.

8

Taking the "Basic" out of "Basic Writing"

Susan Wyche

No academic program generates more assumptions about its students and curriculum than does "Basic Writing." No matter the choice of title—basic, remedial, or developmental—nor whether it is offered at a research university or community college, in the minds of students, faculty, administrators, and legislators alike, the course becomes unofficially "bonehead English." Cherryl Armstrong, who has taught basic writing in such diverse places as Harvard and City University of New York (CUNY) on the East Coast, and California State University (CSU) and University of California (UC) campuses on the West, reminds us that "*basic* is a relative term" (Armstrong, 1988, p. 76). Each institution defines the term, sets the standards, and determines the method by which students are identified and assigned to the course. At Harvard, she points out, they had no basic-writing students until they created a course called basic writing.

Though it may be easy to accept that assessment and instruction artificially construct basic-writing students at an institution like Harvard, schools with less competitive admission standards engage in the same process. Once constructed, however, these labels exert a social grip that

makes transformation difficult. Few basic writing programs are disman-
tled except in the face of budgetary cutbacks or legislative intervention.

This chapter is unusual in that it describes a set of events leading to the
voluntary abolition of a basic writing program. It explains why it wasn't a
single motivation—practical, pedagogical, or political—but a complex of
factors that ultimately convinced faculty at one institution to pursue an
alternative path. It also demonstrates how the existence of a strong assessment program can encourage faculty and administrators to pose questions
about a curriculum that cannot be answered without the feedback that
assessment provides, therefore, highlighting the dynamic circle of assessment and instruction that ideally form a self-reflective writing program.

THE FIRST STEP: ACCURATE PLACEMENT

Until 1991, WSU's basic writing program enrolled a mix of students,
some self-selected, some advised. Though it was not the easiest group to
teach, because the range of skills and experiences varied dramatically, it
did not generate the resentment of a required course. There were older
returning students who self-selected Basic Writing (English 100), though
their skills were more than adequate for the regular freshman course.
There were athletes (including a small contingent of Hawaiians and
Samoans recruited for the nationally ranked football team) and equally
small groups of first-generation and special admissions students, all
encouraged by their respective program advisors to take the most basic
level of composition offered. The majority of students in English 100,
however, arrived fresh from urban, suburban, and rural high schools
across the state and voluntarily signed into the course on the basis of low
Washington State Pre-Collegiate scores after receiving a letter from the
English Department suggesting this placement.

The advent of the English Placement Examination in 1991 changed all
that. The multiple paths into English 100 were eliminated and replaced by
a single, mandatory placement process. Gone were the students who
brought a greater mix of skills and attitudes to the course. The new populations were more uniformly in need of help with writing, and more
resentful concerning that need because it was now required. In the first
year after the placement exam was implemented, 41 percent of the
English 100 students indicated on a survey that they felt "misplaced"
(Haswell, Wyche-Smith, & Magnuson, 1992, p. 15). A survey of English
100 instructors, on the other hand, showed that they believed the exam
had greatly improved placement and that virtually all students had been
appropriately placed (p. 14).

STEP TWO: REVISING THE COURSE

Concurrent with the implementation of the assessment program, the
English 100 director overhauled the program's curriculum, exchanging

two decades of schoolbook grammar lessons and rhetorical modes for a "rehearsal" approach that drew on the materials and methods of the regular composition course (English 101). That course utilized a shared anthology of readings loosely linked to World Civilizations 101 (also a required first-year course at WSU), emphasized academic discourse, involved peer-response groups, and required submission of a portfolio evaluated by a reader other than the course instructor.

The rehearsal structure exposed English 100 students to the substance of English 101 with two significant differences: (1) they prepared and received feedback on a portfolio, but did not have to pass the portfolio to pass the course (as they did in English 101), and (2) they received credit instead of letter grades. Essentially, the rehearsal structure gave students two semesters to complete English 101 (similar, though without the administrative structure to the "Stretch Program" at University of Arizona, where students take a two-semester version of English 101, see Glau, 1996).

Though students initially resented their placement in the course, the rehearsal approach seemed well received. Students told their instructors that they liked knowing what to expect in English 101. By the end of English 100, they had already purchased and read much of the English 101 anthology; produced a portfolio of written assignments, some of which could be revised and expanded in regular course; and had been initiated into the mysteries of portfolio assessment. For the instructors of English 100, a mix of temporary faculty and English graduate teaching assistants who had cut their teeth on English 101, the content and activities were equally familiar. Their prior experience teaching English 101 gave their advice and comments credibility with the English 100 students, and, without the burden of preparing for a new course, instructors could focus on students needing more individualized attention.

According to research that tracked English 100 students as they moved into English 101, the approach was not only well received, it was also successful. Though no statistics had been collected in previous years, by any measure the completion rate looked respectable. At the end of the first year of mandatory placement and curricular revision, 92 percent of the students enrolled in English 100 passed the first time, 80 percent of those enrolled directly into English 101, and 83 percent of those passed the English 101 Portfolio successfully (Haswell, Wyche-Smith, & Magnuson, 1992, p. 19).

STEP THREE: QUESTIONING THE "BASIC" IN BASIC WRITERS

The sweeping changes of 1991 also produced an unanticipated effect. Because English 100 students were doing the same work as students in English 101, and the teachers were experienced or actively teaching in both programs, there was a new basis for comparison beyond the initial placement. Historically, teachers had always noted a significant percentage of students in English 100 whose work exceeded expectations, students whose skills made dramatic improvements in the space of a single semester. Before 1991, this would have been attributed to the lack of systematic placement. When the phenomenon persisted despite the new placement exam, those of us involved in the program were puzzled. We tracked samples of student work back to the original placements but found no signs of hidden potential that the readers had overlooked and no evidence of misreading. At the beginning of the semester, the writing samples clearly indicated that the students were best served by English 100; at the end of the semester, their work was on par with the work of students in English 101.

For the next two years, the transformation of our nonbasic basic writers was a recurring topic of conversation. In the weekly teachers' meetings, we tried to pinpoint when this change occurred. The midterm portfolios provided valuable clues. We ranked English 100 portfolios using the same standards and categories used for English 101: failing, borderline pass, and clear pass. As one might expect, the difference between English 100 students and students in English 101 was significant. Seventy-nine percent of the students in English 101 received a passing score at midterm compared to only 18 percent of the students in English 100. At midterm, the transformation had not yet taken place.

Between 1991 and 1993, we lacked information about final portfolios because the midterm portfolio had been included only to walk English 100 students through the Portfolio process. English 100 did not have a program-wide final portfolio. Still, most English 100 teachers assigned a final course portfolio and so had a reasonable idea as to how their students might have fared had portfolios been read by external readers. In their opinion, a third of their students would have passed the English 101 portfolio with ease, and another third may have been borderline.

We tentatively concluded that somewhere between the tenth and twelfth weeks of the semester—after midterm but before the final portfolio, many of our students' learning curves took a sharp turn up. We speculated that the primary difference between the basic writers and their peers in English 101 was the extent of their experience with school-sponsored writing and reading. From questions that teachers routinely asked in the first weeks of the course, we knew that many did little reading at the high school level—school- or self-sponsored—and few had written more than a handful of papers in their final year of high school. The first few weeks of English 100, then, provided an opportunity to catch up; that's why the midterm portfolio, occurring as it did at the seventh week, showed little progress. But final papers, after students had had several more weeks in which to internalize what they had learned, were noticeably improved.

STEP FOUR: IDENTIFYING AN ALTERNATIVE FORM OF SUPPORT

The rehearsal approach had already moved the English 100 program closer to its English 101 terminus. Our hypothesis concerning the magical period between the seventh and twelfth weeks pushed us to ask, if with no special attention nearly a third of the English 100 students could pass English 101, what could they be expected to accomplish if they received supplemental support?

This question was prompted, in part, by the new one-credit Tutorial Workshop (English 102) offered through the Writing Center that we thought might be appropriate for the English 100 students. It had originally been developed to help students enrolled in English 101 whose placement exams suggested that they might be at risk there. Students met once a week in small groups of four or five with a Writing Center tutor trained in group-facilitation techniques. The students focused on the writing assigned in their English 101 course, reading and responding to one another's work and sharing difficulties they were experiencing with the materials, assignments, or activities of the main course.

We knew that students placed in these workshops were almost unanimously positive in their end-of-the-semester evaluations. They noted that the workshops improved their grades, helped them to meet people, and increased their enjoyment of and confidence in writing (Haswell, Wyche-Smith, & Magnuson, 1992, p. 19). This was not empty praise, as enrollment doubled with voluntary participants in the program's second semester (a percentage that continues today, even though the program has grown to over 10 times its original size).

Interestingly, the popularity of the new program among English 101 students did not immediately inspire us to extend it to the English 100 program. Though placement readers steadily increased the number of English 101 students assigned to English 102, and volunteer enrollments increased in parallel, the percentage of students placed into English 100 remained relatively stable. Perhaps we were overwhelmed already with the changes we had set in motion. Perhaps we, too, were locked into a perception of the basic-writing students that prevented us from seeing immediately the possibilities that this new program presented. It took two years before we wondered whether an additional instructional hour per week for all English 100 students could boost their performance enough to justify placement directly into English 101. Could we, by mainstreaming the students and providing support via the Tutorial Workshop, abolish English 100?

STEP FIVE: SAGE ADVICE

Our question, it turned out, was not a local one. At the time, abolition of remedial programs was becoming a cause célèbre. Periodicals with broad readership, such as *The New Yorker*, were publishing articles about the failure of remediation. Compositionists were hotly debating the politics of placement exams and basic writing programs at conferences and in the professional journals. City University of New York was poised to launch tighter admissions policies for its four-year colleges, severely cutting funding for basic writing programs (Mutnick, 1996, p. 27). There were even rumors that conservative politicians in our own state of Washington were discussing whether remedial programs should continue to be funded at four-year universities. We were not oblivious to these events, but local conditions seemed far more pressing, and from our isolated perspective in the hills of eastern Washington, legislative mutterings on the other side of the Cascades seemed little more than distant thunder.

Then two external voices entered our debate. The first belonged to Peter Elbow, who was researching an article on alternatives to basic-writing programs and contacted us because he had heard about our tutorial workshops. His questions, his interest, and his knowledge of other institutions with similar programs awakened us to changes taking place beyond our province. The questions he posed, both about our existing program and our longer-range intentions for the tutorial groups, tapped many of the issues with which we struggled. In the article that grew out of his inquiry, "Writing Assessment in the 21st Century: A Utopian View," Elbow (1996) identified three other universities that at the time had made the abolition leap successfully—University of South Carolina at Columbus, Berea College in Kentucky, and Cal State Chico. He described WSU as having developed the means for full mainstreaming with the tutorial workshops but not yet taking the radical step.

If being publicly positioned outside the gates of utopia weren't motive enough, a second push came shortly afterward from Edward White. We had invited White to our campus to update a program review that he had written as a member of an external writing program evaluation team several years earlier. That review had laid the political groundwork necessary for much of the curricular revision we had undertaken before 1991 (McLeod, 1991). With the revision of the English 100 and 101 programs and the implementation of the new assessments, it seemed an opportune time to have White conduct an interim evaluation—one that might push our administration into better funding of our rapidly growing programs.

Impressed by the tutorial workshops, White, like Elbow, encouraged us to take the next step.

> Everyone involved with the freshman program sees the development of the Tutorial Workshops as a more appropriate vehicle for assisting students with weak preparation than Basic Writing [English 100], and that belief has been reflected in the increasing number of placements in the Tutorial Workshops. If the energy now used for placement and instruction in Basic Writing can be redirected to Tutorial

Workshops, tutorial assistance can be provided to all who need it. Further, this assistance will be provided in a more positive and flexible context than in a remedial course. (White, 1993, p. 10)

Ironically, White was debating Peter Elbow nationally on the abolition of basic writing—the two representing equally concerned but opposing camps on how best to respond to the political threat that basic writing programs faced. That both individuals urged WSU to push ahead with mainstreaming clinched the decision that we had been wrestling with locally. That they had also spoken in powerful venues—keynote presentations at national conferences and external program evaluation reports—gave us the influence we needed to obtain the blessings of our administration.

STEP SIX: TESTING THE WATERS—
A PILOT STUDY OF MAINSTREAMING

The next semester, we launched a test of our hypothesis on mainstreaming. We invited students enrolled in English 100 to submit portfolios in both the midterm and final English 101 Portfolio readings, with the possibility of receiving credit for English 101 if the final portfolio passed. There were two sections, 29 students in total. (This was spring semester, when far fewer students enrolled in English 100; annually about two hundred students passed through the program.) To find out whether supplemental instruction made a difference, we asked students in one section to sign up for the tutorial workshop.

The English 101 Portfolio readings were read without students' name and home course. The English 101 teachers were not told that the English 100 portfolios were to be folded into their reading—an easy sleight of hand, as over a thousand portfolios were read each semester in English 101, and the English 100 portfolios averaged less than one additional portfolio per reader. We conducted the pilot at both sessions—midterm and final. Although we expected a respectable number of English 100 students to pass, the results astonished even the most optimistic among us.

Of the 29 students enrolled in English 100, 26 volunteered to participate. At the midterm evaluation, only 24 percent of the basic writers passed unequivocally—a poor but predictable performance in comparison to the over half who passed in English 101. At the final portfolio reading, 23 students submitted portfolios (three turned their portfolios in too late to be included). Of those English 100 students who attempted, 91 percent passed; this compared to a 95 percent pass rate for English 101 students. When withdrawals and failures to submit were factored in, 72 percent of the students initially enrolled in English 100 passed the evaluation compared to 85 percent of original enrollments for English 101. Though the pass rate of the English 100 students was not fully comparable to the passing rate for English 101, it was far higher than we had anticipated.

Interestingly, the tutorial workshops did not appear to be a major factor in the results. We had expected that students enrolled in the tutorial courses would pass at a higher rate than students in the "control" group, but the pass rate was identical. However, the number of students in the control group, 13, was too small from which to draw much in the way of conclusions.

STEP SEVEN: MAKING SENSE OF THE RESULTS

These results, and the consistent observations of the English 100 teachers over the years, suggested that the majority of English 100 students were capable of catching up to their better-prepared peers within a few weeks, at least enough to pass the minimal competency requirements as determined by the English 101 Portfolio assessment. Two pressing questions emerged: what had happened to the students who had not submitted, had submitted but failed, or had withdrawn from the English 100 program (that is: what happened to the students who didn't make it) and why hadn't the Tutorial Workshop made a difference in the passing rates between the two groups (however statistically insignificant)?

We first considered the question of the students who hadn't passed. Because the pool was fairly small, we interviewed their teachers, tutors, and advisors. In every case, we heard the same story: these students had a record of problems with coursework and attendance across the curriculum. Advisors reported that several students had struggled with personal matters: financial aid, illness, family conflict. Three had withdrawn from the course in the first weeks of the term. Two had left the university midsemester. From this information, we concluded that some of these students faced problems beyond the scope of university resources or required support beyond the scope of any single academic program. If students attended the course and participated in course activities, the odds were that they would pass. This analysis suggested that broad-based retention efforts rather than curricular revision would be necessary to improve success rates among the students who either had not submitted or had submitted but not passed.

The role of the tutorial workshops was not as clear. At face value, the comparison between the experimental and control groups—those who received the supplemental instruction and those who did not—suggested that it was time on task (the late-blooming learning curve) rather than the addition of the tutorial program that had made the difference in student performance. The obvious conclusion would have been that mainstreaming alone was adequate; we need not include the additional support.

Our interpretation of this data was complicated, however, by what we knew of the dynamics of the experimental section. In the first weeks of the course, the teacher of the experimental group (an experienced and enthusiastic teacher of English 100) described her students as "challenging." By midterm, she labeled the experimental section "dysfunctional" and had written a memo to the director of the program, saying she feared that this particular group of students would "skew the study" because they had created a poisonous class dynamic. Three tutors interviewed these students and kept detailed journals of their tutorial writing sessions during the semester. They concurred with the teacher's concerns—the group of students were providing challenges that exceeded problems tutors and teacher were used to. While the comparison of midterm and final portfolios graphed a neat picture of developing writing skills, the tutors' journals provided a contrasting perspective. So pronounced had some of the behavioral problems become by the second half of the semester that the teacher finally abolished class meetings and worked with the students in individual conferences.

Though the performance of these students rendered the comparison between the experimental and control groups inconclusive, both the teacher and the tutors strongly felt that the tutorial workshops had saved the class. Moreover, the experience of the dysfunctional classroom dynamics argued the case for mainstreaming even more strongly. "These students, grouped as they are in tutorials together and the same class," the teacher wrote in frustration midway through the semester, "can compare themselves only to each other and no one is doing very well."

STEP EIGHT: MOVING FROM REFLECTION TO ACTION

Our pilot study generated more questions than answers, and in an ideal world would have served only as a basis for further research; however, we were developing a sense of urgency because of financial strain on the Tutorial Workshop program. Despite experiencing tremendous growth, it was being run on hours of volunteer time, both by tutors and administrators—a consequence of development during years of budgetary cutbacks. Now in its third year of expansion, the lack of resources was taking a toll. As White had pointed out, downsizing English 100 would allow us to shift resources internally to provide more support for the innovative program. This would allow us both to mainstream the English 100 students and provide them (and other students) support from a strengthened Tutorial Workshop—a system that we now believed to be the *best way* to supplement writing instruction.

In summer 1994, we took our results to the dean of Liberal Arts and the director of General Education. We argued that all students deserved an equal shot at completing English 101 in one semester. We shared the professional literature from K through 12 studies that made strong arguments in favor of mainstreaming—arguments that we pointed out applied to first-year college students as well. Drawing on our recent experience with the dysfunctional English 100 class, we argued that segregation into basic writing courses negatively affected motivation, self-esteem, and attitude.

We argued that we had an effective means of support, the Tutorial Workshop, and that this was more cost effective for the university, because a full three-credit course of remedial instruction would be reduced to one credit of supplemental instruction offered by less-expensive peer tutors. In short, we used every argument that we could think of. The administrators were convinced, and the English 100 program was closed down. We decided not to take the course out of the catalog, but it wasn't staffed and students would not be placed into it at the next placement exam.

STEP NINE: A SUCCESSFUL DISAPPEARING ACT

After years of talking about mainstreaming, suddenly it was fact. Because the decision was made precipitously, and we all felt more than a little nervous about the outcome, we agreed to retain the English 100 designation as a descriptor (and not a functional category) in the placement readings the following year. This allowed us to track students through English 101 who would have been previously placed in English 100. We need not have feared. The success rate in the second year was an improvement over the pilot study: of the 56 students identified as English 100 students by the exam, 84 percent passed, 12 percent withdrew, and 4 percent failed. This was virtually identical to the performance of the other 1,369 students placed into English 101, of whom 85 percent passed, 12 percent withdrew, and 3 percent failed.

If we were uncertain about the timing of the change, in the end it proved serendipitous. The distant thunder of legislative politics was less distant than we realized. A month into our mainstreamed program, a memo landed on the director's desk, asking for information on remedial courses. The request from the provost explained that this survey originated in the state legislature, and materials with the survey offered a helpful description of what kinds of courses should be included in the report. According to the guidelines, English 100 would have been categorized as remedial and would have raised a red flag for conservative legislators interested in shifting remedial students from four-year to two-year colleges. The Tutorial Workshops did not qualify, however, because they were open to all students, used writing assignments from a college-level course, and generated baccalaureate credit.

Under the survey's question, "Number of students enrolled in 'remedial' English?" the Director penned a satisfying "0." And in the report to the state, the provost's cover letter noted: "The number of students in the 'remedial' courses is relatively small, . . . and do not constitute a problem for the university at this time." Just like that, WSU's basic writers had disappeared safely into the ranks of English 101.

STEP TEN: THE CIRCLE KEEPS REVOLVING

Of course, the tutorial workshops were not without their difficulties. University software couldn't handle the complexities of scheduling small groups, so Writing Center tutors hand-scheduled hundreds of students in the first two weeks of each semester. Tutors weren't always reliable. Training was developed on the fly, because Writing Center staff couldn't always anticipate problems until they occurred. Students didn't know what to make of a course that operated with peer tutors who facilitated rather than taught and often had to learn the hard way that attending and participating still mattered, even though they were not in a classroom with a teacher at the front taking roll. As those who have worked with similar programs elsewhere have discovered, however, when students and teachers finally grow accustomed to the structure of small-group tutorials, they realize that it changes the lens through which the students are viewed and view themselves (Grego & Thompson, 1996; Rodby, 1996).

The students who entered WSU in 1995 were innocent of the institutional label basic writers. When they met with their tutorial groups, they were joining nearly more than a third of the English 101 population, many of whom had elected to enroll because they believed that doing so would help them meet deadlines, give them useful feedback, and improve their grades. Indeed, the tutorial program had a higher percentage of sign-ups in the honors version of English 101 than it did in the regular English 101 sections. Any sense of shame, embarrassment, or marginalization that students might have felt when told by placement exam results that they needed the workshop was quickly diminished by the experience of seeing lots of other students enroll who were not required to take them.

Still, questions lingered as to whether this was enough support for some of the students, and teachers would occasionally say, "this student could have used the full three credits of English 100." It was inevitable that problems with students, student writing, and teachers' abilities to respond to those problems would demand review, and the circle of assessment and instruction would undergo another revolution. Times would change, the school would change, and student populations would change. Our experience was not so much about finding the ideal program as establishing a process in which assessment and instruction could exist in a dynamic cycle of feedback and response (see Chapters 2, and 4 to 6).

ANOTHER TURN

The rest of the story has two endings: one at WSU and one at CSU Monterey Bay (CSUMB), an experimental institution founded in 1994.

The director of Composition completed her term at WSU, overseeing a year without English 100, and a new director got ready to take over. He possessed a different and far more positive view of basic writing programs.

Concerned that the loss of English 100 could close down an important option for students in the program who needed more time and support than the tutorial workshops provided, he asked that English 100 be reactivated. At first it was used only for students with severe writing problems, who were placed on the recommendation of English 101 teachers in the first two weeks of the semester. Each year, however, enrollment increased.

Less than two years later, he commissioned the assessment program to develop a better definition of the basic writing category. Old placement exams were reviewed, and assessment administrators decided that the definition needed to be developed by the body of faculty that would, in effect, determine the label: the more experienced teachers-readers of the placement examination (the tier-two readers, see Chapter 4). The reading corps is now changing the way it reads and places writers into English 100. Simultaneously, the English 100 program is under consideration for another curricular and structural revision, based on the Stretch Program at Arizona State University (an option that was not available in the early 1990s; see Glau, 1996). Thus a new cycle of refining and redefining is under way.

In the meantime, the former director of Composition moved to CSUMB where she was given responsibility for designing a writing support program within a new institution—*tabula rasa*. Unlike WSU, where no more than 20 percent of the population was ever placed in basic writing, about half of CSUMB's incoming first-year students are designated remedial by a statewide placement exam. Mainstreaming would obviously mean something very different in this context. Drawing on the experience at WSU, she designed a writing support program that uses tutorial workshops exclusively, mainstreaming all students into writing-intensive courses (CSUMB does not have a traditional freshman composition program). In addition, she expanded the program to serve not only first-year students, but all students, at all levels. In its first three years, the program grew from an initial pilot to a full-blown tutorial program, serving one-third of the entire student population. The workshops for writing have in turn inspired small-group tutorial support for other areas of the curriculum including math, science, and technology.

Many of the same questions that arose at WSU, however, are asked at CSUMB. Are tutorial workshops enough? Do some students need the traditional structure of the basic writing classroom and curriculum?

Unlike WSU, however, CSUMB is still in the process of setting up the other half of the circle—the assessment program. There are some challenges that WSU didn't face. The placement exam (known as the English Placement Test, or EPT) is produced and administered statewide by the CSU system, lacking connection to CSUMB's interdisciplinary, multicultural curriculum. The readers for the exam are drawn statewide from CSU faculty and selected high school teachers and, therefore, lack the obvious link to CSUMB's classroom teachers. Program portfolios and junior-level assessments are under development but haven't been implemented fully. These gaps need to be addressed; otherwise, a potentially successful program will develop without the feedback that keeps it honest.

Obviously, neither of these endings is really an ending. At WSU and CSUMB, as at other institutions of higher learning across the country, the argument for the presence or absence of a basic writing course will go on. Experimental mainstreaming of basic writers will spread. Some programs will last, some won't (Gleason & Soliday, 1997; Grego & Thompson, 1996; Rodby, 1996), The presence of internal and external pressures will continue, and conscientious administrators will find themselves on one side of the fence or the other. Whether an institution chooses to offer a basic writing course or not, no one should argue for the presence anywhere of an unexamined one.

9

Value-Added Studies: Defending the Circle

Richard H. Haswell

At WSU in 1990, the precipitous need to install a writing assessment examination system, described in Chapter 2, had one benefit that was appreciated even at that anxious time. Because both an entry placement and a junior "qualifying" examination had to be devised, and devised simultaneously, we had an opportunity to write into the framework of the two tests the capacity for value-added studies. Such studies were not part of the official agenda, which centered, at least sub rosa, on the enforcement of writing competency. Those of us charged with constructing the examinations were more interested, however, in curriculum and learning than in surveillance. We were aware of the value-added talk that was generally in the assessment air around the nation in 1990. With the addition of a value-added design, Washington State University's (WSU) intended examination structure would take (for better or worse) the shape of well-advertised state programs already in place in Florida, Georgia, New Jersey, and South Dakota. All those programs "emphasized the use of mandated basic skills assessment for entering freshmen, rising junior examinations, and value-added approaches to assessment" (Sims, 1992, p. 53).

In the area of undergraduate composition, value-added inquiry, or the attempt to measure educational impact over time, concerns itself with two interlocked queries. How do students change in their writing during the undergraduate years, and what effect does the curriculum have on that change? Although at WSU the undergraduate writing curriculum itself was not under any concerted attack, we had deep and abiding questions about its success in fostering and maintaining continued growth in student writing after the first-year, English-department writing course, and so did the All University Writing Committee (see Chatper 1). To both our agendas, we saw the added value of value-added studies.

So we built into the examinations several features that would assist such inquiry in the future. We made the first-year and third-year examinations comparable in writing prompt and composing situation, allowing the kind of pre-post design basic to value-added investigation (Boyer & Ewell, 1988). We gave the four rhetorical frames used in both examinations (Appendix B) a developmental shape, in the sense that the frames all applied cognitive, social, and affective frameworks that have been shown as undergoing active and qualitative change in many people during the college years. One frame asked for a resolution of several conflicting views (Basseches, 1984), one required establishing and then solving a problem (Arlin, 1984), one required assessing accuracy or truth in the representation of a complex situation (Schaie & Parr, 1981), and one required choosing pragmatically from among several approaches to an issue (Labouvie-Vief, 1982). Finally, we made both exams a point to collect information about the examinee, information that, after several years of databank collection (see Appendix C), would allow easy selection of participants in value-added studies, whether longitudinal, cross-sectional, or case-study. In short, we were accomplishing what later student-outcomes proponents would recommend, creating inside a program the framework by which the program itself could be tested (Sims, 1992, p. 118).

More important, as it turned out, the framework became another way that an undergraduate testing apparatus reaches beneficially beyond itself, beyond the outcomes that it generates, and interacts with the instructional program that it is testing.

SKEPTICISM

One must understand, however, that even in 1990 value-added studies were viewed with a good deal of skepticism. These reservations as to the worth of the value-added approach apply specifically to efforts to quantify undergraduate education and generally efforts to measure growth of writing competence. The problems raised are numerous, the solutions not readily forthcoming. Attrition of research groups is inevitable when the participants are beginning college students and the study follows them into later college years. Because the outcome criterion is improvement, there is established an uneven playing field that gives the advantage to the weakest students at the start, the strongest students having the least room to improve (it is possible for a weak student to gain more than a strong student over a given span of time yet end up still a weaker writer). Cohort effects, or the influence of particular historical years, cannot be controlled no matter how and when participants are selected. Similarly, the particular impact of writing curriculum on student writing also cannot be isolated, because other kinds of effects—other courses, extracurricular experiences, and normal human maturation—cannot be unconfounded from findings. Pre- and posttests cannot be made equivalent because they will be interpreted differently by students of different ages or by the same student at different ages. Testing instruments may be too crude to measure subtleties of writing gained over the course of a few years or too shallow to measure anything but superficial writing traits. Results cannot be generalized easily, from one year to another within an institution or from one institution to other institutions. Finally, value-added testing across college years is difficult and time-consuming. (For these and other problems, see Astin, 1993; Jacobi, Astin, & Ayala, 1987; Pascarella, 1987; Warren, 1984.) All these problems radiate from a central paradox in value-added inquiry. If the end point turns out essentially different from the start point—the effect that educationalists wish—then how can one validly be compared to the other?

It is not surprising that since 1990 the academic interest in value-added inquiry has waned rather than waxed. Few institutions have started new studies. Some, like the University of Connecticut, have seen promising initiatives fall quiescent. The few schools that have maintained studies have long made value-added investigation an integral part of the curriculum itself (e.g., Truman State University and Alverno College) or have been reluctant players in a state-mandated "rising-junior" examination system (e.g., Miami-Dade Community College in Florida). The one major exception is Harvard University, which continues a tradition of value-added undergraduate "Assessment Seminar" reports begun by Whitla in 1977 (see Light, 1992; Sommers, 1994). In composition circles, the situation is even more bleak because of a long history of resistance to empirical studies in general and to a special disaffection with pre-post gain inquiry (White, 1990b). It is likely that some of the reluctance of current compositionists to engage in value-added studies of their programs may also stem from a still-healthy underground myth that student writing skills deteriorate during college (Haswell, 1991, pp. 44–53). There is also a discouraging history of past studies that have found no statistically significant gains, either from beginning to end of a course or from first year to some point later on. No one wants to spend time and energy on an investigation that is likely to find the very outcomes one fears.

This chapter argues that those fears are poorly grounded and that value-added study of writing in college is, despite all its problems, an enterprise in which many college writing programs can well invest. The chapter shows some results of value-added studies at WSU and recommends some of the inquiry methods. It shows that coordinated exams alleviate some of the logistical problems of value-added study, especially problems of participant attrition and investigation time and costs. It does not deny that most of the methodological troubles with value-added inquiry remain but does argue that within the institutional ecology of an exam system, some of those problems can be bracketed while, at the same time, new benefits may emerge—benefits that go beyond the empirical outcomes that the study discovers.

Perhaps the bottom line is simply that a college writing program must be based on the premise that it has lasting benefit for the student (Chapter 6) and that one benefit cannot be otherwise than an improvement in the writing performance of the students. Testing difficulties should not be an excuse for a program to avoid testing one of its basic premises or reasons for being. Despite all its troubles, value-added study has the virtue of looking this premise right in the face.

LONGITUDINAL GROUP INQUIRY

There are two keys to our value-added approach, to study groups and to use a longitudinal design. The focus on groups (randomly selected) rather than on individuals fits best the nature of value-added methods and information (Ewell, 1985). In value-added studies, longitudinal research is usually preferred over cross-sectional research and, as we can illustrate, its findings are more persuasive to an institutional audience. Longitudinal study compares performance of the same student across time, whereas cross-sectional study compares different age-groups of students at the same point in time. In cross-sectional investigation, change over time must be inferred, and it cannot easily answer the charge that it may be comparing two groups different in essential ways (Rest, 1979). The charge cannot be lightly dismissed, especially in investigating students in college, where it is fairly normal for a quarter of the first-semester class to be missing by the junior year (Tinto, 1987). In longitudinal investigations, because the pre- and the postgroups are composed of the same students, change over time is more directly manifested, making interpretation of the results much more intuitive, and, therefore, better for an audience that may not be versed in inferential statistics.

In the last decade, composition study has wisely turned to longitudinal research, avoiding the problems of comparisons of groups from which earlier cross-sectional studies suffered, studies such as Gebhard, 1978; Haswell, 1986; Kitzhaber, 1963; and Whitla, 1977. Unfortunately, although longitudinal value-added studies of college students are uniquely informative, they are few in number and they investigate few students. During the first nine years of the 1990s, writing researchers saw over 10 million students complete their undergraduate degrees around the nation, and case studies recorded and combined the writing progress of a mere 25 of them beyond the span of one semester (Chiseri-Strater, 1991; Haas, 1994; Herrington & Curtis, 2000; Spack, 1997; Sternglass, 1997; Wolcott, 1994).

These studies suffer from other limitations. Because they are case studies, they suspend investigation into group traits, which forestalls application of the findings to pragmatic contexts such as the construction of academic courses or the revamping of programs. The studies tend to focus on self-selected and exceptional students—basic, English as a second language (ESL), or unusually committed students—which further limits generalizability of findings. They also take a Herculean amount of time to gather their data, at least as long as the period of change studied. In short, and in worldly terms, while all of these studies find longitudinal improvement in student writing over the college years (especially Sternglass, 1997), and sometimes locate improvement where critics and even advocates of current writing instruction might not expect it, their findings and methods lack institutional viability or political clout. If a campus faculty, central administration, board of regents, granting agency, higher-education coordinating board, or public at large asks for evidence that students improve in their writing within an undergraduate writing program—not a Philistine request, as this chapter argues—a writing-program administrator would find in these studies only a very shaky defense.

In this sense, the assessment program at WSU set itself up in 1990 to defend itself. It can use the first-year and third-year examinations as pre- and postsampling points, it can set up longitudinal comparisons because the rhetorical tasks were coordinated, and it can readily sample any number of students with the data-intake system. What this defense looks like will be illustrated shortly, with three empirical studies of WSU students, all three of which find improvement in writing from matriculation to the start of the third year. The approach, with its appeal to normal trends and group traits, may not be *de mode* in the current era of marginality, deconstruction, and situatedness. But then it does not challenge these current preoccupations. It merely offers a method that may help composition administrators navigate certain political waters. As we will see, some of those politics involve their own teachers.

THREE VALUE-ADDED STUDIES AT WSU

By 1997 there was a large pool of WSU students with first-year and junior-year essays on the shelves and personal data on computer file. The databank made selection of participants for a longitudinal study, as well as location of their writing, very expeditious. A total of 64 students were randomly chosen for the study, half males, half females—a sample large enough to make group judgments persuasive and small enough to make analysis manageable. Each student had written the argumentative impromptu essay as an entering student and then as a junior with between 60 and 65 hours of credit. Random selection of the research group started with the juniors, so the population sampled was not entering students but rather students who have lasted into their junior year. As it turned out, the random sample of 64 compared well with the population of juniors as a whole, in terms of pre-matriculation verbal skills, high school and college grades, and intended major. (For full analysis of the research, see Haswell, 2000.)

First Study

The 128 essays (two written by each student) were rated using a standard holistic procedure. The rubric gave equal weight to ideas, support, organization, diction, sentence construction, and mechanics. Raters judged typed essays blind to name of rater, academic class of writer, and knowledge of the nature of the study. Using an 8-point scale for their rating, they achieved an interrater reliability (alpha) of .86. The difference between first-year and third-year essays was highly significant (t-value 3.06, $p > .003$). The essays written when the students were juniors averaged one full point higher than their first-year essays, an increase by nearly one-fifth of the scale range that the raters made use of.

Second Study

One problem with holistic rating is that performance on subskills is lost in the final holistic score. The second study compared the same set of essays but kept subskills distinct. Readers worked with pairs of essays, knowing that they had been written by the same student, but not knowing which essay had been written earlier. They judged which of the two essays was a "little better," "obviously better," or "greatly better" than the other in terms of each subskill and then in terms of an overall judgment. The six subskills were the same ones identified in the holistic rubric: ideas, support, organization, diction, sentences, and mechanics.

Table 9.1 summarizes the results. Nearly 80 percent of the time, the student's junior essay was judged overall to be better than his or her freshman piece. Only three of the 64 students had their freshmen piece judged "obviously better" than their junior piece (none were judged "greatly better"). In terms of the subskills, the weakest improvement in the junior essays was in mechanics (with about 70 percent judged better than the freshman essays), the strongest in support (78 percent), ideas (80 percent), and diction (83 percent).

Third Study

A third study of this same sample of 64 students turned to objective, countable measures to avoid the charge that the first two studies rely on subjective impressions. It first used factor analysis to locate nine nonredundant components of change in college undergraduate writing. The factors included syntactic skills, elaboration and substantiation of ideas, coherence, establishment of logical boundaries, fluency, and vocabulary. The study then determined on nine measures which best represented the factors and, at the same time, stood as defensible, traditional, and feasible measures of writing development. Measures were chosen that had a history of recording undergraduate change toward postgraduate or professional levels of competent writing performance. When there were several equally qualified measures, the choice went to the one that lent itself to computer count via word-processing software, in the interest of cost-efficiency of the study.

Table 9.1
Comparison of Pairs of Essays, One Written as a Freshman and One as a Junior, by Washington State University Students (N = 64)

Comparison of freshman and junior essays: overall quality

78.1% of the time, the student's junior essay was judged, *overall*, to be better than her or his freshman essay.

Comparison of freshman and junior essays: *little better, obviously better, greatly better*

32.8% of the junior essays were judged a *little better* than the freshman effort
35.9% of the junior essays were judged *obviously better* than the freshman effort
9.4% of the junior essays were judged *greatly better* than the freshman effort

17.2% of the freshman essays were judged a *little better* than the junior effort
4.7% of the freshman essays were judged *obviously better* than the junior effort
0.0% of the freshman essays were judged *greatly better* than the junior effort
100.0%

Comparison of freshman and junior essays: diction, ideas, support, sentences, organization, mechanics

Diction	82.8% of junior essays better than freshman
Ideas	79.7% of junior essays better than freshman
Support	78.1% of junior essays better than freshman
Sentences	76.6% of junior essays better than freshman
Organization	71.9% of junior essays better than freshman
Mechanics	68.8% of junior essays better than freshman

Table 9.2 shows the nine quantifiable measures selected to represent these factors (one was the holistic rating of the first study) and the results when they were applied to the 128 essays. All nine measures show a change from first to third year in the direction of professional, postgraduate writing (Haswell, 1986). Only one of these shifts did not reach statistical significance. In sum, this present longitudinal study arrived at an unusually robust documentation of improvement from first-year to junior-year writing (see Haswell, 2000, for a full discussion).

Table 9.2.
Longitudinal Data on Nine Measures of Writing, Comparing the Essays of Students Composed at Their First and Junior years (N=64).

Measure	Spearman Correlated T-test (N = 64)			Comparative Performance of First and Junior Year
	T-Value	Confidence	Correlation	
M1—Mean length of sentences in words	3.06	.003	.483	Junior averaged 1.41 words longer
M2—Mean length of clause in words	2.75	.008	.399	Juniors averaged 0.64 words longer
M3—Holistic rating mean (8-point scale)	4.96	.000	.406	Juniors averaged 1.0 scale points higher
M4—Percent of words in final free modifiers	5.24	.000	.011	Juniors averaged 4.2% more of essay
M5—Percent of words in introduction	2.25	.028	.128	Junior averaged 2.9% more of essay
M6—Mean coordinated nominals per clause	1.04	.302	.415	Junior averaged 0.01 more per clause
M7—Percent of words in free modifiers	5.87	.000	.466	Junior averaged 5.3% more of essay
M8—Length of essay in words	7.21	.000	.428	Junior averaged 149 words longer
M9—Percent of words nine or more letters	2.23	.029	.030	Junior averaged 0.8% more of such words

THE PERSUASIVENESS OF VALUE-ADDED STUDY

Administrators

Together, these three studies offer evidence that WSU juniors have better writing skills than they had when they first entered the university. The evidence is not without question. Although it would be a temptation for local writing administrators to use the findings to defend existing curriculum or to recommend changes (e.g., encourage more work in mechanics), they would be wise to resist the temptation. They must take seriously White's position that a causal relationship between instructional program and writing improvement is very difficult to establish (1994a). Who can say from where the one-fifth jump in holistic rating of the impromptu arguments of WSU juniors came? On the other hand, the answer that it probably came from not one course (i.e., first-year composition) but from the discursive pressures and interplay of many courses only supports a writing curriculum, such as WSU's, which is strongly Writing Across the Curriculum (WAC) based and has required writing components in its lower-division general-education classes (see Chapter 1). Similarly, administrators could answer the statistician's caution that longitudinal designs inflate educational gains with effects from maturation (Pascarella & Terenzini, 1991) with the argument that the curriculum evidently is interacting positively with student maturation to have generated such a group-wide advance. A writing administrator can still send the findings up to higher administration with pride and some good reason to be proud.

Indeed, higher administrators may be the group most readily persuaded by the methods and the results. It is likely that they would approve of the empirical nature of the studies and be gratified to hear of outcomes generalizable to the majority of nontransfer first-semester junior students, studies with a selection of measures partly based upon a factor analysis, with statistically significant outcomes on most of the measures selected and with measures and the direction of change they record positively identified with successful postgraduate writing performance by previous research.

Administrators might also be pleased with the relatively low cost of these studies (an estimate of total hours for the third study, easily the most time-consuming, comes to about 180) and with the knowledge that the efficiency was in part attached to an initiative they had earlier supported. While higher administrators would acknowledge the methodological problems in the findings, they would also sense their argumentative force, which switches the burden of proof to the other camp. They have evidence that instruction is working at WSU—let someone else try to find evidence that other factors caused these outcomes. Few administrators would hesitate to report these findings to governing entities such as regents or state coordinating boards. (That, in fact, is exactly the route taken at WSU by a report of these three studies.)

Writing Faculty

The political use of value-added findings is neither something of which to be ashamed nor is it entirely alien to the way writing faculty will respond. As Jacobi, Astin, and Ayala note, teachers are apt to erect "political barriers" to a value-added finding when it threatens their status quo, barriers often taking the form of a critique of research methodology (1987, p. 11). With writing teachers, the status quo may be a course long taught or a belief in backsliding juniors that inspires them to teach upper-division courses, and the critique may be that numbers can't be trusted. On the other hand, teachers may distrust these findings on perfectly valid grounds. They might note the artificiality of using testing situations to produce writing for study. They might caution that students should not be judged on timed, impromptu performance, which may be their worst writing (Sternglass, 1997, pp. 144–151). They might also suspect that countable indicators such as sentence length or even holistic score, real enough for the analyzer, are dubious to the teacher because they are leveling abstractions that usurp the kind of concrete rhetorical distinctions used by writers at work. And they might certainly be skeptical or befuddled how the underlying realities of growth in writing expertise, or the impact of writing instruction, or even the quality of written products could be detected, in the third study, by such esoteric measures as mean clause length or percent of total words devoted to a final free modification. Intuitively, teachers are likely to echo White's criticism of value-added studies in general, that they tend to be "trivial, difficult to make sense of, and peripheral to most instructional purposes" (1984, p. 10).

There are reasonble answers to these reservations (see Haswell, 2000), but for teachers of writing, and for thinking administrators who would like to be convinced that the measures used to support value-added allegations are meaningful, perhaps the most compelling way to legitimize these three value-added studies would be to call up the original essays as witness. The empirical measures of the third study, alledgedly trivial, could even be used to select examples. Teachers, for instance, could be asked to compare the following two essays written by a student whose change from first- to third-year writing on the nine measures is close to the normative change for the whole group, including an increase in average sentence length by over four words, an increase in length of essay by 142 words, and a rise in holistics score of over one full point on the 8-point scale.

Here is the first year essay, a response to a paragraph by Barry Lopez describing a professional wolf hunter:

> When I think of a sport I think of hard physical work that is not only exhausting to your body, but also to your mind. When I think of a sport I usually think of basketball, soccer, football, or tennis,

but it's very rare that I think of hunting as a sport. Hunting has been around for years, just as basketball has, and it can be physical to both your body and your mind, same with basketball. Hunting even has an object, to kill the animal, and in basketball it's put the ball in the basket. Well then, why do some people say that hunting is not a sport? This has been a question asked for many years "is hunting a sport?"

I feel that Barry Lopez did a great job of express his opinion in his essay. He took us right into the mind of a hunter and we read what he is feeling when he kills an animal. He described how it was not the kill, "it was the moment when the blast of the shotgun hit the wolf and flattened him." He said that the wolf fought back till the end. The hunter spoke of the animal with high respect because he believed that now that he had seen this 400 times he would be like the wolf and never quit until the last minute. The hunter spoke of the animal with high regards yet he wanted to kill him? Lopez's opinion of hunting was that he thought it was strange that you could kill something you highly respected and wanted to be. It's like killing yourself.

I would of wanted to say the say thing Lopez wanted to say to the guide. I don't see how people can see killing another animal as a way of life. Many people have different views then Lopez or me, some see hunting as a way of relaxing, such as I see basketball. They feel that there are so many animals, whats one less? Other people see hunting as a way to survive. Not as much anymore, but there was a time when hunting was how you ate dinner at night. All three of these views have arguments that back them up.

I think that how a person thinks of hunting, as a sport or not, is their personal opinion. I just hope that the hunters take responsibility of "their sport" and are not endangering animals.

For comparison, here is the junior essay, on a paragraph by David Guterson in support of home schooling.

Some people around the world feel very strongly about having their children taught at home. Whether it be because of religion, tradition or disbelief in the school system these people feel that their children will benefit form at-home teaching. David Guterson is one of these people. David and his wife teach their 5, 7, & 9 year old boys at home because "homeschooling is a life their family likes." Even though David feels this way about his own children he is a high school teacher at the local high school. After reading, I became very interested in why the Gutersons feel so strongly about teaching their children at home and why Mr. Guterson is a highschool teacher himself?

David and his wife have explained, in the paragraph, that they teach their children in a non-competative, non-stress environment. The boys are taught that learning is not separate from life. They also feel that learning should never stop; it should start when the boys wake up and continue through dinner, if necessary. I got the impression, from reading what David Guterson wrote, that he and his wife like to teach the boys because they feel that only they know how the boys learn and they want the boys learning experience to be theirs and not some strangers method of learning. David mentioned that he felt that the boys education was "tuned to their hormones" and that it was "theirs." I feel that this is a very selfish way of teaching his children because an education is something that is to be shared with everyone. David is a very intelligent man to be bale to teach his children all they need to know at home, along with all that the neighbors children need to know at his high school. Mr Guterson must feel that his method of teaching and his information is all that <u>any</u> child should learn, that is why he also teaches at the high school. The fact that Mr. Guterson teaches at the high school is probably beneficial to his children because he can hopefully bring home new knowledge and modern teaching methods.

Since Mr. Guterson is a certified teacher I am suprised he does not know what his kids are missing out on. I am an education major here at Washington State and I am taught that their is much more to learning than just facts and memorization. There is a social aspect to learning that is very important. David and his wife are holding their children back from the social aspect of going to school. The children will never know what its like to be away from your parents for a whole day, or to meet a new friend. It is also not practical to have all the boys learning together with the different ages. Children can also teach other children at school or modeling or peer teaching.

Teaching children at home is a subject that has many pro's and con's. I believe that David and his wife have their reasons and are teaching their children well yet they need to really need to look at what the children are missing. The school system in the United States is not perfect but just think what life would be like if we didn't have one?

Even non-English personnel can see the difference. The most striking change is in the quality of the ideas. In his earlier essay, poised on the brink of college, the student lets slip inanities ("Hunting has been around for years, just as basketball has"), takes up a question with no stated purpose ("Is hunting a sport?"), and after two more paragraphs summarizing the quoted passage, declines to try resolving the issue ("how a person thinks of hunting, as a sport or not, is their personal opinion"). As a junior, the student first hones in on a contradiction within the author's position and, in subsequent paragraphs, offers a rationale for it (David Guterson is such a good teacher he wants to make sure his own children receive the best education) and a critique of it (Guterson is, unwittingly, depriving his children of learning through social interaction with other children, through modeling or peer teaching).

It would not be hard to show that this improvement in thinking accompanies improvement in other rhetorical skills. As a junior, the tone is more formal and under control, the vocabulary more exact. Note the verbs "benefit," "interested," and "teach," whereas the first-year verbs are restricted to "think," "be," "have," "say," and "ask." The logical categories are more carefully drawn ("religion, tradition or disbelief in the school system"), the given information more elaborate ("Some people," "their 5, 7, & 9 year old boys,"), and the sentence length more artfully varied. The conveyance of the contradiction with a coordinated final free modifier clause in the last sentence has an especially sophisticated ring to it.

When students make large gains in the two years—and there are a number of the 64 whose improvement is little short of astonishing—a face-to-face comparison of first-year and junior-year effort is very compelling. Here is just the introductory parts of the essays written by a student whose holistic gain was three full points. First-year introduction:

"Time waits for no man." Life can be described as the time one spends on our ever changing Earth. As one grows, he or she becomes more knowledgable of things and events in his or her lifetime. Many people see age as a sign of decrepity. I see age as an instrument of knowledge. As man gets older, he realizes the importances of life. He often reflects on his past experiences. This is not a sign of decrepity. It is a sign of a generation of history revisited. It is knowledge.

Junior-year introduction:

The issue presented in Postman's article has provided society with a weighty dilemma for years. Students tend to be shaped socially and culturally by the images shown on television. Postman implies that advertisements on television have molded students into people who are entirely dependent upon the television media's portrayal of life to achieve acceptance in mainstream society. Also, he believes students find it more difficult to read a piece of writing than to have images placed in front of them to achieve similar results. Postman feels educators are in continual competition with television to gain student's attention. In addition, Postman tends to agree that advertisements are preeminent factors in developing students' socialization skills.

I, personally, would include more factual data and statistics to solidify my argument concerning this issue.

The first-year introduction may have the appeal of terse expression and an interesting idea, but the junior succeeds in many more ways, in its classic introductory shape, its authoritative phrasing ("weighty dilemma," "preeminent factors"), its expanded grasp of complex categories ("people who are entirely dependent upon the television media's portrayal of life to achieve acceptance in mainstream society"), its control of cohesion, its strong verbs, its varied sentence length, its shift in focus from background to essay topic, its careful logical restrictions ("mainstream society," "shaped socially and culturally"), and its nonredundant coverage of points—all while producing an essay more than twice as long.

In working with writing faculty (cross-disciplinary or otherwise), one strategy will especially help turn resistance to value-added studies into open discussion and program enhancement. That is to make the student writing elicited by the studies a topic for faculty workshops. All kinds of knotty issues can be put on the table. The concern over using impromptu compositions to test improvement in writing skill, for instance, may dissipate on seeing students actually improve in unrehearsed and largely unrevised writing. The issue of junior backsliding can be openly discussed and illustrated. In the WSU studies, 15 of the 64 writers received a lower holistic rating on their junior essay. Yet as Clark (1987) found in her case study of six juniors with first- and third-year impromptu essays, most of these 15 regressing students had written better than average essays in their first year. It is possible that students who write comparatively well on entering college do not find in the curriculum as much of a motivation to improve their writing in their first two years of courses. At the faculty workshop, it would be important to discuss the presence of regression because, among other implications, it helps teachers read the longitudinal record as partial evidence of programmatic outcomes, not purely as a trail left by some inevitable developmental migration uninfluenced by teachers or courses of study. Whatever the topics of discussion, the advantage of using a longitudinal group design for the studies will become apparent. Data from the randomly selected group will show where individual student writing is eccentric and not representative, and direct comparison of the same student's writing at two points in time will keep intuitive obvservations about change in student writing concrete and grounded.

Other Institutions

At first glance, value-added studies seem the least likely candidates for transportation from one institution to another. It's true that the three small studies reported here support the general-education program at WSU, and not in trivial ways. The random sampling of students is straightforward; the description of writing improvement includes aspects of writing skill that cover a range of features; and the high majority of outcomes show solid levels of statistical confidence. But, as with all but the most complex value-added study (Astin, 1993; Pascarella & Terenzini, 1991), the findings evidenced no direct causal path from particular writing courses or even from a university-wide, general-education writing system. Causes of the writing improvement from first to third year remain as obscure as they were. Furthermore, if value-added investigation doesn't much help make sense of the curricular situation at WSU, how will it make sense elsewhere? The central benefits of value-added study emphasized in this chapter—confirmation of existing practices, political leverage, in-service discussion—are site specific, and may not extend to other situations. There is even no guarantee that replication of these measures with programs at other schools will generate the same positive outcomes as at WSU, with its robust interdisciplinary writing requirements in all lower-division general-education courses.

This is not to argue, however, that other institutions should forgo value-added studies. Other writing programs have their unique virtues. Contrary to received knowledge, the evidence from the literature is that studies with value-added shape can be devised sucessfully to document those virtues. Most of the investigations that have recorded no evidence of improvement in writing across the undergraduate years or, worse, evidence of regression (e.g., Curry & Hager, 1987; Graham, 1987; Kitzhaber, 1963; Scharton, 1989), have fairly obvious flaws in design that can account for the discouraging findings. Where studies are longitudinal or use carefully matched cross-sectional groups, they record gain (Haswell, 1986; Light, 1992; Sternglass, 1997; Whitla, 1977). Sommers (1994) even found improvement in writing over the sophomore year (despite its notorious "slump")—found it at Harvard with its strong second-year "teaching fellow" program, in which students receive many essay assignments along with writing-tutorial advice in subject-based courses. All it might take is a small but steady stream of value-added studies around the nation to eradicate the common belief that skills gained in first-year composition are largely lost not long after students leave the course (e.g., Sosnoski, 1997, p. 171: "With luck, an improvement or two survive").

One part of value-added studies, however, can be transferred with profit from one institution to another. That is method. Just as Chapter 8 recommended a theory for transport, this chapter recommends certain research methods: longitudinal design, groups randomly selected at junior year or later, collection of writing and data for later use, coordination of writing exams when they are given at separate points, and creation of prompts with a developmental cast. Were such methods used elsewhere, then findings could be compared. With comparisons of findings between institutions will come an improvement of interpretation of findings within an institution. Certainly without replications, without contrasting outcomes from other sites, the use of the local findings will not only remain localized but will remain poorly interpretable even there. Designed first to convince local administrators and to instruct instructors, value-added studies will become more convincing and informative to everyone the more they have similar outcomes with which to compare and conjecture. Just as local writing tests become useful beyond the testing itself by circling back to instruction, so local research will acquire a second life locally as it is applied elsewhere.

10

Validation: Part of the Circle

Richard H. Haswell

Validation of an academic program is any effort to supply evidence that any part of the program is working. That definition is broad as a barn. In this chapter, however, I want to argue that the validation of writing programs should be broad. This is especially true of validation of programs such as the one at Washington State University (WSU), programs that are open, complex, and generously based—barnlike, not to put too fine a point on it. It follows that a persuasive validation will use multiple methods of investigation. "Multimethod validation" is a good strategy with writing programs for several reasons. In part it is good not only because it takes varied outcomes from a validation study to better a varied program, but also because the act of investigation itself becomes a part of the program, and it is not wise to enhance a complex structure simplistically. Just as assessment of student writing circles back to enhance the instruction of students, validation of a program circles back into the ongoing activities of the program. As Chapter 6 points out, self-study itself is a creative or formative step. This is why—my final point in the chapter—the best validators of a writing program may not be outside reviewers with limited knowledge but the administrators of the program with inside knowledge.

MULTIPLE INQUIRY IN THE VALIDATION OF
WRITING PROGRAMS

Multimethod approaches (as they are called by experts in program evaluation) have seen few applications in the small province of writing-program validation. Witte and Faigley (1983) call for a "confluence" of qualitative and quantitative methods to evaluate the complex interactions of whole writing programs. So does White (1989), although his reason is more in the spirit of program defense than program enhancement: "You will measure everything possible, in the hope that something may possibly work out" (p. 204). More recently Scharton (1996) has called for triangulation designs in the assessing of student writing and Hughes (1996) for "multiple methods" in the evaluation of Writing Across the Curriculum (WAC) programs. However, actual mulitmethodological studies of writing programs are hard to come by.

Why is this so? One reason may be that in composition studies, theory of the social apparatuses that support instruction in writing, such as writing programs or formal writing tests, has not advanced as rapidly as theory of the writing itself. Consider a test of writing. Today, writing is widely assumed to be a social act, contextual, deeply embedded, even constructed; however, the testing of writing does not enjoy the same currency. It is still widely assumed that language tests measure an underlying capability or "aptitude" for language use. So with indirect tests of writing, the standard test validation is still internal, through item analysis, because the main question is how well the items on the test work in discriminating among degrees of that assumed aptitude among test-takers. With direct testing of writing, say a portfolio of writings, item analysis is impossible, but still the pieces of the portfolio often are taken to reflect fragments or aspects of some internal writing capability, and assessment theorists still search for ways that raters can agree independently on one rate for the whole portfolio (e.g., Nystrand, et al., 1993).

In a laudable effort to bring our conception of formal writing-test validation up to date, Camp defines writing assessment "as a set of contextualized performances and procedures" (1996, p. 139). Let's be more specific and define an institutionalized writing test as a social apparatus that applies a nomenclature (specialized and provisional language) to classify and label people for certain public uses. By this definition, it is largely irrelevant whether or not a score (e.g., "87th percentile" on the SAT Verbal) actually measures some universal writing aptitude. What is important is that the score operates as a bit of language with useful social effects, temporarily attached to a person who has been through the complex institutional routine that determined the label ("took the SATs") and then used it for various social ends ("accepted into Kansas State").

Now once we take a writing test as a social apparatus producing a nomenclature for public use and then ask how should such a process itself be tested, major contrasts appear with validation practices of 25 years ago. Suddenly everything is problematic, everything under question. If the apparatus is social, then what (fallible) humans run it for what (debatable) ends and (more or less) how well, and how do the (vulnerable) people who are labeled by it feel (they think) about the process? If the product of the apparatus is a nomenclature, that is, a language system constructed by professionals for specialized and temporary ends, then how well do its labels match up with performance of people in the world outside the test? If the nomenclature is also a classification, then what is the value system that underlies it? If the nomenclature is provisional, then how long before the historical motives for the original construction change, or how long before the labels drift out of use, attached as they are to people who are also changing? Finally, and most crucially, what *are* the uses that are made of this labeling, by the people who constructed the test, by the people who run the apparatus, by the institutions that use the labels, by the people who acquire the labels? If the essential question of test validation is whether the test works for society, then the overriding issue pertains to public benefit and not to universal "aptitude" for writing or to internal validity of testing, both of which in a social apparatus are provisionally constructed just like everything else and serve only as long as they serve the ends of the apparatus.

For validation, one upshot of all of this seems fairly evident. Once the notion of a universal or "true" competence in language is written out of our definition of "writing examination" and the notion of fluid social ends written in, then we can no longer be satisfied with a single-measure follow-up of the examination. We commit ourselves to multiple-measure validation. All this is to repeat the current dictum, that language acts are social acts, but it adds the perhaps not so common but still commonsense assertion that writing tests themselves are language acts. So essentially a test of a writing test should be no different from a test of writing, which evaluation experts have been saying for decades requires, as a socially embedded activity, multiple samples and multiple readers. Another way of putting this is to say that the validation of any writing *test* is really a validation of a writing *program*. The program stands as the first-level social matrix in which the test act is embedded. For models of validation, then, writing-program validators might well turn to program evaluation.

Indeed, if they do not they will continue to look outdated (Moss, 1998). Within the discipline of program evaluation, this last quarter century has seen no approach receiving more attention than multimethodological ones (for useful syntheses, see Brewer & Hunter 1989; Fiske, 1982; Mark & Shotland, 1987). Program evaluation offers writing-test validators four powerful rationales for multiple inquiry:

1. *Use.* Focus on social utility pushes validation beyond just some alternate method to supplant traditional quantitative designs. For any single validation, a variety of different methods are needed because any testing apparatus and any educational program is composed hierarchically of different people with different needs and, therefore, with different uses for the results. No one study is going to satisfy all stakeholders, and no one stakeholder is going to find useful all validation studies, unless it is the chief administrator of the assessment program (a point to which I will return).

2. *Perspective.* Partly because different people in a program have different needs, they will work out of different perspectives. Yet, any one validation measure tends to privilege the perspectives of certain people and suppress the perspectives of others. Testing the predictive power of the SAT Verbal by correlating it with college grades privileges the teachers who give the grades. (It privileges them because it does not test the validity of the grades.) Even the most carefully constructed survey of stakeholder attitudes privileges the perspective of the researcher, who has to make decisions about survey questions and target groups.

3. *Cross-Checking.* Inquiry is "triangulated" in multimethod validation so that the blindness or bias of one study may be illuminated, corrected, or balanced by the angle of view of other studies. In a validation of the SAT Verbal with college grades, as I have said, the value system of college teachers is uncontrolled for. Those values could be tested in second study, a holistic appraisal of end-of-course writing with program administrators as evaluators. Because teachers and administrators may share the same biases, an exit survey of student self-assessment of their writing might help balance information. I am unaware of any writing-test validation designed to reap the advantages of a cross-checked or "multiplistic" design.

4. *Probing.* Multiple studies are needed in writing-test validation because no one answer is ever complete. Validation studies of something as empirically squirmy as a placement examination cannot be expected to prove anything. Rather they probe something. They bring back partial returns from partial samples that must be synthesized with samples from parallel but not exactly replicating probes. Two of the most direct values of multimethod validation is the way it augments the interpretability of findings and deconstructs the certainty of superficial interpretations (Mark & Shotland, 1987).

With its emphasis on pragmatic use, participant perspectives, cross-checking, and probing, multiple inquiry has a large potential for writing-test and writing-program validation.

In a sense *Beyond Outcomes* is an instance of multiple inquiry. The studies reported in Chapters 2, 4, 6, 8, and 9 certainly scrutinize the WSU writing program from different and sometimes clashing perspectives, and studies in Chapters 11 and 12 add even more radically divergent views. The present chapter tightens the inquiry, however. It focuses on the two placement examinations and somewhat self-reflectively explores how the activity of inquiry itself operates as a motivating part of the whole writing program. I do not present the following validation history as a model of multiple-inquiry method, which does not recommend conducting too many studies without careful planning (Mark & Shotland, 1987). Moss (1998) provides a critique of the following studies *as* a validation project. Here I am not centrally intent on showing how multimethod validation might defend WSU's writing tests. Mainly I am interested in the ways multiple studies *function:* how angling in on one part of a writing program illuminates that part as a social apparatus, with connections to the whole writing program and with uses that serve individuals throughout a university (and beyond) in complex and often conflicting ways—and how the act of conducting the studies serves similar varied ends.

STAKEHOLDERS

There is no doubt that writing tests at WSU serve a variety pack of ends: to place students in writing courses, to support a WAC initiative, to support a general-education reform of the undergraduate curriculum, to send a message to prospective employers of degree-holders, to soothe faculty, to help fulfill a mandate for outcomes assessment from the state higher-education coordinating board, and to serve as a form of writing instruction in itself. Stakeholders in the program are numerous. Potentially benefiting are not only the students, teachers, and administrators of the writing program but also teachers across campus (who assign and evaluate the course submissions for the junior portfolio), faculty serving as raters (who feel committed to a procedure, the effects of which they can see around campus), local administrators (who want to see clear benefit for their majors and their faculty), central administrators (who backed the general-education reform and the WAC initiatives and the tests themselves), the Board of Regents (who approved the testing package under pressure from the state coordinating board), and the designers of the tests (who see implemented a large-scale testing scheme with new and risky features). Each of these people is asking of the program, is it working? They ask, of course, from their particular perspective. I organize the following selection of validation studies and results around these stakeholders, faithful to my working definition of a writing test as an apparatus whose final end is public use.

Students

The immediate use of placement exams is to put students into courses that prove beneficial to them. From the vantage point of students who place into basic courses, the benefit may be hard to see; but that particular student opinion is subject to change, and it will take more than one inquiry to see it. Four weeks after being placed by the first-year placement examination into the one-hour tutorial (English 102), 39 percent of the students thought the exam was not accurate in their case; yet, at the end of the semester, less than 10 percent of the students believed the course had not been beneficial to them. Similarly with the junior portfolio, a telephone survey of examinees found that although all students awarded "pass with distinction" thought the exam accurately reflected their performance, the numbers drop to 70 percent for those receiving a simple "pass" and to 35 percent for those receiving "needs work." Yet an exit survey of students in the upper-division, one-hour tutorial (General Education 302), into which most needs-work students are placed, showed nearly all of them pleased with the course and more than a few stating that it was the most beneficial writing course of their college careers (Haswell, 1995).

Student opinion about their own progress in writing, of course, may not be borne out by their writing performance. Another inquiry took advantage of the fact that in the first-year writing courses, students submit a midsemester folder, which is rated "pass," "questionable pass," or "fail" according to end-of-the-semester standards. Students in the basic course (English 100) have their folders mixed in with the others. The assessment of midsemester folders (Table 10.1) helps support the validity of the placement test. Students placed into regular composition received fewer fails and questionable passes than did students placed into regular composition with the tutorial, who received fewer fails and questionable passes than did students placed into basic writing. Further support for the placement exam comes from the fact that the few students who enrolled in regular composition without having taken the placement test had a worse midsemester record than that of students in the tutorial (see Chapter 8 for further analysis).

Student self-assessment and exam results can sometimes be quite at odds and need to be cross-checked. For instance, in telephone interviews many international students who had earned a needs-work on the junior portfolio said that they had felt doomed to failure because they knew that nonnative speakers almost always fail. Exam results (Table 10.2) easily dispel this myth. Nonnative writers who began their postsecondary education at Washington State pass at exactly the same rate as do native writers. Combined with other probes, the figures in Table 10.2 enhance—revise and complicate—interpretation of the writing program in other ways, as Chapter 6 notes.

Table 10.1

Results of Freshman Composition (English 101) Midsemester Writing Folder with Placed Students

Placement History	Pass (%)	Questionable (%)	Fail (%)
Placed in regular English 101	78	9	13
Placed in English 101 with the one-hour tutorial	63	15	22
Placed in English 100	18	32	50
Did not take the placement examination	58	14	27

By way of another instance, some WSU administrators would like to believe that as a group, transfer students write worse than nontransfer students. Again the evidence suggests that this is not the case, not at least with native speakers, whose performance on the exam shows little difference according to transfer status. As Table 10.2 shows, it is second-language *transfers* who show questionable preparation for the exam; however, about 80 percent of the interviewed transfer students, both native and nonnative speakers, said they felt at a disadvantage because they had been poorly informed about the exam and had had trouble finding teachers to sign off on their papers, some of which originated from other schools. Add to this another twist: 93 percent of second-language transfer students felt that their portfolio rating reflected their performance on the exam accurately, compared with 67 percent of nontransfer, second-language writers. Together the various validation probes converge to show the transfer ESL students very much at risk and very conflicted about the exam and diverge to show that the kinds of assistance already in place for this group, outlined in Chapter 6, will not be simple.

One form of assistance would be to inform second-language students of the results of this validation before they take the test. Comparison of

Table 10.2

Results of the Junior-Level Portfolio Examination According to Language and Transfer Status

Language Status	Transfer Status	Pass (%)	Pass with Distinction (%)	Needs Work (%)
Non-native writer	Non-transfer	81	02	17
Non-native writer	Transfer	62	03	36
Native writer	Non-transfer	81	12	07
Native writer	Transfer	81	10	09

registration for the first-year placement exam with that for the junior exam finds a large number of international students who place into Washington State University's ESL sequence, yet who then do not enroll for it; instead, some years later they register for the junior examination with transfer credit, often from a two-year college writing course taken during the summer. It would be a productive act of advising to show these freshmen the performance distributions above, which demonstrate transfer students performing much worse than students who had undertaken the ESL sequence of writing courses at Washington State.

One of the less appreciated uses of validation studies, in fact, is to recycle the findings themselves back into the test program. With the WSU junior portfolio, even a simple distribution of test outcomes could be extremely useful to students trying to decide how much effort to put into preparation: pass with distinction, 11.5 percent; simple pass, 79.4 percent; and needs work, 9.1 percent. The special language, "pass with distinction," is translated for students by the 11.5 percent, a figure that very well could validate a student's striving for a goal that seems attainable. Students later preparing for the junior portfolio face a special quandary: should they wait to take the exam until they have better papers to submit? They might find informative a breakdown of performance by academic hours earned when the student took the exam. The results in Table 10.3 would show students that the answer is not simple. Taking the exam early does not put them at risk, but waiting a semester or two beyond the recommended time (60 to 75 hours) is risky, except for the slim minority of students who wait until their senior year (which has its own special risk). Administrators of the exam, of course, may not like all of these figures nor like having them accessible to students.

Teachers of Writing Courses

A placement instrument works for teachers when it puts into their courses only students who fall within instructional parameters imagined by the teachers. Yet there is a natural tendency for teachers to resist placement procedures per se. It is difficult to convince them that they can't bring along any student who ends up in their section. At WSU this allegiance to students surfaced when teachers of the first-year writing courses resisted a request from placement administrators to check their rolls for students who had placed in one course and registered for another. Such teacher attitudes question the results of an end-of-semester survey that otherwise appears to support the placement test. Regular-composition teachers judged only 4 percent of their students misplaced, basic teachers only 3 percent, and tutorial teachers only 6 percent. This possible teacher bias should be checked with other probes. The relative success of students on the midsemester folder reading (see Table 10.1) argues that the placements stratified the writing skill of students roughly in line with the var-

Table 10.3
Credit Hours Earned When Taking the Junior Examination and Results

Hours Earned	Percent of N	Simple Pass (%)	Pass with Distinction (%)	Needs Work (%)
Up to 60 hours	23	75.7	17.2	07.1
61-75 hours	42	79.2	12.4	08.4
76-90 hours	22	79.8	09.2	11.0
91-105 hours	10	77.3	13.3	09.3
Over 106 hours	03	76.3	23.7	00.0

ious courses. End-of-semester grades add further support, because they showed withdrawals, in both the regular and the basic courses, declining from the level of years before the placement exam was installed.

Further cross-check, nonetheless, may add information. After all, because all of these probes operate within the milieu of the first-year writing program, they may share bias. What happens to this support for the exam after students leave that milieu? With the databank, it was easy to take a quick look at this issue by correlating performance on the first-year placement with performance on the junior exam. Rankings were formed from the outcomes of the two exams: first-year placements were ranked exemption highest, English 101 second, English 101 plus English 102 third, and English 100 fourth; portfolio placements were ranked pass with distinction highest, simple pass second, one-hour needs work third, and three-hour needs work fourth. The correlation (Spearman rank) was significant ($p<.05$) and positive, but very low: .24. There is not much argument here for the lasting validity of the first-year placement. Rather the argument is for the presence of the junior exam, because it seems to elicit a quite different writing performance, perhaps to tap into a writing skill that over two years has changed with students in different ways.

Three parallel probes into subgroups, however, do show some predictive value of the first-year placement.

1. As we have already seen, nonnative writers who evaded their placement into the university ESL writing sequence performed far worse on the junior exam than did any other group.

2. Students who are exempted from first-year courses by the placement exam—around 1 percent of exam takers—do exceptionally well on the junior portfolio. None of them earned needs work, and exactly half of them earned pass with distinction, compared to 11 percent for the population as a whole. Upper-division teachers often

aver that some of their worst writers were exempted as freshmen, a belief that these figures document as largely a myth.

3. The value-added studies reported in the previous chapter show over three-quarters of a random selection of juniors writing impromptu better than they did as entering students. All in all, the disparate findings about the longitudinal performance of groups of students may converge at one useful generalization for writing teachers, that writing change during the first two years of college may be generally one of improvement, but it also is deeply nonuniform across student groups.

Teachers of Other Courses

Across the WSU campus teachers had been asked to play a difficult role in the new junior placement process. They had to reread and evaluate papers brought in by their students, either rejecting the papers as unsuitable for submission for the portfolio or rating them as "acceptable" or as "exceptional" ("within the top 10-percent of student performance on the particular assignment"). Their problems with this nomenclature quickly became apparent when during the first year of the exam they handed out the "top 10 percent" exceptional rating at a 43 percent clip. Here validation took a nontradition form: a workshop of teachers across campus who had been signing off on the largest number of student submissions. Many problems were voiced during the session. The term exceptional was too loose, criteria for evaluation drifted from teacher to teacher, and responsibility for the evaluation was not clearly perceived (could teaching assistants sign off on papers in large classes?). Comparable to other stakeholder groups in the program, however, the teachers showed complex and self-contradictory perpspectives, as Chapter 12 will detail. Although the workshop participants highly supported the general format and goals of the junior portfolio, a great many other teachers had hardly heard of it.

Administrators

Heads of departments and programs, of course, might not support the examination if they felt that it was taking up too much of their faculty's time, but they might support it if it provided them with useful information about their programs. Here validation could well have taken the form of report-and-response, though little of this has been done. For a while department chairs were sent a list of the teachers most active in signing off on portfolios, largely so that credit for the work would return to the teachers. There was no response to this list from the chairs. More response could have been expected had they been sent Table 10.4, which orders departments by the percent of their declared majors who received needwork placements.

Table 10.4

Performance on the Junior Examination According to Declared Major

Major	N	Pass (%)	Pass with Distinction (%)	Needs Work (%)
Communication Broadcasting	64	91	6	3
English General	157	73	24	3
Communications General	349	86	10	4
Teaching and Learning	385	85	11	4
Communications, Advanced	104	86	10	4
Environmental Science	77	84	12	4
Nursing	162	84	12	4
Biology	209	80	16	4
Agricultural Econonomics	44	86	9	5
Humanities General Studies	41	80	15	5
Pharmacy	74	81	14	5
Political Science	116	79	16	5
Architecture	74	84	10	6
Agribusiness	46	83	11	6
Natural Resource Sciences/Wildlife Management	47	79	15	6
Psychology	331	83	11	6
Human Nutrition and Foods	47	87	7	7
Animal Science	104	81	12	7
Foreign Languages	58	74	19	7
Civil and Environmental Engineering	130	84	8	8
Speech and Hearing Sciences	83	81	11	8
Mechical Engineering	117	85	7	8
History	114	75	17	8
Zoology	102	77	14	9
All Exams (Mean)	6747	81	10	9
Criminal Justice	218	82	9	9
Sociology	191	84	7	9
Recreation and Leisure Studies	77	87	04	9
Microbiology	61	72	18	10
Human Development	157	80	10	10
BA Marketing	209	85	5	10
Construction Management	37	86	3	11
Sociology General Studies	198	82	7	11
Interior Design	59	81	7	12
Business general	286	82	6	12
Horticulture	39	77	10	13
Exercise Science	45	80	7	13
Fine Arts	68	80	7	13
BA Management	195	81	6	13
Applied Merchandise and Textiles	53	85	2	13
BA Accounting	231	81	6	13
BA International Business	87	78	8	14
Undeclared	91	79	7	14
Electrical Engineering	95	68	15	17
Hotel and Restaurant Administration	264	79	3	18
BA Information Systems	69	77	1	22
Computer Science	36	67	8	25
BA Finance	169	69	4	27

The figures are provocative. The range in performance of major is quite broad, even within units. The College of Business, for instance, might well take notice that all their majors score below the universal mean, and that 22 percent of their information-systems majors and 27 percent of their finance majors earned needs work, compared to only 10 percent of their marketing majors and 13 percent of management and accounting majors. Similarly, chairs could also use a ranking by department on the mean credit hours that students had earned when they stood for the exam, because they are concerned about time-to-graduation of their majors. Such a ranking, which appeared in the third validation report (Bonnema, Haswell, & Norris, 1997), shows substantial differences among departments, with nursing and zoology students, for example, taking the junior examination at an average of 68 hours credit and communications and finance students at an average of 80 hours.

The reality is that for validation such data sets are not useful until they are interpreted by the parties involved. The chair of the Finance Department, whose students seem to come out poorly on both of these measurements, might argue that the kind of writing tested by the junior portfolio is not relevant to finance majors, or that the department has large numbers of international and transfer students who have good reasons to delay taking the exam. Then again, the chair's dean might not agree. An illustrative case in point occurred when I presented some of the portfolio results of Education majors to a teacher professional advisory board. I showed a list of all courses in the School of Education that had been the origin of papers submitted to the examination. It was a very unevenly distributed list: 26 courses were represented by only 1 submission, 17 more by only 2 to 4 submissions, 8 more by 5 to 9 submissions; then 1 course had 19 and another course had 54. Several members of the Advisory Board were disturbed, seeing that the bulk of submissions came from only 10 courses or a fifth of the School's offerings. The dean of Education, who was more aware of faculty workloads and assignment of faculty support, pointed out how many different courses apparently required extended writing. The chair of Teaching and Learning expressed pleasure that most of the courses listed were in her department. I consider a meeting such as this as test validation, because it elicited perceived value of the test from several different perspectives.

Higher Administrators

By way of validation for the testing program, higher administration might look at several distinct outcomes, among them costs of maintaining a new system and compliance with any new general-education requirements for graduation. Because exam administrators could show the provost that student fees for the two exams were steadily reducing the initial start-up debts and that student subscription for the exams was growing pretty much as expected, both verbal and financial support for the program from the central administration continued. That support, of course, is a kind of validation in itself. Seeking validation from higher administration, however, is a risky business, as Chapter 13 illustrates at length.

Board of Regents

At the end of the second year of implementation of the junior exam, I reported on its progress to the Board of Regents at their semiannual campus meeting. Again, I construe the encounter as another validation probe. As might be expected, the regents, who function sometimes as a public relations board, were favorably impressed by the moderate but not insignificant rate at which upper-division students were required to take more writing. They were also interested in the list of departments whose students had performed exceptionally well (animal science, biology, English, electrical engineering, history, pharmacy, political science), perhaps because it contained some entries from the sciences and professional schools. If this response sounds typical, even stereotypical, this particular board of regents resisted easy categorization. They approved most openly two outcomes of the testing program that had gone largely unappreciated by other constituents. One was the fact that to date the corps of raters had come from 29 different academic units, and the other was that after two years of implementation, students had submitted papers from 616 different courses around campus, taught by 880 different teachers. It may be that better than anyone the regents had an understanding of the program as an institutional apparatus, with active participation across the university as a sign of health.

THE ROLE OF THE VALIDATOR

Of necessity the role of the validators will be complicated in a multiple-inquiry investigation. As probes multiply, opportunities to maintain that old image of a distant observer standing beyond the fray dwindle. Instead the validator must strive toward a different sort of distance. It will be a kind of oversight, but not in the governmental sense of the term. While various stakeholders are validating the testing program largely through their perceptions of its use to them individually, the validator is listening to everyone and imagining the larger picture and eventually recommending changes that will enhance the utility of the program as a whole.

That is not an easy role, because it entails holding two sometimes contradictory conditions together, intimate knowledge of the program (Patton, 1986) and proactivity (Leviton & Hughes, 1981). For instance, when the validator is also the chief administrator of the testing program—

as was my case at WSU—simultaneously the validator has strong insights into problem areas, strong motives to find payoff measures, and strong temptations to table certain recommendations for change. Multiple inquiry begs for multiple validators. A team of validators simply offers more chance of cross-checking within the validation process itself (I am now talking about testing the test of the test). Nevertheless, I feel that with multiple inquiry into most writing programs it would be a mistake to exclude the administrator of the testing system from the validation team.

There are good reasons for this. In the first place, if any one person on campus has a complex understanding of the existing test and, therefore, the motivation to seek a complex enhancement of the test, it is the test administrator. Have no doubts, an honest multiple inquiry will end with a mixed judgment on any writing test. The more probes sent out, the more perspectives heard from, the less is the chance for a unified assessment. It is stakeholders with peripheral connections to the test who have reason to wish for a single-strand validation. The test administrator may be the stakeholder with the most desire to take a full look.

A test administrator is also in the best position to imagine and effect some of the more innovative and powerful forms of validation, those going beyond the traditional one of formal, quantified experiments (Patton, 1986). More than any stakeholder, it is the test administrator who wants to go beyond outcomes. In my short stay as coordinator of the exams, the inquiries that led to the most change were two administrative initiatives: the workshop with faculty over the problem of portfolio course-paper submissions (which resulted in a handbook for faculty at large) and information sessions with dorm groups (which changed the way the examinations were advertised). Some of the most interesting validation issues were hardly accessible except through inside, day-to-day experience with the program. Has the junior portfolio been a learning experience for students? I believe it has been for some students but not for the majority, yet I can validate that belief only in two roughshod ways. One is through some 50 or 60 office conferences I had with students who were pleading to be allowed to retake the exam, during which 20-minute sessions I often saw a rapid change in some cavalier notions about writing, for instance about the need to convince readers with a balanced argument. The other way is through the mundane task of taking in portfolio submissions, when large numbers of students could be seen occupying a space somewhere between utter indifference to the test and frustrated misconceptions about the test. Such was the source of my encouragement for studies of student attitudes toward the exams, of the kind reported in the next chapter.

Finally, test administrators are in the best position to convert validation recommendations into realities because they may be the people most committed to making use of the validation. This returns to the central argument for multiple inquiry in validation. In the end it seems a very simple point. Multiple inquiry multiplies recommendations for change. During my term, my recommendations for the junior portfolio alone were numerous: that ways needed to be found to reduce student procrastination in taking the exam, that transfer students should be better informed about the exam, that the second-language writer's plight needed immediate attention, that standards and procedures for signing off on student papers should be made more available to the faculty, that information about comparative performance according to college and major should be used to improve writing instruction across campus, that certain paragraph prompts used on the exam should be discarded, that the procedure of rater consultation during tier-two readings should be studied and improved, and that a forum should be developed through which students can voice their feelings about the exam and gain a better understanding of its uses. Most of these proposals have now been bettered and implemented by subsequent test administrators. What could be categorized as a shotgun approach to validation may have its problems, but clearly no single inquiry and arguably no more controlled inquiry would have led to so fruitful a course for future action.

Part IV

Beyond Outcomes

Washington State University's rising-junior writing examination cannot be considered especially long lived, not yet. Many midstream proficiency writing examinations have been around longer, some much longer. Rising-junior exams have been implemented by the University System of Georgia in 1972, Eastern Oregon State University in 1975, City University of New York in 1975, Northeast Missouri (Truman) State University in 1976, South Dakota state universities in 1977, Florida state universities in 1983, the University of Arizona in 1983, Ball State University in 1987, the University of Southwestern Louisiana in 1988, the California State University campuses in 1989. This list is highly truncated. A 1988 survey of 675 colleges and universities found 79 with a proficiency test in writing, "usually at the junior level," and that leaves out of the count the two-thirds of the schools that did not respond to the questionnaire (Daniel & Ludgewalt, 1988).

Also left out of the count are schools, such as Brigham Young University and the Catholic University of America, that have run a mid-course proficiency exam and then eventually abandoned it. No one has put that topic on their survey. An informal response from faculty at colleges where rising-junior exams still exist often sketch a sad picture. It's one of apathy, frustration, distance, silence. Faculty appear alienated from the exam. "Most folks just want students to take it earlier and to pass it." "We try to pay as little attention to the test as we can." "Many say they hate it but see no point in doing anything about it." "We don't consider these tests as our business." Administrators seem aloof and unresponsive. "The chair can offer no reasons for giving the test." "Many teachers think it is futile to speak out against the authority of the Board of Regents." "They are not providing resources to keep faculty involved in developing and evaluating the exams." "It suffers from a lack of institutional commitment." Meanwhile students, who take the tests and the consequences, are not spoken about or are described in terms of their silence. "It is a moribund assessment program, due to general disdain among students, faculty, and administrators."

These kinds of comments come chiefly from colleges in which the requirement of the examination has been mandated from above and, worse, in which the results of the examination are unconnected with instruction. The state orders the test, the students take the test until they pass it—the college records the results. There is nothing much that students, faculty, or administrators can do before the test is taken, and nothing much happens after the test is completed either. If little leads toward outcomes, less leads beyond outcomes. Outcomes are isolated from the living institution of learning in which they are not embedded but merely suspended. Such writing assessment would fare poorly against Catharine Lucas's touchstone of ecological validity, which she defines as "the extent to which a test reflects (and hence reports results from) the whole writing environment of the learner, and the extent to which it impacts the environment in positive rather than negative ways" (1988, p. 12).

Part IV of *Beyond Outcomes*, more even than other parts, explores and interrogates the ecological validity of WSU's Junior Portfolio. Chapter 11 breaks the silence of students and listens to how they say the exam has influenced their education afterward. Chapter 12 surveys faculty and finds none of the hatred or disdain reported from other schools but still less understanding and awareness than the WSU Writing Program would like. Chapter 13 asks how the Writing Program can best educate and influence higher administration about the results and the impact of the test.

In asking what should lie beyond outcomes, Part IV could have focused on any other parts of the Writing Program, the WAC system, perhaps, or the Writing Center. The message would have been the same. Unless an assessment-instruction program find ways to extend itself vitally throughout the whole ecology of the university—students, faculty, and administration together—it will become a moribund part that eventually will be sloughed off. The assessment system will not last beyond its own outcomes.

11

Students as Stakeholders: Maintaining a Responsive Assessment

Jennie Nelson and Diane Kelly-Riley

Administrators of large-scale writing assessment programs often take students' views for granted. The exams are constructed for the benefit of the students as placement mechanisms into first-year composition courses, as midcareer demonstrations of their writing proficiencies, or as exit devices proving their readiness for real-world writing challenges. These exams and their interfaces with instructional aims have been carefully constructed by "experts" to uphold fairness, validity, reliability, and curricular goals. As we considered the variety of writing assessment programs in higher education, we wondered about the degree to which students play an active role as stakeholders in their ongoing maintenance. There have been programs, such as the now defunct portfolio assessment at State University of New York (SUNY) Stony Brook, which attempted to integrate students into the "power circle of assessment" (Belanoff & Elbow, 1986), and inquiries into students' conceptions of a particular portion of an assessment such as the prompt (Ruth & Murphy, 1988; Murphy & Ruth, 1993), and rarely an organizational structure to deal with students one-on-one who fail a formal exam, such as the counseling system for San Francisco

State University's junior English proficiency test (Freedman & Robinson, 1982). Not surprisingly, though, we were unable to locate any systematic inquiry into students' views of large-scale writing assessment programs.

Most often, as administrators of writing assessment programs, we take a reactive stance to students. We depend on them to initiate contact with us when things don't work by filing petitions, crying in our offices over the unfairness of the exam, or taking us to hearings at grievance boards. But "what kind of proof do we have that students are wrong when they say, 'I don't belong in this dummy class'?" (Elbow, 1996, p. 93).

This reluctance on our part to solicit student views on the Writing Portfolio began to undermine the integrity of the program, resulting in numerous misunderstandings of our purposes, misconceptions, student myths about the exams, and general distrust in the process. Misconceptions about the purposes of assessment programs are not unique to Washington State University (WSU). Catherine Palomba states that at Ball State University "students were also very vocal about the writing competency examination. They thought this exam duplicated assessment in their writing courses. It has taken a steady stream of messages to help them see the relevance of the test" (Palomba, 1997, p.43). Our goal to maintain a responsive assessment program prompted us to venture into new territory, seeking out the students' perceptions of our writing assessment program. This chapter explores and follows some at-risk writers' experiences with WSU's writing assessment program to highlight the importance of asking students about their impressions of the program and the types of information that students can yield in the effort to maintain a viable and dynamic writing assessment program.

A HISTORY OF NEGLECT?

In September 1995, to the relief of its administrators, the junior Writing Portfolio demonstrated itself as "firmly entrenched and healthy" (Haswell, 1995, p. 2) in the WSU culture. Students complied with the new requirement, and the submissions of papers from almost every department on campus helped promote extended writing assignments across the curriculum. In the first two and a half years into the implementation of the Portfolio, 11 percent of undergraduates earned the pass-with-distinction rating, 79 percent demonstrated competency in meeting upper-division writing requirements at WSU, and only 10 percent demonstrated a need for additional writing instruction.

Over time, the stability of the program continued to prove itself. In June 1997, "the Writing Portfolio [checked] out, basically, as a sound writing-assessment program" (Bonnema, Haswell, & Norris, 1997, p. 2). Performance outcomes stabilized: students receiving passing or pass-with-distinction ratings equaled 90.7 percent, and those requiring additional writing instruction decreased to 9.3 percent. Small studies were conducted on the reliability of the readers and the topics. Most performed at acceptable rates. Recirculation of portfolios receiving simple pass placements achieved 95 percent repeat of the original placement. Most of the topics were fair in gender and language status; those that didn't were tabled.

The Portfolio was linked to instructional goals. Most students demonstrated that their writing abilities were competent to meet the challenges of the upper-division Writing-in-the-Major courses. Best of all, the Portfolio identified students with problematic writing abilities and required additional writing instruction. In the initial years, this amounted to roughly two hundred students each year between 1995 and 1997 (compared to the two thousand who passed or earned a distinction rating). Most of these students were required to take General Education 302, a one-credit, upper-division writing tutorial taken concurrently with the writing-intensive courses within the student's major. These students simply had to complete the coursework in General Education 302 and then their Portfolio ratings reverted to pass. The needs-work rating would not be permanently recorded on the students' transcripts and so, in the eyes of the Portfolio administrators, would not haunt these students in future job or school prospects. The only information recorded was the class taken, and many students volunteered to enroll in General Education 302, so it did not carry the stigma of remediation.

The administrators of the Writing Portfolio felt that the needs-work students were happy with the instruction they received in General Education 302, based on anecdotal evidence. Students had to complete only one credit to fulfill the Portfolio requirement, and this was done in a friendly, small group, tutorial setting. From time to time individual students complained about their Portfolio results or that they had already completed all of their upper-division writing requirements and felt the one-credit course served no purpose, but those complaints were written off as typical student objections about meeting graduation requirements. These grumblings seemed inconsequential when compared to the achievements of the Writing Portfolio. The Writing Assessment Program had proved the Portfolio's worth to central administration and had provided the university with tangible data on student learning outcomes, which were used in the recent university-wide accreditation review. Over two thousand students a year demonstrated competent writing abilities as defined by the faculty!

As the number of Portfolio submissions increased, however, so did the number of student complaints about their needs-work ratings. Because procrastination to complete the exam was so high, these protests were attributed to the fact that students had delayed the exam by their own choice and were complaining about a situation they had created for themselves. By submitting the Portfolio late, students turned the midcareer diagnostic assessment into a barrier exam to graduation, actually resulting in the delayed graduation for some who had to complete one final credit of General Education 302 before earning their degrees. These students' strident voices were often heard in the hallways around the Writing Assessment office, but their views as legitimate stakeholders in the Writing Assessment program remained largely unexamined.

In short, the initial success of the Writing Portfolio overshadowed the needs-work students' concerns. The designers and administrators of the Writing Portfolio were justifiably proud that they had secured the investment of faculty, central administrators, the state legislature, and wider academic circles in the Portfolio Assessment. Many faculty and administrators were excited at the prospect of having a real solution for the problem of student writing.

The needs-work student writing, however, has been difficult terrain to define. Initial studies of rater reliability for the Portfolio focused solely on the one-reader, simple-pass rating at tier one, assuming that this would be the most controversial component in the two-tiered evaluation process (see Chapter 3; Haswell, 1998a), and solid rater reliabilities for this rating have reassured test administrators. Subsequent studies of the tier-two decisions were buried in an in-house report (Haswell, 1995). Recently, however, in a small investigation, the Writing Assessment Program determined the reliability of the needs-work rating to dip as low as 28 percent. (The study, explored earlier in Chapter 6, details the difficulties our assessment program has encountered in making consistent needs-work ratings.) This information supported the students' complaints about the validity of their needs-work ratings and called for a closer look at their experiences.

According to Pamela Moss, "It is important to study the actual discourse that occurs around the products and practices of testing—to see how those whose lives a testing program impacts are using the representations (interpretations) it produces" (1998, p. 119). The students who were most negatively affected by the assessment program were those whose writing was labeled needs-work. Their experiences with the program were most important because they, at least according to some faculty and administrators, were the primary reason for our existence. If our program was not meeting their needs, then our program's long-term viability was at stake.

AN EFFORT TO RECOUP: CASE STUDIES

In 1997, to investigate the Writing Assessment program from the students' perspectives, a faculty member and a researcher from a nearby university conducted a series of case studies, recruiting a number of randomly selected students who had received needs-work ratings on their Portfolios and were required to enroll in the one-credit writing tutorial (General Education 302) before they could graduate. Students who agreed to participate in the study met with the researcher two or three times over the course of a semester for brief interviews and provided weekly log entries describing their experiences with the Writing Assessment program and General Education 302. This inquiry yielded a much less rosy picture of the Writing Assessment program than its administrators and supporters had envisioned: students were not happily complying with their additional requirements. In fact, many of them expressed confusion about the purposes and outcomes of the Portfolio and were frustrated at the seeming disconnection between the assessment and the required coursework. From this study, it became apparent that the needs of the students most negatively affected by the Portfolio assessment required a different approach.

We turned to Fourth Generation Evaluation for an alternative approach. Egon Guba and Yvonne Lincoln describe this as a "form of evaluation in which the claims, concerns, and issues of stakeholders serve as organizational foci" (1989, p. 50). Their assessment practices are hermeneutic in nature, involving a significant amount of negotiation. According to Guba and Lincoln, "five arguments seem...to be compelling reasons for insisting upon the use of stakeholder claims, concerns, and issues as focal organizers for evaluation":

1. The fact that stakeholders are placed at risk by an evaluation and, thus in the interest of fairness, deserve to have input into the process.

2. The fact that evaluation exposes stakeholders to exploitations, disempowerment, and disenfranchisement so that they, in the interest of self-defense, are entitled to some control of the process.

3. The fact that stakeholders represent a virtually untapped market for the use of evaluation findings that are responsive to self-defined needs and interests.

4. The fact that the inclusion of stakeholder inputs greatly broadens the scope and meaningfulness of an inquiry and contributes immeasurably to the dialectic so necessary if evaluation is to have a positive outcome.

5. The fact that all parties can be mutually educated to more informed and sophisticated personal constructions as well as an enhanced appreciation of the constructions of others. (p. 57)

Because the original intention of the Portfolio was to design a student-centered examination, the philosophy supported in Fourth-Generation Evaluation seemed the most logical to embrace. The improvement of the assessment program for the students most adversely affected by it became our main purpose in gathering this information. Students going through our assessment represented an untapped source of information about our progress.

FINDINGS: AN ASSESSMENT PROGRAM THAT "NEEDS WORK"

The case studies focused solely on students who were deemed as having problematic writing by the Portfolio evaluation. These students were asked to address the following topics in interviews and written logs:

1. Describe your experiences with the Portfolio requirement. Once you received your needs-work assessment, did you have any expectations about General Education 302?
2. How are things going in General Education 302, thus far?
3. Overall, what do you think of the Portfolio requirement and General Education 302?

Naturally, students' feelings about the portfolio requirement and General Education 302 were mixed, but every student expressed confusion about the apparent contradiction between their own teachers' largely positive evaluations of their writing and the Portfolio committees' seemingly negative assessments. For example, Dan—who had already completed two Writing-in-the-Major courses and earned an A and a B— explained that Portfolio readers had said that his writing lacked focus, when, in contrast, teachers' written comments on two of the papers he had submitted praised his writing for its focus. Dan challenged the Portfolio assessment, pointing out the contradictory assessments to a Portfolio administrator: "I said, how come it says right here, in the notes, good focus? . . . and then right here again—why, it's an English paper—I did this paper in English 101—good focus!"

Another student praised her General Education 302 course but questioned the validity of her Portfolio assessment: "The class is great, but the reasons I was given as to why I did not pass the Portfolio never seem to come up as a problem in this class. For instance, I was told I needed to work on concept of topic, focus of direction, logic, support and integration, and clarity of ideas. I have written over three papers in my Writing-in-the Major class and none of these problems seems to show up. In a sense, I am confused as to why I didn't pass the Portfolio."

Other students questioned the reliability of Portfolio readers' evaluations because, as one pointed out, "The people who are doing our Portfolio aren't exactly from an English background. How come they can say if I write good or bad? What did they do to be able to do that?" This student had received A's on most of her English 101 papers, and she asked "Who should I believe—my teachers or the committee?"

Many students praised the Writing-in-the-Major courses because they recognized the value of developing writing skills in their own fields, but they questioned the value of the timed writing test. An ESL student said, "If the purpose [of the Portfolio requirement] is to develop students' writing skill, then we don't need the timed writing. We don't usually practice timed writing in our classes." Another student, who was certain that she had "failed the Portfolio" based solely on her timed writing, wished that she could have a second chance to take the test. She explained that she had recently completed a psychology class in which students were required to develop outlines for essay questions on weekly quizzes: "I got really good at it . . . I was so proud . . . because I never liked to do outlines, but I can see where it does organize my work a lot more. I just wish I had that chance to try again on the timed writing." The same student argued that English 101 and 102 should "focus on Portfolio targets [so that] all that is assessed in the Portfolio will be covered" in first-year writing courses. Students felt that their courses should have prepared them more overtly for the Portfolio requirement.

Even though students questioned the validity of Portfolio readers' judgments and the value of the timed writing test, many still praised the required General Education 302 course. Specifically, students who were able to take General Education 302 concurrently with their Writing-in-the-Major courses reported that they found the class helpful: "Working with another peer and [the teacher] has become an asset to my writing. They let me know when my writing is too wordy and now I try to use more concise words. . . . Overall, I believe this class has helped me identify and strengthen weaknesses in my writing. Now that I look back at some of my writing, I can see improvement. The class was a tool that I was happy to take advantage of."

While a number of students over the course of two semesters shared their experiences concerning the Portfolio requirement, the following two case-study students' responses reveal the worst-case scenarios and, most clearly, the frustration that many labeled students felt with the process. The Writing Portfolio is a requirement for all undergraduates at WSU, including transfer students. This population in particular finds the requirement frustrating because they enter the university as juniors and are expected to complete it the following semester. The two case-study students' responses are reproduced at length below to provide the worst-case scenarios in terms of things that can go wrong in an assessment process if the students are not consulted on their experiences with the program and its aims.

Q1. DESCRIBE YOUR EXPERIENCES WITH THE PORTFOLIO REQUIREMENT

Janey: "I kind of scrounged up some things."

I like to think my circumstances were fairly unusual. I'm a transfer student. I went to my [major] professor and asked her what kinds of things. . . . I didn't even know about the writing portfolio, how it worked or anything and then I applied for graduation. So my professor told me I needed to take the test because time was running out.

I went to take the test and I knew I did really bad on that. . . . I don't remember what my topic was but it was just some obscure topic that was really kind of difficult to write about.

I had already taken the "Writing in the Major" Class. Got a B+ in that. Wrote the final paper and had really good comments—teacher thought it was professional writing. . . . And my advisor, the head of my department, said that I couldn't turn that in [with my Portfolio], so being a transfer student, I didn't save anything and I didn't have much to turn in. . . . She was incorrect, I found out later, which is unfortunate for me. And so, I had been at WSU like a year and a half, and I kind of scrounged up some things. I had an abstract I did for one class and a really short assignment for another, and, I don't remember what it was, but a one-page something.

I like to think my circumstances were fairly unusual. I had taken English. I went to a community college and to Central Washington University and I took English 101 and 102 and did really well in those classes. Never had a problem with writing. Then all of a sudden, I turn in those things and get this letter in the mail saying that my writing, they thought that my writing needed further instruction and I needed to sign up for class.

So it was kind of like a blow. So I went in to talk to the person in the writing portfolio office, and I told her I just didn't understand and that I wanted to know why. . . . She told me that the one-page thing I turned in was really good, but that one of them was too short for them to even judge and one of them was a summary. . . . She said that just judging on that one thing wasn't enough and that I needed to take the one-credit class. . . .

I went back to the head of my department and told her, and she
wrote a letter over there telling them that she didn't approve of
the whole process. . . . [Of how] I went in there [and they said
they] don't have enough to judge me on, but can I turn in more?
[The writing assessment] woman said "We can't do that."

Bev: "I think my writing skills are excellent."

I'm a transfer student. I have my AA degree. I'm not taking any
English classes here; I haven't saved any of my papers because I
was unaware of [the Writing Portfolio requirement].

Well, I had one paper from the community college that I had
saved because I just thought it was a cute paper. I liked it. It was
more of a personal experience than a research paper. And so I did
turn that in with my writing portfolio to show how I had progressed from my freshman year. I turned that one in along with
two papers that I had written that year. One was business law—
it was a tort reform paper—and when I had my teacher sign off
on that (on the original paper she gave me 25 extra credit points
for it) she marked it Excellent, which I had been told she never
does. And then [I turned in] an introductory letter about myself
for Management 350. And I went and got that signed off and he
also put Excellent on it and I got an A on that paper. . . .

I had a real problem with the timed writing test because of
the questions. It was something about . . . America's society
and traditions. . . . It was pretty biased to middle class, upper
class, traditional, Caucasian society. It was based on traditions,
and in our family we didn't celebrate Christmas, not because of
religion. We just didn't do it—you know, we didn't do the birth-
day thing . . . so traditions was not part of my upbringing. . . .
So I said how I felt that traditions weren't as important in soci-

ety as the respect and the bringing up of the children. . . . And then the second part [of the timed essay] was how you evaluate your own writing. I said in that that I did go off on a tangent on, you know, society, respect and all that stuff, because I wasn't aware of traditions and I had never been brought up in that. . . .

I won the English merit award in high school. I never had a problem with English or writing. And they [the Writing Portfolio staff] said I didn't pass it, and I was like "you gotta be kidding." I was extremely upset, humiliated. I couldn't understand how I could pass all my English classes—never got anything but an A in English. . . . In the dorms and stuff, because I was a junior, my friends would come in and have me reread their papers and we'd go over them and fix them. . . .

I was so humiliated and really angry, and I asked the lady [in the writing portfolio office] and she said "Well, they said that you needed to clarify your point or that what you wrote didn't pertain to the question" and I said "well yeah, exactly."

I was really upset, just about crying . . . and she was like "You seem really upset; maybe you should go talk to somebody." I'm like, "That's why I'm here talking to you, and you obviously don't have any good answers for this." I asked her about [an appeal process] and she said there is an appeal. And I asked has anybody ever gotten past the appeal? She said no, or that one student out of so many had and that it wasn't even worth it—just take the class.

I think my writing skills are excellent. My teachers have told me they are excellent. I do writing for my job [at Sears], for announcements over the intercom and other stuff.

Q2. HOW ARE THINGS GOING IN GENERAL EDUCATION 302?

Janey: "There's something else that needs to be evaluated."

You go in there [to sign up for General Education 302] and put your name down and you put your schedule and I think they took my major and what semester I was in, if I had already taken the writing class, so that they can put you in a small group with people who have a similar situation. . . . In my group, all of us are either graduating this semester or next—we've all taken the writing in the major class.

[The teacher] is a grad. student and the first session he didn't show up until late; the second session he never showed up. It's just I feel like we're having to make this commitment and no one else is, and it's kind of not taken seriously. . . .

I understand that the purpose of [the course], ideally, is to help students who in fact do need support for their writing, especially while they're taking those writing in the major classes, but when it's after the fact, it kind of defeats the purpose.

For us to get this far and there be a problem with our writing, that says something about the whole university. You know, for us to get past the "M" class and there be a problem with our writing still, there's something else that needs to be evaluated.

Bev: "It's humiliating to me."

[After signing up for General Education 302] I missed the first meeting because no one notified me about it, and [when I called the portfolio office] they said it didn't really matter because actually the guy who was supposed to tutor it showed up late and nobody was there. So I showed up for the second meeting and he never showed up, again. . . . So, obviously, we weren't that important.

I got a description of the Gen Ed 302 program and its goals and it is supposed to support people who are taking the writing in the major course at the same time. There are five people in my 302 writing group, including me, and everyone has already taken their M courses.

When you [the researcher] called me I was really excited to be able to tell somebody . . . that this is just crap.

We're not doing any writing in there—someone brings their resume and we just check it over.

It's humiliating to me—only a few people know that I'm in it.

Q3. OVERALL, WHAT DO YOU THINK OF THE PORTFOLIO REQUIREMENT AND GEN ED 302?

Janey: "I feel this is a waste of my time."

While talking with other students about the 302 course require-ments, I realized that we were all unclear about what we needed to do to get a "pass" out of the class. Although we knew we had to write a two page evaluation of the course, we were not sure what criteria had to be met to fulfill our writing portfolio require-ment. When the tutor came to class, we asked him to explain the evaluation. . . . He did not bring any information, but said that it was very informal—it was not going to be graded on mechanics, spelling, or structure.

I immediately countered by asking him to explain the tools they were planning on using to evaluate if we met our writing portfolio requirement. He said that was it. I was flabbergasted! I am taking this course because I am told my writing is not profi-cient. Yet, what have I learned from taking this class that will supposedly meet all of my writing needs and fulfill my requirement? In class, we review punctuation (which I've learned since 1st grade) and evaluate each other's current writing projects. I don't understand how we can effectively evaluate each other's writing if we all have problems with our writing.

Our teacher responded by saying that he feels you cannot teach writing. I told him that I feel this is a waste of my time and have yet to learn anything out of this class which I did not know prior to taking it. He said there are many controversies over the process by which writing should be taught. He agreed with me and told me that numerous others, like me, had gotten caught in this trap too.

Bev: "I think this course needs to be directly related to the writing portfolio requirement."

The 302 meetings continued, but most of the time we left early because we didn't have anything to do. Attendance began to fall as the course went on, and one student dropped out.

My frustration increased during one of the classes in which we had a substitute tutor. He gave us a worksheet containing sentences and a definition about the "funny little thing called a comma." I was absolutely furious! This was absolutely degrading! Here I was, a senior in college who already had one degree, had taken three previous writing tests, passing all, and I was being taught what a comma was! I did pass third and fourth grade, where I learned about punctuation and sentence structure. My group wasn't very cooperative with the activity and later discussed how ridiculous it was.

Reluctantly, we all showed up for out next meeting, and our anger and frustration began to surface. We started bombarding our tutor with questions regarding what this class had to do with

our writing portfolios. We were told that this class was not directly related to the writing portfolio, and that our tutor had not read
our portfolio to find out our weaknesses in writing. I was furious
that this course, one which I was required to take, had nothing to
do with why I was required to take it. I asked our tutor if there
was a syllabus and who had written it. The syllabus consisted of
activities and worksheets on sentence structure, grammar, and
punctuation. All of the things outlined in the syllabus we were
required to know before we could pass elementary school. We also
learned that the individual who wrote the syllabus and designed
the course was not directly related with the writing portfolio
either. Our tutor told us that the individual was qualified to design
the course because he shared an office with the head of the writing portfolio program.

I do not think this qualifies him to design this course. He needs to
know exactly why students are required to take the course, and
design the course to improve the skills each individual is lacking. . . .

I think this course needs to be directly related to the writing
portfolio requirement. The tutors need to know why every student
in their group did not pass and design the class around those
needs. If someone would have gone over my writing portfolio and
told me exactly what I did wrong, how I could improve my writing
skills, then I would have benefited from this class. At this point, I
feel I have wasted ten hours of my time, time that I could have
been doing something actually productive, such as the dishes.

QUALITIES OF A RESPONSIVE ASSESSMENT: KEY
CONSIDERATIONS

The case studies underscore Guba and Lincoln's assertion that stakeholders' concerns and issues should serve as focal points for organizers
for assessment programs. Several problems for student stakeholders were
identified in the WSU system: First, they faced a nonexistent or rigid

appeals process. On receipt of their scores, the needs-work students had few options open to them, and the Portfolio administrators were reluctant to question the validity of the raters' evaluations. Second, in the eyes of the needs-work students, the connection between the Portfolio assessment and the subsequent coursework required in General Education 302 was tenuous at best. The administrators and tutors of General Education 302 struggled to work with students who were not enrolled in a class that assigned writing. The design of General Education 302 was predicated on the fact that students enroll in classes assigning writing, and then use those assignments for the course content in General Education 302. Without writing to work on, the students and tutors were left to design and generate the content of the tutorial. The final problem resulted from a combination of factors. Students who waited to submit their Portfolios until their final semester and who received needs-work ratings, transformed the Portfolio from a midcareer diagnostic exam into a high-stakes barrier exam. This perhaps resulted in the most anger and frustration for all parties involved.

CHANGES IN THE PROGRAM

Since our study, and in part because of it, the administration of the Writing Portfolio has now changed to be more attentive to the needs-work students' concerns. First, a three-option appeal process has been implemented. Students can now choose to resubmit the entire Writing Portfolio; they can contest the original decision and have the entire second-tier, interdisciplinary corps of readers re-evaluate the Portfolio; or they can file a senior petition if extenuating circumstances prevent them from completing the requirement. As Guba and Lincoln note, "stakeholders are placed at risk by an evaluation and, in the interest of fairness, deserve to have input into the process" (p. 57). These choices now allow students to have more control over the outcome of the Portfolio process.

Likewise, students who are required to take General Education 302 must do so concurrently with a class that assigns writing, an "M" course or other class. Other students, who have no writing to bring to the tutorial, must enroll in a three-credit writing course. This shift intends to tie the Portfolio evaluation directly to the subsequent instruction, and to make the required writing instruction more meaningful. While the Portfolio administrators intended the one-credit writing tutorial to satisfy the requirement, the students enrolled in the class without concurrent writing courses did not view it this way. They were happier to be in a well-defined, three-credit course—even though it meant more work, the class itself generated the assignments making them feel like they were improving their writing.

The appeal process not only allows students more control in the Portfolio process, but also it serves to educate the evaluators about difficult and problematic ratings. Needs-work ratings that are contested by students are turned back to the second-tier evaluators as a norming device. They see the original ratings by the evaluators and review the contents of the Portfolio for discussion of the characteristics of the submitted writing. The Portfolio administrators considered a "third" tier of evaluation composed of the faculty of the Writing Program who could override an erroneous rating. Turning the contested ratings back to the faculty evaluators, however, helps them become "mutually educated to more informed and sophisticated personal constructions as well as [providing] an enhanced appreciation of the constructions of others" (Guba & Lincoln, 1989, p. 57). By turning the evaluation back to the second tier, the faculty evaluators' learning increases as they struggle to define "problematic writing."

BALANCING ACTS

The continuing challenge of a writing assessment program is to resist entrenchment (see Chapters 2 and 7). Administrators who want to create a responsive writing assessment must find avenues that allow them to tap into different stakeholders' experiences with the assessment. The following questions posed by Pamela Moss (1998) offer useful starting points for program administrators: "How [can] the perspectives of different stakeholders [be] elicited and used to improve the program"? (p. 118); and "How coherent are course goals and activities with the assessment of students' needs that underlies the placement decision?" (p. 117). To find these answers, we made simple inquiries—surveys, interviews, and phone interviews—into what students knew about our program and what they thought about it. We focused on the at-risk population in the Writing Portfolio: the students who received needs-work ratings and were required to complete additional writing instruction. In the initial start-up years, we were convinced by the "numbers" that the students should be happy with the assessment process, but when we finally asked them about their experiences with our program, we received an unexpected response. As a result, we were able to gather useful information about our program that we could not have obtained from other stakeholder populations or from our regular data collection. The information allowed us to identify easily solvable problems in our assessment.

Another important question in this search is to find out "how do the (vulnerable) people who are labeled by [the program] feel . . . about the process?" (Haswell, 1998a, p. 111). Viewing students as legitimate stakeholders can dramatically improve the assessment by seeking out their experiences, and it can begin to adequately address their concerns by making changes in the system. The WSU case studies present the contradictory picture of strong statistical data with adverse students' experiences. Statistical data and surveys alone could not have revealed the problems in our system. By taking a proactive approach to hearing student concerns, we have been able to take steps that will ensure a better assessment program in the long run.

However, an assessment program that solicits perspectives from all its stakeholders opens itself to the sometimes burdensome task of perpetual negotiation. Perhaps, in the end, this negotiation yields meaningful and positive outcomes for certain stakeholders, but the process can be frustrating and difficult. The Writing Program administrators face the challenge of incorporating the desires of many stakeholders, which for vulnerable populations, may be at odds with others (see Chapter 10). In the reality of most writing assessment programs, standards have to be met and bars set; procedures are established to help make the program run efficiently; financial realities affect the extent to which the stakeholders' concerns can be considered. The variety of converging forces surrounding an assessment program can be overwhelming. Currently, students are afforded a great amount of freedom in WSU's Portfolio evaluation, and sometimes they use this freedom to their own detriment (as in the case of the late Portfolio submissions).

Peter Elbow argues that "the main influence on learning" is probably "the dimensions of freedom and coercion" (1996, p. 97). Negotiating the balance between freedom and coercion is one of the trickiest balancing acts assessment program administrators face. Nevertheless, a responsive assessment program continually raises questions about its assumptions and practices and continually seeks out the perspectives of its most vulnerable stakeholders in attempting to answer them. While these questions will be unique to each program and the stakeholders involved, vulnerable stakeholders must always have a voice.

12

Faculty Opinion and Experience: The Writing Portfolio

Fiona Glade, Diane Kelly-Riley,
Susan McLeod, and William Condon

A discussion of faculty opinion is appropriate in this volume, because the impetus for Washington State University's (WSU) Writing Across the Curriculum (WAC) program came from the faculty. Specifically, the Writing Across the Curriculum (WAC) program began with a pained question: "What are we going to do about student writing?" In the mid-1980s, faculty at this institution, as elsewhere, were distressed at what they saw as a serious decline in student writing skills. Whatever the reasons for this apparent decline (Russell, 1991, pp. 274–76), faculty distress was serious enough to galvanize a vote in the faculty senate to do something—institute a gate-keeping test, perhaps—about the sorry state of student writing. In the fall of 1985, the Faculty Senate did what such bodies usually do: they called for a committee to study the problem and make recommendations.

The All-University Writing Committee received its charge that spring; the members worked for a full academic year (1986–87), reading everything that could be found about how students learn (or don't learn) how to write. Many of us who wrote chapters in this book were involved in those discussions; we also brought in outside experts, including Edward White and Toby Fulwiler, to discuss possible assessment designs and WAC program elements, and a state mandate for assessment of writing (among other areas) at entry, midcareer, and end of program added impetus and urgency to our efforts. Over the next few years, as WAC workshops began and the English Department tinkered with the first-year composition curriculum, committee members became increasingly convinced that we needed a fully integrated set of writing programs.

In the plan that emerged by 1990, assessment would be part of a larger program, one that also involved curricular change in General Education (including first-year composition), student support (in a writing center), and faculty support (in the form of WAC workshops). The entire program as conceived would begin by assessing students' writing skills as soon as they walked through our doors as first-year students, using this information to place them in the appropriate level of first-year writing. We would then add writing-to-learn assignments to all General Education classes, instituting a rising junior portfolio as a diagnostic tool to assess both transfer and our own students to make sure they were ready for upper-division work (and require more writing coursework if they were not), and creating in each major at least two Writing in the Major (M) courses in which students learned the discourse of their particular discipline. Along the way we completely rethought and transformed the way we taught first-year composition, expanded our writing center almost beyond its capacity to serve students (a familiar role for writing centers), worked with the General Education Committee to infuse writing throughout the curriculum, and invented new ways of doing writing assessment. We also convinced the administration to create a new position, Director of Campus Writing Programs, and hired someone to help us keep this elaborate system running. After more than a decade of phasing in various elements, the program is now complete, as shown in Figure 0.1 in the Introduction to this book.

The centrality of writing to thinking has become part of the vocabulary of our campus—faculty in the disciplines now accept the WAC program as part of what we do well here; they also accept student writing as something they themselves can have a hand in improving. The various essays in this book demonstrate that although we did not know it at the time, assessment is central to our endeavors. Besides just giving us placement information on the student at entry level and diagnostic information at midcareer, allowing us to do what is best for that particular student, our assessment instruments give us longitudinal data that allow us to examine how student writing has improved over time. Perhaps most important of all from the administrative point of view, assessment gives us important information about our program—the rising junior portfolio allows us to track the kinds of writing going on in the university, where it is taking place, and who is assigning it. This important information provides us a feedback loop into the program through which we are able to examine both curricular and support elements of WAC on our campus. We began this program in the mid-1980s with what seemed a fairly straightforward faculty question: "What are we going to do about student writing?" The faculty answer at that time was "assessment." They were right.

TRACKING FACULTY OPINION

The preceding might be called a faculty member's history of the WSU Writing Program. It is the way teachers see it generally and may be contrasted with an administrator's history (Chapter 1) and a writing assessor's history (Chapter 2). Faculty ideas about assessment have changed, however, since those early days, in part, we think, as a result of the program. As faculty have become more involved with our program, and as a result more savvy about issues surrounding assessment, we have had to listen to their changing notions and assumptions. Tracking changes in attitude is a bit like chasing a rainbow; nevertheless we will try. During 1998–99, we conducted interviews with faculty who, in one way or another, have been involved with the WAC program, either as WAC workshop participants or as readers of the WSU Writing Portfolio (occasionally as both). We also distributed two surveys: one in the fall of 1996 that questioned the general instructional faculty at WSU, and the other in the spring of 1998 limited to tenure-line faculty. Both surveys asked for their perceptions of the Writing Portfolio requirement. We have also been conducting interviews of faculty who have attended our WAC faculty seminars, many of whom (not surprisingly) are involved with the Portfolio, either as readers or as faculty who sign off on student papers for the Portfolio.

When we began our discussion of student writing on campus in the mid-1980s, faculty opinion was heavily in favor of a writing assessment instrument that would function as a gatekeeping device. The sentiments expressed in the faculty senate debate that accompanied the passing of the WAC principles were most heated on this point: weak writers should be weeded out. It was an embarrassment to the institution to continue to graduate students whose communication skills were so lacking. A "test" was what the faculty thought they were ordering.

The All University Writing Committee had other ideas, however. Inspired by a number of compositionists who encouraged us to think beyond what others were doing, as a subcommittee we put together the rising-junior portfolio as the equivalent of this "test." Of course, the portfolio did include a sit-down, timed-writing portion, which was what the faculty originally had in mind—that part is certainly a test. But the rising-junior portfolio in its entirety—consisting of three course-written papers and two timed essays—was conceived by the subcommittee as a diagnostic tool in the form of a midstream placement exam rather than an exit exam. The purpose is not to weed out students but to flag students who need more help and get them that help when they need it. It would not have been surprising for some faculty to react negatively to the portfolio solution as a bait-and-switch device. After all, it is not exactly what they ordered. We were prepared for this reaction; what was surprising was that we didn't get it. To the contrary, faculty opinion of the Portfolio has been overwhelmingly positive.

The majority of faculty participate by signing off on course papers that students submit in their Writing Portfolios. According to internal reports compiled by the WSU Writing Assessment Office, in May 1995, 880 teachers had signed off on Writing Portfolio course paper submissions. In June 1999, this figure had increased to 2955 instructors—representing all of the departments on campus signing off on course paper submissions. Faculty members have also participated as paid evaluators of the Portfolio. To date, 150 faculty members, representing 50 departments, have completed the Writing Portfolio reader training and have served as paid readers in the two-tiered process. These faculty members are recruited from the ranks of those who have signed off on the course paper submissions in the Writing Portfolios. Initially, they are trained as first-tier readers to evaluate the timed-writing portion. Experienced readers, who often also are instructors of Writing-in-the-Major courses, are promoted to second-tier readers, who make the final diagnoses on the problematic portfolios. At the second tier, they determine whether a student requires supplemental writing instruction (designated as "needs work") or whether the writing represents the upper 10 percent of undergraduate writing at WSU (designated as "pass with distinction").

The training of the portfolio readers has helped extend our faculty development efforts. Faculty members are recruited to be paid readers of the Writing Portfolio from the ranks of those who have signed off on course paper submissions or those who have attended the WAC workshops and have indicated an interest. The method of recruiting and hiring from the faculty ranks was based on common sense and was incorporated into the two-tier system of reading placement essays (Chapter 4): the more experienced teachers would be able to identify problematic writing and to diagnose students' needs better than less experienced teachers. This method developed concurrently with William Smith's "expert reader" model at the University of Pittsburgh, although we did not know about that model when we were developing ours. Smith's studies (1992, 1993; Calpas & Smith, 1995) demonstrate that experienced teachers of writing make more valid and reliable placement decisions based on their expertise, because they recognize the qualities in the writing that differentiate the writers needing supplemental writing instruction from those who don't.

In the training sessions for tier one, we provide the faculty readers with an overview of the evaluation process and walk through a discussion of the possible placements (pass, pass with distinction, or needs work).

The "real" faculty development occurs in the actual evaluation sessions where the readers first discuss a piece of writing in a norming session and then consult with each other on problematic pieces of writing. The cross-disciplinary conversation in the norming session assures the constant redefining and refining of the standards for acceptable writing at WSU, standards that, within this process, are actually defined by the instructional faculty as they discuss characteristics, perceptions, and issues of the student writing. At the same time, the reading and scoring process raises faculty awareness of the variety of perspectives from which student writing can be viewed. The Writing Assessment Program relies solely on the expertise of the faculty raters to evaluate the Writing Portfolios. If a student contests an evaluation, that writing sample is turned back to the readers to discuss as a group to make a final judgment. This conversation helps clarify the boundaries for the readers between competent writing and writing requiring additional help.

Such widespread faculty involvement in the Portfolio process has also—at least in part—served the purpose of educating faculty about the process. In several Likert scale questions in the 1998 survey, faculty indicated that the Writing Portfolio was not their primary motivation for assigning writing in their courses. That faculty do not perceive the campus writing initiative, including the Writing Portfolio, as the primary reason for assigning writing comes as no surprise. Rather, teaching students to write well within the discipline is a valued quality across campus and, as faculty responses to the survey indicated, is supported largely by the departments. We believe this attitude is in part a result of the success of the WAC faculty seminars over the years, but it also reflects the fact that teaching, as well as research, is valued at our institution. Getting good teachers to see that assigning writing is important to their students' learning processes is hardly difficult. In fact, the WAC program overall has served not so much to encourage more writing in the curriculum (as we found in a 1987 survey of all faculty, it was already there), but to work with teachers on how to incorporate writing and learning more effectively in their classrooms.

Our longitudinal ethnographic research agrees with the information we gathered from the surveys. For example, one series of faculty interviews we conducted asked participants how the rising-junior portfolio has affected their teaching in terms of how they look at writing. The majority responded that their teaching has not been influenced by the existence of the portfolio. Indeed, many used their response to this question to confirm their commitment to teaching writing within their own fields: a teacher of a large general education class explained that she was "already convinced that having good writing skills is indispensable for success in university work and in a career," and an agriculture economics professor maintained that he has "always asked [his] students to write extensively and that expectation has not, nor will it, change." Many faculty members pointed out that neither the nature nor the number of their writing assignments has altered as a result of the portfolio; still others listed grading as another aspect of their pedagogy that has not changed. One anthropology professor who assigns only "essay questions or projects involving written narratives" in almost all of her classes states that she finds it difficult "to imagine what [she] would change if [she] were to consider doing what we might label 'teaching to the portfolio.'"

Although the rising-junior portfolio is most definitely a presence for faculty across the disciplines—several interview respondents mentioned the high numbers of student requests they receive to sign off on portfolio submissions—it is clear that many believe it is a positive presence that serves to reinforce the work they are doing in their own classrooms. A number of those faculty members who teach upper-division classes spoke with especially marked enthusiasm about the effectiveness of incorporating the writing process in their assignments to help students gain the most from writing to learn and, by extension, to learn to write well and to feel adequately prepared to submit papers for the junior portfolio.

An overwhelming majority of faculty who responded in interviews to the question about the effects of the rising-junior portfolio on their teaching also mentioned the positive influence of the WAC faculty workshops, several having attended more than one. In fact, many of the strategies they now use successfully for teaching writing in the disciplines—pre-writing and revising, workshopping, and Haswell's "Minimal Marking" system (Haswell, 1983), for example—are strategies they incorporated into their teaching after having attended a WAC workshop. Having articulated their own teaching philosophy as a result of attending the workshop, many faculty felt empowered to take more risks with their teaching, especially with regard to allowing for the process of writing in their classrooms, as well as to encourage their students to take more risks with their writing. These strategies appear frequently on the student papers in the portfolio. As a result, we have evidence from the portfolio that faculty now demonstrate a much more sophisticated understanding of assigning and assessing writing than they did in the 1980s.

The fact that so many faculty members have participated in the Writing Portfolio apparently has not affected the general understanding of the requirement, however. In our 1998 survey of faculty, 63 percent of the respondents did have a general idea of one of the purposes of the Writing Portfolio, that it provides instructional support; however, the other intentions of the Writing Portfolio were not as well known. A mere 9 percent indicated an awareness that the Writing Portfolio evaluated the General Education curriculum. Thirty-nine percent of respondents knew that it determined students' writing proficiency, while 37 percent acknowledged it as a midcareer assessment of writing. Finally, 33 percent indicated that it was also used to recognize exceptional writing abilities. These low percentages suggest that many faculty members are still unsure of the multiple intentions of the Writing Portfolio. In fact, a few of the respondents stated that the survey informed them about the requirement: they had never heard of it before. We believe these figures demonstrate how difficult it is to pass on to the faculty what the rationale is behind assessment efforts, even in an assessment program as large and pervasive as ours. No differently than students (see Chapter 11), faculty tend to operate on a "need-to-know" basis; if they are not directly involved in the Portfolio assessment by virtue of serving on the All-University Writing Committee or as a Portfolio reader, their understanding of the Portfolio's larger purpose is slender indeed.

EFFECTS OF THE PORTFOLIO ON FACULTY

Our interviews have shown that the Portfolio has had some effect on the faculty in two areas: awareness of the more public nature of their students' writing, and an acceptance of the need for revision of student work (sometimes even after a grade has been given). When the Portfolio was first instituted, those of us on the All-University Writing Committee got a number of calls from concerned faculty member who were being asked by students to sign off on papers for the Portfolio; the concerns were always the same—who would be reading these papers and their own comments on the papers? What if the paper were acceptable as a class exercise, but the teacher felt uncomfortable signing off on it because it still needed some editing? In all these cases, we reassured teachers that they were in fact the first readers of student papers and that those reading the portfolio would accept them as the experts. We then invited them to become Portfolio readers themselves. Many of them accepted that invitation.

This ongoing conversation among our faculty has also become part of our faculty development program, bringing together teachers and practitioners from all disciplines to discuss student writing. Also, what was initiated as a conversation about the difficulties of teaching writing has evolved into a network of conversations about writing in general: not only students, but instructors and faculty members are getting together in groups to discuss the process of their own compositions. As such, our concerted long-term, university-wide efforts have created what we might call a community of writing: although effective assessment of student writing has been a focus of this community, this has happened only within the larger framework of allowing for the process of students' writing—both on short- and long-term levels—to take place.

13

Working with Administrators: A Dialogue on Dialogue

Richard H. Haswell and
Susan McLeod

In the spring of 1995 we received word that higher administration would like a status report on the junior portfolio examination. We shouldn't have been surprised. The exam had been planned since 1989, and students had been sitting for it since 1993; however, we were still caught somewhat unaware. University writing-program personnel may exaggerate how much stock the faculty put in our enterprise (Chapter 12), but we communicate with them on a daily basis. We may ignore or be ignorant of the feelings of students about our enterprise (Chapter 11), but we talk and work and wrangle with them on a daily basis. Higher administration, however, disappears from our immediate concerns for long periods of time, semesters even, if economically the enterprise is faring smoothly. Ironically, it is higher administration who at any moment, by simple fiat, can disenfranchise us—and have done so to entire programs in the past (Anson & Brown, 1991).

The two of us sat down to talk strategy. Rich was coordinating the Writing-Assessment Office and would write the report. Susan was associate dean of Liberal Arts and had advice, both practical and theoretical (McLeod, 1992). We knew what we were talking *about* from the beginning: the status report. But what we were *talking* about dawned on us only gradually: the rhetorical nature of writing-program evaluation within an academic institution. In this chapter we will use the first, the report, as an example. The second is our principal topic.

THE RHETORIC OF INTERNAL EVALUATION

We list some assumptions readily made about the rhetorical nature of university writing-program personnel (UWP) evaluation when it is intended for an internal administrative audience. The assumptions are easy to make but, for evaluators, easier to forget than put into practice. They apply whether the evaluation is in the form of a status or progress report, an audit or accountability report, a validation study, or of any other kind of forensic memoranda sent to higher-ups. The assumptions apply whether the operation is the whole writing program or any part of it, such as the freshman tutorial, the ESL sequence, or the Writing Across the Curriculum (WAC) program.

First, the need for evaluation arises, just as does the need for any piece of discourse, out of both a general and a particular context. The general context is provided by institutions of higher learning, which are large, complex, and thoroughly stratified. The particular context is no less complex but, in addition, never the same from one month to the next; therefore, the rhetorical participants in a UWP evaluation will be varied. Even when there is only one evaluator (rarely the case), there will be multiple readers, and multiple stakeholders (see Chapter 10). Further, each of these participants will have different relationships to the evaluation, different purposes, and different needs. The two main participants, faculty evaluator and administrative reader, often take on diverse motives and roles. All these assumptions mean that UWP evaluation provides ample grounds for communicative conflict, clashes that stem from misunderstandings and that can lead to further misunderstandings. In short, the rhetorical nature of UWP evaluation tests all that the evaluator knows about rhetorical purpose, context, kairos, and audience.

This chapter will explore the rhetoric of UWP evaluation in a very pragmatic way. We will stress—realistically, we hope—the crucial facts of multiple purpose and multiple audience. UWP directors, for instance, need information from ongoing evaluation to know how their programs are working and where they might need to fine tune. In such situations, the UWP directors themselves are the audience, and the purpose is formative. Often, however, UWP directors are asked to evaluate the program for some other audience: a central administrator, a Board of Regents, a legislator. The purpose in such a case may be summative or pleading or political—or merely epideictic, assuring the reader of the program's overall worth. In this chapter we focus on writing to external administrators, taking the perspective of what Michael Patton (1986) calls "utilization-focused evaluation"—a perspective from the needs of the decision makers who have requested and may be using the results of the evaluation. Our pragmatic approach assumes that all points in an act of evaluation have constitutive links with social and political action, from value-construction (Swidler, 1986), validity (Messick, 1989), and methodology (Smith, 1986), all the way to the evaluator's concerns about personal reputation (Gomm, 1981). We agree with these authors that program evaluation is a negotiative process among stakeholders, a way of organizing experience with social and personal consequences and values.

Pragmatically put, our goal is to arrive at some recommendations to assist UWP evaluators in writing reports that will achieve their own goals. Our route is fairly straightforward. We begin by contrasting the typical roles and motives of evaluator and administrator, because these two groups form the core rhetorical dynamic of an administrative report, writer and reader, and because clashes between their respective roles and motives lead to some of the most common rhetorical failures in UWP evaluation. Then we describe our own particular situation of the spring of 1995 in some detail to argue that rhetorically UWP assessment is always located in the particular and always complex. We do so with a dialogue, part transcribed and part reconstructed, between a coordinator of a university writing-examination program with a report to write and an administrator who knows both the program and the intended audience. The dialogue mode is fitting because it will model the ideal spirit in which we believe program evaluation should be undertaken. Dialogue, in a very literal sense, is both the nature of UWP evaluation and the solution to its rhetorical problems. From this specific case, we then extract some general ways evaluators and administrators tend to clash, because we believe that only with attention to these conflicting perspectives will functional evaluation be achieved within an academic institution.

ROLES OF THE UNIVERSITY WRITING PROGRAM EVALUATOR

Typically, the roles of UWP coordinators who are evaluating their own program rise out of a matrix of professional experience different from that of administrators. This is an obvious but crucial point. UWP coordinators *cum* evaluators are entangled, in a direct and ongoing way, with the very programs and personnel they are evaluating. They may be teaching one or more of the WAC courses under scrutiny, or they may be managing a testing office responsible for both the cross-campus assessment procedures and the validation of those procedures. They may even have helped design the courses, the assessments, and the validation studies. Certainly they are experiencing daily frontline encounters with the people who are most immediately affected (and sometimes confused) by UWP programs—students and their relatives, advisors, teachers, department chairs, and clerical staff. More hours of their days than they would like are used up by meetings with statisticians, oversight committees, and technology teams from the computing center. Because they are at the same time teachers and researchers as well as evaluators, usually they persist in the endless task of reading the professional literature, conducting workshops, and writing, presenting, and publishing their own scholarship.

Out of this primordial soup a certain number of roles emerge for the UWP evaluator. The primary motivation—to describe and appraise the UWP program to better it—mobilizes the variety of drives and impulses into a few overriding motives, motives that shape and fuel the roles the evaluator takes on.

What are those basic motives?

- The first is intellectual curiosity, the simple need to learn the truth. Are teachers really following the procedures recommended by the program and reading drafts of student writing? Do students really appreciate or even understand the principles behind UWP initiatives? UWP evaluators want to sound out these and other mysteries, and should want to, as every chapter of this book argues.

- A second basic motive, sometimes at odds with the first, is self-defense. Evaluators, caught up in the formation and implementation of UWP programs, need to defend their positions. They need to justify both the educational practices they are evaluating and the evaluative procedures they are using—and in the process to strut their stuff, to demonstrate their expertise.

- A third motive is to maintain social groups. UWP evaluation may help unify coworkers in the assessment office, bind together a cohort of UWP teachers through self-understanding, or support the self-image of an entire faculty by making programmatic outcomes public. The motivation to further social groups lies behind a spectrum of evaluator actions, from placating oversight boards to gaining budgetary support.

- A final basic motive, it goes without saying, is to better the educational process. UWP evaluation may satisfy some quite self-serving ends of the evaluator, but it never fully lacks, at least for UWP evaluators never fully loses, that essential yearning to find a better way for students and teachers.

These motives set ends to be achieved and expose the need for evaluators to take on certain roles. (Later we will compare the roles of the academic administrator.)

1. *Expert:* one who knows what has been done and what can be done in terms of program evaluation.

2. *Interpreter:* one who serves a constituency outside the program (e.g., administrators) by explaining how things operate and fare from the inside; or one who serves an internal group (e.g., a WAC seminar or an assessment office) by conveying and explaining the position from outside (e.g., the university budgetary office).

3. *Educator:* one whose final allegiance is the learning and welfare of students.

4. *Scientist/researcher:* one whose final allegiance is to the truth as far as it can be determined, one who will uphold evaluation standards of reliability, validity, and fairness.

5. *Team worker:* one who will maintain and further the cohesion and viability of a group, be it validation team, testing office, or UWP faculty.

6. *Apologist:* one whose duty it is to defend historically and theoretically an enterprise, be it a validation process, an ESL initiative, or an interdisciplinary writing workshop.

ROLES OF THE ADMINISTRATOR

It is part of academic culture to grouse about administrators, to construct them as "other," to blame them for the day-to-day inconveniences and inanities of university life. After all, they set and enforce policies and procedures; ipso facto, they are the focal point for dissatisfaction about such issues. The two of us have done our share of such institutional grousing. To write up an effective evaluation of a UWP program, however, we need to think carefully about administrators as audience—what they do, what they want, and what kind of information they might need from evaluators to do their job.

Administrators have different motives than UWP coordinators/evaluators. The primary motive of administrators, unlike evaluators, is to decide where the UWP program fits in the institutional priorities so that decisions can be made about it. Administrators are not devoid of intellectual curiosity and the need to discover the truth, but those motives are always secondary to a primary need, to make decisions about allocation of resources. As the academic equivalent of managers in a corporation, they have the job of maintaining the quality of the institution while working within budgets (these days ever-shrinking). Administrators are busy people. They work on long-range planning for the institution, articulate and enforce policies, monitor (and worry about) such things as enrollments, faculty hiring and retention, and outside perceptions of the university. Like UWP evaluators, they too have particular roles to play.

1. *Generalist:* one who knows a good deal about a number of different disciplines by virtue of having oversight of all departmental units,

but who is not an expert in any but his or her own discipline, and usually not an expert in program evaluation. The description of administrative knowledge, "a mile wide and an inch deep," is useful to keep in mind.

2. *Mediator/Problem-solver:* one who explains various groups in the university hierarchy to each other, conveying the wishes and needs of those above (trustees, legislators) to those below and in return representing the needs and desires of those below to those above. Mediation usually involves resolving conflicts between these needs and wishes.

3. *Manager/Team Leader:* one whose final allegiance is to the health and welfare of the institution or the unit that he or she heads.

4. *Steward:* one who is charged with upholding standards and maintaining quality control and with using resources in accordance with institutional priorities.

5. *Entrepreneur:* one who is expected to meet with possible donors to the institution and to be involved in fundraising.

6. *Spokesperson/P.R. specialist:* one whose duty it is publicly to defend the institution or a piece of it by highlighting its quality and its success.

In summary, on one side the evaluator tends to operate as an expert researcher and educator with commitments to the truth, to student learning, and to various circumscribed groups within the institution, guiding those groups by interpreting the larger academic community and (rarely) informing the community by defending the groups theoretically and pragmatically. On the other side, the administrator tends to operate as a steward and manager with commitments outside the institution to efficiency and to public standards, creating and enforcing policy, solving problems, gaining funding, and in other diplomatic ways mediating between academic groups for the benefit of the whole institution.

Listing their roles helps identify one major conflict in the ways evaluators and administrators see and utilize internal evaluation. When evaluators assess their own UWP programs, they look toward improvement in the program. But administrators, though not unconcerned with program enhancement, are more concerned about the health of the entire institution. They look toward quality assurance, accountability, and public relations. The UWP assessment, therefore, must give administrators only the particular data that fills their needs. An unexpected outcome ripe for further research, for instance—an evaluator's plum—is of no interest to the administrator unless it demonstrates the ongoing health of the program.

Our listing of the different roles suggests many further areas of conflict and potential misunderstanding between evaluator and administrator. Conflicts will arise, however, not simply out of a clash between two divergent academic functions but complexly out of the particular situation at hand. They will depend on the history of the program and the institution, on the current political and economic forces at play, on the organizational channels in operation, on the personnel in place, and on a wealth of other contingencies. By definition, UWP programs are complex, and many of them are youthful. All are in development, or ought to be (see Chapters 3 and 4). Certainly some general areas of conflict can be extracted; we plan to end this article by doing just that. But the very nature of the conflicts, the fact that they exist *as* dialogue among the participants (or lack of dialogue), recommends that they be conceived in context. An understanding or misunderstanding between evaluator and administrator requires a look at its local, messy venue.

A DIALOGUE ABOUT REPORTING EVALUATION RESULTS

To illustrate the interaction of all these roles, we present here a dialogue between an administrator (Susan) and an evaluator (Rich). This dialogue illustrates two things: first, the potential for misunderstanding that we have just discussed, and second, the advantages when the administrator occupies a middle ground between the intended audience and the UWP program. Susan happens to occupy this middle ground, although she is certainly not unique in this advantage. As we have said, this particular dialogue occurred during one particular UWP internal evaluation in the spring of 1995. The provost, who is the chief academic officer of the university, along with the vice provost indicated that they were looking for a status report on the junior Portfolio. What eventually ensued was that Rich, as coordinator of Writing Assessment, produced not one but four reports. Chronologically,

1. A four-page "stopgap" informational report issued five weeks into the spring semester, addressed to the director of General Education and sent on to the provost, to whom the director reports.
2. A five-minute oral report, delivered to the Board of Regents during their annual meeting at commencement, with the vice provost, the provost, and the president in attendance.
3. A six-page "progress" report to the provost and vice provost, via the director of general education, sent a month after the end of the spring semester.
4. A long, formal "internal" report issued at the end of the summer, sent to the director of General Education with copies to the chair of the All University Writing Committee (Haswell, 1995).

The following dialogue took place between the two of us in June, after the first two reports had been issued, but while the third, the "progress" report, was still being written. The dialogue is both a reminiscence of the circumstances that resulted in the first two reports and a working session adding finishing details to the third.

The report under construction has multiple audiences. Besides the usual routing (to the provost and vice provost via the General Education director), other readers will/may be the All University Writing Committee, the dean of the College of Liberal Arts (in whose area most of the writing courses reside), the president, the Board of Regents, and Washington State's Higher Education Coordinating Board. The report may also come into the hands of a stray legislator or two as well as local news reporters. Indeed, it was an awareness of the diversity of needs among these readers that led to the splitting of one report into four.

Rich: This January I heard that the central administration was itchy for a formal account of the Portfolio. That caught me by surprise me since the exam is only two years old and not yet at full steam. From the start I have sent results of student performance (the percentage of "pass with distinction," "pass," and "needs work") to people who needed them at the moment, such as the All University Writing Committee, the director of General Education, various department chairs, the director of Composition, the Student Advising and Learning Center. Of course I thought that sooner or later there would be a validation study, but I didn't imagine the kind of status or accountability report the administrators wanted. Do you know what lay behind that want?

Susan: Yes. I remember that the biennial budget was coming due, and every time that the university's budget request comes before the legislature, there are questions about accountability: What are we spending the state's money on, and what kind of bang we are getting for their buck, what's working, what isn't. The administration needs data, evidence of quality for the budget hearings, to justify the newest request. I think the other driver was the Higher Education Coordinating Board. The HEC Board, like its counterparts in other states, is heavily invested in outcomes assessment statewide.

Rich: My first response was what we are calling the stopgap report. The name reflects my mood at the time. In it I asked six questions, which reflect problem areas, and gave whatever statistics or data I had as answers to these questions. Looking back, would you say this was wise?

Susan: Were they questions or problem areas that you had been asked about, or were they ones you just saw in the material?

Rich: Both. I saw that I had answers to questions that I was interested in, and there were questions that had come out in some conversations that I had with the All University Writing Committee. Like this whole issue of performance: at what rate are we giving out ratings of needs work and pass with distinction? The issue of how well transfer students do is a question that the General Education director had brought up several times. Now in the subsequent report to the regents, I took a considerably different approach, highlighting positive outcomes of the exam and mentioning no areas in need of action. Won't such a radical change of format and content make administrators suspicious?

Susan: No, because the two reports have different purposes. Earlier in the spring the pressure was to give a preliminary report, and it looks to me that there were some very specific questions that people wanted to know the answers to—for instance the success of the transfer students. In fact, one way to approach a report like this is to simply contact the administrator who requested it and ask, "What do you want to know?" Then frame the report as you did, using the questions they want answered. It's a way of getting a quick outline. Administrators don't have a lot of time to research questions they are being asked by their constituencies—they much prefer that the expert craft answers for them. But the presentation to the regents—well, the regents are here for just one day, and they have a lot to absorb. That doesn't give us much time for subtleties. They want to hear that the program is working.

Rich: That brings up the question of what people mean by "working." Everyone seems to have a different take on the outcomes. For instance, after one member of the All University Writing Committee saw the stopgap report, he told me that the figure of 10 percent of exam takers put into the needs-work category was low. He said that he thought 20 percent was more "accurate." On the other hand, the dean of Liberal Arts thought that 10 percent was a good sign, showing that undergraduates are writing well here, better than expected.

Susan: There will be some readers of all your reports who think that undergraduates write very badly, but that notion is based on some comparison with what they remember as the golden days of their undergraduate years. I think of this as a "Paradise Lost" mindset, and it is perhaps more prevalent than you and I might like to believe. What they think they should see and what the report says may be two different things, and we need to be honest.

Rich: Well, *what's honest* has about the same rhetorical status as *what works*—both are equally problematical, though from different sides of the fence. One of the learning moments in all of this was when I first talked with a central administrator about my oral report to the regents. On the phone he said that—he was looking at this stopgap report —"you have some good data here, could you give me five minutes at that meeting?" And then he was very careful, and he said, "Vanilla, nothing fancy." So from that I put together some stuff, most of it positive. But at the time I asked him would it be all right to report the poor performance of the transfer ESL students and the comparative performance of colleges, and he hesitated. Then he said, "Yes, if you want to." Then at the meeting itself, I quickly saw that he was giving me good advice about audience and kairos—what was being reported by other presenters was truly nothing but vanilla.

Susan: Right. The regents technically are at the top of the University's organizational chart—the deans and the General Education director and the vice provost report to the provost, the provost reports to the president, the president to the regents. The regents are appointed by the governor; they are bright, well-educated people who are deeply concerned about the institution, but they are more of a ceremonial body. They must approve all tenure decisions, for example, but that approval is really a rubber stamp. This is not to say they are not an important audience—they are in fact influential in the state and quite shrewd, and they have a veto power they are not afraid to use. But they don't have the decision-making power that the provost has at the local level. They are interested in the overall picture.

Rich: As I was giving this oral report to the regents, there was one piece of the data that they reacted to much more than to the others. It was when I said that Portfolio papers had been submitted from "880 different teachers in 660 different courses in 63 different departments." That seemed to be very impressive to them. You could hear the intake of breath. Why do you think it was?

Susan: You said generally that there was wide-spread compliance. But when you started talking about actual numbers, I think that makes it real to them. They are thinking, wow, this is a big operation. Until you hear those numbers, you don't realize the sheer size of it. That is precisely the sort of fact that the provost will want to quote in his various public presentations, for good public relations. It gives people an idea of how hard we are working.

Rich: As I said, at the regents' meeting I saw they were truly getting vanilla. And so as reports of others kept coming in, I kept marking stuff to leave out of mine. I left out that data on transfer ESL students. I did mention that the portfolio was having a good cross-curricular effect, that a number of departments are doing exceptionally well, and I named them. But I did not name the departments that are having trouble.

Susan: I think that was a wise strategy, because you were talking to regents, who want to hear only about what's working. But the provost and vice provost need to have a more complete picture, since they are the chief academic officers of the institution. Quality control is their job.

Rich: So we are back to what's working. What is the vice provost's take?

Susan: He is first and foremost interested in academic quality. That is his definition of *working*. As vice provost for Academic Affairs, he is charged with general day-to-day quality control of academic programs. He is the Provost's right-hand person and feeds him information. As one of the very first participants in the original UWP seminar I ran in 1986, and as a fine teacher who has always required writing in his anthropology classes, he is very supportive of anything having to do with the writing effort. He will define *working* as improving the quality of our product—student writing.

Rich: How will he use the progress reports?

Susan: To show the folks above him in the administrative hierarchy who hold him accountable—the provost, the president, the regents, the HEC Board and the legislators—that the university is doing a good job with writing on the undergraduate level.

Rich: So that is why you insist that, even with him, we need to emphasize the positive?

Susan: Yes. Not that we don't want to think about how the program can be improved, but things that we can improve ourselves are not his concern.

Rich: What about the provost? Is he different from the vice provost in how he defines what is working?

Susan: Yes, but mostly in the way he wants that information given to him. He is a hard scientist. Where the vice provost is used to ethnographic studies (since that is how he writes up his own research), the provost wants clean facts, to show quality and cost effectiveness. One of the ways I get at the question of readers is to look at the documents they themselves have produced. And if you look at what the provost produces for other people in the university to consume, it is a very short amount of text with a series of bullets, one right after another. Like many public figures, that's also the way he talks, in sound bites, giving nuggets of information. One of the things we want to do with this report is to provide something that then he could translate very easily into one of the overhead transparencies that he uses in his presentations to show what the institution is doing.

Rich: Is that why you recommended in the progress report an executive summary of no more than a page?

Susan: Yes, and not just because the bullets and executive summary are parts of his own administrative style. That format will help him get the gist of the report quickly, and he will appreciate that because he has so much paper to go through. Administrators are overwhelmed by paper—there's always a stack to be read and translated into action. They don't have much time to ponder and reflect.

Rich: Which of these bullets will most attract his attention?

Susan: The bullet giving the ESL data will be particularly interesting because I think there is a general feeling on campus that ESL students have writing difficulties but no one quite knows what to do about the problem. I'm sure you are going to hear about this figure, that 36 percent of transfer students who identified themselves as ESL received the needs-work designation. That's going to be pulled out immediately. And this bullet, "By all signs the Portfolio examination is entrenched and healthy," ought to be pulled out and put at the very beginning. And this final bullet, "Areas in need of further study and improvement," needs to be changed to "Recommendations." What we want them to do with this report is not just learn about what we are doing but take some action.

Rich: The provost will be the one who finally makes the decision to take action. What kinds of action do you think he will take?

Susan: It depends on what the data show, and we need to foreground the data that we think are most suggestive of the action that the provost has the power to take. The data show pretty convincingly that ESL students need support, and at the moment we have no area in the university with the expertise to provide that help. So we may want to recommend that someone in ESL be hired to provide us with that expertise. University administrators are problem solvers; we can help them solve those problems by suggesting solutions.

Rich: Well, since I leave most of the negative information about departments out of this progress report, how is the provost to learn about it? About a month ago, after I had written the stopgap report, you and I talked and decided that for the "final" product I should in fact write two different accounts, this short progress report and then a longer internal report with the data in full–each college and each department and how well they are doing in terms of their students' performance and of their faculty's compliance with assigning writing in their classes. Your suggestion was that the progress report should go up the administrative line, while the internal report should go to the All University Writing Committee, and they should decide what should be done with it. Why do you think that is better than sending negative information directly to the vice provost and the provost?

Susan: Because the AUWC has been the body working directly with individual faculty members on writing-in-the-major courses and on issues of faculty compliance with assigning writing in their classes. The provost and vice provost are decision-makers, but on a day-to-day basis the university committee structure is the machinery by which we get things done.

Rich: So because the AUWC is representative, their decision to do something about it can be more effective.

Susan: They can do something about it in a formative way, working with faculty who are their colleagues, rather than in a punitive way, as the provost might be pressured to do.

Rich: So the question is always, what will administrators make of this data, what will they do with it?

Susan: Absolutely. Administrators are always under pressure in terms of resources and are always looking for reasons to reallocate those resources. The only reason to give them negative information about the workings of the program is if the program really isn't working over all and should be discontinued, or if we thought they should do something about the problem by allocating more resources. For example, in our ESL situation, we have a clear problem and we can't solve it. The administration can—allocation of resources (hiring an expert in this area) will help solve the problem. But if it is a problem we can correct, they don't need to know about it, or if they do, just enough to know that we are correcting it. Any negative information in an otherwise positive report can be easily misunderstood and misused by those who have their own agendas. What would happen if we said in our report that rater reliability could be improved? Administrators might respond by saying, "OK—then we will discontinue the Portfolio and put in a machine-scored multiple choice test, which will be reliable." Ouch. We have to be honest in the overall picture, of course. If a program is not doing what we thought it would, we need to come clean.

Rich: So it's a matter of including in a report only the information that administrators can use, can show to their constituencies, or take particular action that we can't take.

Susan: Yes, utilization-focused assessment.

Rich: With the progress report, you recommended listing the various departments that Portfolio raters come from. Why did you think this information would be useful to administrators?

Susan: I want to make sure that they understood that this is not an English Department operation—that it is a broad-based assessment effort involving people from all disciplines on campus. I think that this is important politically. Because you have been so proactive in getting people from all different disciplines involved in the reading of the portfolios, the word has spread among faculty that this is an effort that includes all who wish to be involved. But administrators tend to be isolated from such general campus understandings. It's hard for them even to attend faculty meetings in the departments with which they are officially affiliated. Your report then serves an important informational function; you are telling them what the general campus already knows.

Rich: And telling them in a substantive form, with figures, so they can test the information against what they have heard.

Susan: Yes, so if Prof. Indignant marches in and says "This is an English Department plot against the rest of us!" the administrator can pull out the report and say, "Well that's not what these figures show."

Rich: As I was preparing the stopgap report, there was one area where I began to sense that I had a different concept of this assessment than the central administrators had. I have always wanted the Portfolio to be primarily instructional, a diagnostic tool to get students the help they need in order to succeed at the upper-division level. But administrators seem to see the Portfolio as a test showing student outcomes or a hurdle showing quality control. Their and my notions of the basic motives behind the Portfolio clash.

Susan: I think that as long as the people in charge of the Portfolio understand that its function is diagnostic rather than punitive, there's no need to explain the niceties of that distinction to the administration. Administrators are involved in two things that may make it better for them to think of this as a test: quality control and public relations. Their job is to let people know that yes, we have standards and we are doing something about student writing. We're testing it. And furthermore, few institutions of our size have been able to make this sort of test work but (trumpets, please) *we* are.

Rich: So this is one area in which the display of data can get around those conceptual issues.

Susan: Yes. And the understanding of the Portfolio as a test might even work in their favor—when they are talking to legislators, or potential donors, or to the regents or the HEC Board. Some segments of the public have a rather punitive notion of what education is all about, and the notion of a test might fit their schema of an institution with high standards.

Rich: One last question. It was my idea to make this progress report the first of a sequence, one every two years. Does that make sense?

Susan: Yes. You have managed to coordinate it with the biennial budget request that the director of General Education has to send forward. You want to make sure that if you are asking administrators to do something with the information you give them, then you must do it at a time when they have the resources. It's very savvy of you to know what the budget cycle is and coordinate your report and accompanying recommendations with that cycle.

Rich: Well, there is a difference between savvy and lucky. So two more years and another progress report?

Susan: The administration will hope so. Administrators are always being held accountable by all of their constituencies—above and below them. The information we give them is information that they want to use. Especially these days when authority of any sort is under fire, they are constantly scrambling to find data that show the university is really doing its job—that professors are not just a bunch of drones and that we are teaching students something useful. They are eager for information, especially when we have programs that are really working and can prove that they are.

CONFLICTS BETWEEN EVALUATOR AND ADMINISTRATOR

As we hope our dialogue shows, the possibilities for conflicts between UWP evaluators and administrators are legion. Within the arena of UWP programs, however, there are six common conflicts that warrant special attention. These conflicts may appear to be simplifications and even abstractions, but they have served to help troubleshoot or clarify encounters between UWP evaluators and administrators in the past.

1. *The clash between a vision of a part and a vision of the whole.* Almost by definition, evaluation of a program requires a restricted gaze. An evaluator who studies an upper-division, writing-intensive program, say, is constantly tempted to disregard the relevance of that program to the university as a whole. The attention is to certain courses, certain teachers and students, certain outcomes. The nature of empirical testing and inferential statistics further circumscribes that attention, and the evaluator may

investigate only a sample of sections and test for a small selection of outcomes. When all is done, it is hard to resist speaking in the time-honored words of many a validation study and refuse to vouch for the implications of the conclusions beyond the few variables measured. Yet the administrator, however sympathetic, needs to go beyond outcomes. Decisions need to be made about the entire program, with constant attention to the ramifications of those decisions in terms of the university as a whole.

2. *The clash between description and action.* Indeed, when administrators rightly complain that the evaluation report lacks clear relevance to the formation of policy or fails to recommend a clear course of action, the evaluator may easily fall back on the researcher's defense that the study is purely descriptive and that it is up to others to decide on its implications. Descriptive findings, however, can be more or less useful. The evaluator can measure the number of pages submitted in intensive-writing courses, from which it is difficult to recommend further action, or assess the value of the writing from the students' and the teachers' point of view, from which viewpoints recommendations for change are more readily seen. A wise evaluator designs the need for final recommendations right from the start.

3. *The clash between problem-discovery and problem-solving.* It is a temptation for program evaluators to think of internal evaluation as a search for problems. Comparison of syllabi from intensive-writing courses *across* disciplines probably shows some departments weaker than others in the integration of writing assignments with subject matter. This is a problem, however, for which the administrator wishes the evaluator had included other findings indicating a solution. Of more use to the administrator might be the identification of especially successful teachers and techniques *within* disciplines, in which case recommendation for improvement is clearer. Again, evaluators could well be aware of the need to shape evaluation toward solutions from the beginning.

4. *The clash between expert and public understanding.* Evaluation of human performance has become a highly technical field. Every part of it has a professional history of unresolved debate. It is easy for knowledgeable evaluators—the more knowledgeable, the easier—to direct their reports to their own kind. Administrators need to send evaluation findings to persons and groups who may have little professional understanding of evaluation and even personal bias against aspects of it such as data collection and statistical analysis.

5. *The clash between the need for truth and the need for usefulness.* By nature and certainly by the creed and procedures of assessment methodology, the evaluator presents all the findings, the whole findings, and nothing but the findings, no matter how negative, discouraging, or confounding. There is even a commitment to report conclusions that suggest the methodology itself was flawed or incomplete. The administrator often has a very difficult time making use of such an approach. Some of the

most difficult standoffs between evaluator and administrator occur because of the imperative of one to report negative findings and the need of the other to have findings that are convincing, supportive, or persuasive for a particular constituency.

6. *The clash between abstractions and personalities.* Formal evaluation asks that the evaluator move toward objectivity and generalizations whenever possible. The evaluator is looking for regularities that lie underneath the confusion of surface input and is trying to set the eccentricities and individual agendas of the individuals involved in evaluation—students and teachers—aside. The administrator, on the other hand, must deal directly with personalities because they are a means by which and an avenue through which things in a complex organization are accomplished. And the administrator must deal with them on a case-by-case basis, knowing that each person is unique and that uniqueness often is the key to successful action through that person.

RECOMMENDATIONS

Having presented our own dialogue, which illustrates some of these clashes, we would like to follow our own advice and close with some recommendations for those asked to produce evaluations of UWP programs.

1. Ask as many questions as you politely can about the needs of your primary audience (who may or may not be the people requesting the evaluation report). Who is your most important audience, and why does that person/committee want this evaluation? Is the purpose to find out how well the program works, to find out how cost-efficient it is, to justify funding (or slashing) the program? Your report will no doubt have multiple audiences, and you should not ignore them, but you should focus on the primary audience, usually central administrators, and the use they will make of the report.

2. Examine the sorts of documents that are both consumed and produced by the office to which your report ultimately goes. Use these documents as models.

3. If at all possible, before or while you draft your report, carry on your own dialogue with an administrator who knows the stakeholders and is willing to help you think through the issues. This dialogue works best, we think, if that person is a midlevel administrator—not someone to whom the report goes, but someone who knows the personalities and the motives and who has experience writing similar reports and can help you phrase things where necessary in administrationese.

4. Focus on recommendations and action. Administrators rarely ask for reports so that they can file them—they are decision-makers.

They need evidence that they have made good decisions and evidence on which to base new ones. Think carefully about what you want to have happen as a result of the information you are presenting. Do the data suggest that you need a bigger budget for the program? Is the program growing at such a rate that you need a new computer to track it? Don't expect administrators to figure out what you need. Tell them the problems your data illuminate, and then suggest a solution. For this audience, do not ignore the need for public relations.

5. Find out about the budget cycle at your institution and what relationship your report might have to that cycle.

If we may return to our opening point, writing up an assessment of a UWP program tests all that the evaluator knows about rhetoric. We should take the advice we give our students: Figure out who the audience is, what the purpose and situation are, what particular readers will do with what we send them and what formats will serve them, what models should guide us, and how much feedback we need on our drafts. This kind of audience awareness is less difficult than it may seem. After all, the distance between evaluator and administrator is not that great. While we have contrasted their motives and roles, we also think it instructive to remember that both usually started out with the same experiences, as faculty members. Where there are commonalties in experience, there are ways to communicate.

Part V

Program Future: Eight Questions

Here is an encapsulation of this book's advice on creating, implementing, and keeping healthy a long-lived university writing program that integrates assessment and instruction. Following the habit of a short-lived provost at Washington State University (see Chapter 13), bullets are used to show that the order of items has no significance.

- Integrate programs in as many ways as you can. Especially integrate assessment and instruction.
- Assess ultimately for the sake of instruction; instruct incidentally for the sake of assessment.
- Develop a sense of ownership in participants, especially students.
- Respect and involve stakeholders, especially students.
- Build sanctuaries where participants can tell stories.
- Support a strong, central university writing center.
- Encourage grassroots changes, discourage top-down changes.
- Publicize goals early, but privately leave them flexible.

- Treat program development, including formal assessment, as an adventurous space, open to explore.
- Innovate.
- Seize the reins because often nobody else really wants them.
- Let the local scene shape the assessment; eschew marketed tests.
- Indebt but don't enslave yourself to the scholarly literature.
- Don't let innovation fossilize. You need it to beget further innovation.
- Let the people who will maintain the program help build it. Let the people who will maintain it help keep building it.
- Make assessment and instruction each shape the other into an evolving whole.
- Self-study and validate without compunction.
- Be as creative in program maintenance as you are in program creation.
- Give authority to those who feel ownership and show expertise.
- Make the maintenance and the unit that maintains fit, especially fit according to the temperament and the skills of the people in the unit.
- Expect poison from standing programs. With academic programs, modification is the staff of life.
- As the institution changes, change the instructional-assessment program.
- Don't ever imagine that an examination rating system is handmaiden to the exam or that the exam is handmaiden to the instructional program.
- Don't be too concerned if operational aspects of the program lack theory, but remember that theory sells the program to the skeptical and explains it to the interested.
- Assess both the individual student and the local instructional surround. Always the final goal is improvement in student writing.
- Self-evaluate with an eye to better as well as to defend the program.
- Know that critique of one's own program is energizing and creative.
- Organize writing-center systems and assessment systems to complement not counter each other.
- Within hybrid academic units, help teachers, students, and even administrators follow natural learning cycles. Synchronization is wholly timely.
- Never transform one entire part of a writing program—strong change—without self-evaluation of the whole program.
- Have faith in value-added studies to the extent that you have faith in your writing program. The success of the second justifies the trial of the first.
- Articulate assessment examinations that are administered at different times in a student's undergraduate career. Forearticulated is forearmed.
- Validate, every single time, with multiple measures.

- Let the stakeholders shape the validation; let the parties involved interpret the outcomes.
- In program validation, never forget that students and their feelings and opinions are the most valuable to explore because they are the most vulnerable to exploitation.
- Don't study the program unless you are willing to act on the findings to improve the program.
- Energetically instruct the students about the assessment-instructional program; energetically instruct the teachers about the assessment-instructional program.
- Don't forget that the best way to make faculty aware is to make them a part of every aspect of the assessment program: innovation, design, implementation, maintenance, development, validation.
- Be aware that program administrators and higher administrators have different motives and different outlooks, though they have the same roots.
- With higher administration, shape discussion more in terms of future action and less in terms of outcomes, unless the outcomes have political use.
- Assess for placement, not for competency; validate for program development, not for program outcomes.
- And in case you missed it: Make assessment and instruction each shape the other into an evolving whole.

One last advice might be that because a functioning writing program is alive and changing, one should always keep an eye on the changes, which appropriately is the subject of our final chapter, Chapter 14.

14

Whither? Some Questions, Some Answers

William Condon, Fiona Glade, Richard H. Haswell,
Lisa Johnson-Shull, Diane Kelly-Riley,
Galen Leonhardy, Jennie Nelson,
Susan McLeod, and Susan Wyche

1. Postsecondary assessment-instruction writing programs sometimes lead brief lives. What are the chances that a system like Washington State University's (WSU) will enjoy a long one?

What ensures the viability of a testing program is difficult to define—whether it is the actual shelf life or the responsiveness of a program that makes it long lasting . Certainly, the length that a testing method has been used does not indicate its effectiveness or usefulness in assessing students' writing as these notions themselves are open to interpretation. Many would agree that a Scholastic Aptitude Test (SAT) or Collegiate Assessment of Academic Proficiency (CAAP) style of exam has been long outdated, but this form of evaluation continues to thrive as an acceptable and widely used assessment measure for college entrance, proficiency, and exit examinations. This type of exam's viability seems akin to Dracula:

any reflection by students or administrators on the meaning of the results yields nothing, and no one has quite been able to find a sufficient wooden stake to put this invalid use of the exam to rest.

Fundamentally, this style of exam is the most distant from the instructional and curricular needs of students, faculty, and administrators. The exam offers a quick solution to the daunting task of determining where hundreds or thousands of students should begin or end their academic careers. Ultimately, indirect exams function as mechanistic sorting devices that herd students into or out of the bureaucratic maze of an undergraduate degree program, providing little information except a numerical quantification. Assessment programs designed to serve as an end, whether as a placement mechanism or as a gatekeeping device, tend to become quickly ineffectual because the population outgrows it. These psychometric measures, narrow in scope, attempt to measure a static entity. Students and the systems in which they exist, however, are not fixed enterprises.

Forms of assessment that serve as a means to a larger context, which adopt fourth-generation evaluation principles, operate with a different notion of viability. In this sense, the life of the testing program depends on the investment of all stakeholders in the process—from students to faculty to administrators to legislators and their constituents. Responsive assessment offers a local, dynamic, human-centered, accountable practice whose survival depends on the ability to change and adapt to the ever-evolving system in which it exists.

Diagnostic assessment practices are naturally more involved, messier, and more difficult, but they provide an institution the opportunity to combine assessment with instructional practices, empower the local populations of an institution, and yield a variety of data more representative of its populations to engender a response. All this would argue for an enhanced longevity of the assessment system.

Recursive assessment practices are currently in their fledgling stages—some have been short-lived, like the SUNY Stony Brook first-year portfolio assessment, while others continue to grow and evolve into established programs, such as Alverno College's assessment/advising system. These practices are changing the notion of viability in testing programs, shifting the focus from labeling students to providing them with useful feedback that can inform their instructional choices. Hopefully, the stakeholders—the holders of the stakes—have the power to finally lay the indirect exam to rest never again to see night or day. *DK-R*

2. Will the integration of the writing assessment and the Writing Across the Curriculum (WAC) system help ensure longevity of the two programs?

The answer, I think, connects to the fact that writing assessment has been around for a long time in higher education, but what is new (and continuing) is the national movement by legislators, trustees, and others to tie all assessment to accountability. One of the reasons the Writing Portfolio has been so successful at WSU is the need for central administrators to show the legislature and our Higher Education Coordinating Board that we are in fact doing what we say we are doing—improving student writing. The danger of all assessment initiatives in education is that they become reductive; legislators and the general public have a good deal of misplaced trust in standardized tests and in the resultant tidy charts, graphs, and percentiles.

If anybody knows that student or faculty outcomes in a WAC program cannot be reduced to a number, it is the WAC director. The challenge for WAC, then, is to find assessment instruments for both students and programs that satisfy the stakeholders and avoid positivist measures that do not adequately reflect the complexity of both student learning and the WAC programs that are structured to facilitate that learning. The portfolio as an instrument of authentic assessment, therefore, fits nicely with the goals of WAC programs, and each helps keep the other healthy. *SM*

3. How much will research methods need to change to meet the ecological concept of a university writing-assessment program fully embedded in the life of the university?

The notion that an assessment program has its own ecology requires us to expand the research terrain. Historically, researchers examining assessment programs have focused solely on students—their preexam status, their performance, and occasionally, but not often, their thoughts and feelings about the assessment. Other components of the exam situation have not been studied. For example, how do teachers and advisors feel about it? What do students tell their parents about the assessment? How do administrators at all levels view the assessment program? How do they describe the assessment to new faculty, to outsiders?

When novel methods of testing are adopted (such as a portfolio of course writings for the junior-level exam), then new questions for inquiry are raised. How much time does a typical student spend preparing the portfolio? How do students decide which writing samples to include? What kinds of conversations take place when students bring in a paper for a teacher to sign off on? What do students tell each other about the portfolio requirement? Do their task representations for the junior placement exam differ from their representations for the freshman placement? What strategies do students rely on for writing the impromptu essay? How do students' academic advisors describe the portfolio requirement? What kinds of questions do teachers ask themselves when they are requested to sign off on students' papers? How do portfolio readers negotiate the tricky terrain of overturning another faculty member's evaluation of their students' writing? How much value do departmental administrators attach to the assessment process—to their students' performance, to their faculty members' participation in the program? How are these views and values transmitted to a departments' members? New research questions and innovative methods for answering them must evolve as an assessment program's ecology continues to grow and change.

Traditional research tools, such as surveys or questionnaires, may not be effective in tapping into the perceptions and daily conversations that are part of a testing ecology. Ethnographic research methods may be more appropriate for exploring this new research terrain. For example, longitudinal case studies of new students and faculty members would reveal how their views of an assessment program evolve over time. Graduates could be asked what they remember of their participation in the program, one or several years after graduation. No doubt future researchers will devise methods of research that would amaze us today. At Western College of Miami University in Ohio, enterprising researchers attached beepers to participant students and asked the students to note in a log precisely what they were doing when the beeper sounded (it was turned off when they went to bed) (Amiran, Schilling, & Schilling, 1993). Just as the methods may shock us, so will the findings. In this case, many faculty may be pleasantly surprised to read that the logs revealed that students were devoting nearly 40 percent of their waking time to academic matters. JN

4. Part of the current ecology of the examination system at WSU is a certain amount of resistance to it from both students and faculty. What steps ought to be taken to reduce that resistance? How can WSU's response to resistance influence future assessment practices?

Assessment processes, if they are democratic, must be reliant on and responsive to the stakeholders invested in the process. Responsive assessment is necessarily collaborative and multidimensional. It is many things to many people, so it seems natural to suppose that some of those people will be resistant. That resistance will be both reasoned and unreasoned (support can be both reasoned and unreasoned, too). Because democracy and fairness are foundational elements in responsive processes and because both are dependent on reason, assessment programs must remain open to all forms of resistance for the simple reason that resistance facilitates critical reflection and growth in ways that compliance cannot. Fear of resistance (regardless of whether the resistance is reasoned or unreasoned) may disrupt the need to reflect. In short, resistance is a natural and constructive part of any assessment ecology. The hard part is recognizing resistance and listening to the stakeholders who are actively resisting.

Resistance is important because it is directly related to reflection and growth. That is, reflection allows for constructive change. Both resistant and supportive stakeholders can contribute to the ongoing process of con-

struction. Responsive writing assessment programs rely on critical examination to promote a reflective awareness of the process in its context. Of
course, not all assessment processes are open to critique or change, both
forms of resistance. And the sad fact of the matter is that responsive
assessment practices have not become as commonplace as one would
hope. So in the future, it would be beneficial if the process of responding
to resistance at WSU could be extended to elementary and secondary
assessment practices.

To get at the potential of future developments, at what our experiences
say about how college assessment might change in relation to the idea of
resistance, it seems reasonable to first examine something other than the
ideal, to use a negative situation to examine future potentials. For example, until my wife and I spoke with our daughter's teacher, it took one
and a half to two hours for our nine year old to finish her homework. Our
daughter's teacher, as it turned out, was responding to the pressures associated with an assessment process that will be used not only to judge our
daughter's progress in the public school system but also to determine the
teacher's standing in relation to other teachers across the state.

The first question my wife and I asked was how could any assessment
of fourth graders, especially a decontextualized assessment, reflect on
specific fourth grade teachers? We reasoned that an assessment of fourth
graders' writing could not reflect the abilities of a particular fourth grade
teacher because there is a history of instruction and life happenings experienced by each student that is not controlled by the teacher. That is, students can be influenced by teachers, but students are not their teachers.
Unfortunately, our daughter's teacher, like other teachers at the school,
has not been resisting, something we did not think strange until we were
told that no one knew exactly what our nine year old would be writing
for the written portion of the state-wide test. At best, there were rumors
that the fourth graders would be expected to write an academic summary (newly changed from a persuasive business letter). We supposed that
college professors were behind the choice of a summary and business
professionals had chosen the persuasive letter. Regardless, we knew that
nobody had asked us what we thought.

Of course, my wife and I attempted to make our concerns apparent,
but our resistance (or willingness to contribute) to the process has thus far
been ignored. For example, our attempts to become involved have met
with unreturned phone calls, misinformation, and scowls from principals
more invested in Pavlovian experiments in cavity making than in examining the effects of a decontextualized assessment process on underrepre-
sented and unrepresented stakeholders. Unfortunately, these and other
oppressive aspects that emerge in a closed assessment process can con-
sign some stakeholders to subordinate or dehumanized positions. That is
how we started to feel, powerless and subordinated.

As alienated stakeholders, my wife, my daughter, and I decided to make ourselves human by objecting (a form of resistance). Our daughter, who was never asked what she thought about the assessment process, will not be participating directly. Collaboratively, we decided that she could best contribute by objecting, which has caused her teacher no small amount of confusion. In fact, the teacher's only comment was "I'm not sure you can do that." The problem is that she sees our resistance as something negative, something that breaks an unstated and unquestioned set of rules about compliance.

The assessment process at WSU provides examples of how resistance and people who resist can find affirmation. First, the doors of those directly involved in overseeing the assessment process are always open, and the people behind the doors are more than willing to accommodate stakeholder interests. As our collaborative narratives make apparent, writing assessment that is responsive accepts ongoing change from a variety of resistant sources (see Chapter 11). In short, the assessment is affirming because it is an educative process, which as explained by Guba and Lincoln (1989), is a process in which "all have the opportunity to confront and develop criticisms of their own constructions as well as the constructions of others" (p. 139). Stakeholders who resist are necessary to any assessment process because they aid in the construction.

In the future, assessment administrators learning from the assessment at WSU might begin their constructions by simply affirming the idea that resistance is not negative. Without it, people involved in assessment are less able to reflect on their practices. In the future, those striving towards or maintaining responsive assessment programs might simply ask "Why?" and "What do you think we should do?" when a student or teacher (or any other stakeholder) voices his or her objections. The point is that resistance (even from oppressive perspectives) should not be diminished so much as focused and contemplated because it stimulates the process of critical awareness. Without critical awareness, the process of assessment becomes more domesticated than transformative, more authoritarian than democratic. *GL*

5. Distance learning facilitated with computers is an inevitable future. Think of WSU's English 102 or General Education 302 on-line. Can tutorial writing groups survive in cyberspace? Can the instruction-assessment hybrid program survive on-line?

The success of the WSU Writing Program rests in large part on the creation and sustenance of communities of "knowledgeable peers" who work together to develop ideas and discuss the implications of the ideas they generate. The structure of the program emphasizes group interactions ranging from the assemblage of faculty raters to discuss problematic placement and portfolio essays to the gathering of students enrolled in credit-based writing tutorials to discuss the writing they are doing in their coursework. These groups negotiate knowledge and its presentation through conversations and consultations that occur in carefully facilitated physical space. However, given that a growing percentage of WSU students (and faculty) do not reside on the main campus and do not have convenient access to their peers, ways in which these learning communities might be successfully reproduced in cyberspace warrant consideration.

Multiple technological avenues exist for individuals to engage in communities within carefully designed computer-mediated spaces. The recent popularity of MOOs, MUDs, chatrooms, newsgroups, email exchanges, and virtual classrooms clearly indicates that communities in cyberspace are capable of serving both social and instructional needs. Regardless of the proliferation of such sites, research on the functionality of interpersonal relationships in cyberspace indicates that there is little agreement on how well these interactions create and sustain meaningful associations. Currently, opinions on computer-mediated communication (CMC) exist within a spectrum encompassed by two extremes: (1) the belief that on-line communities are substandard and cyber-interactions shallow and potentially antagonistic (Stoll, 1995), and (2) the conviction that computer mediated communication has the ability to supersede the limits of face-to-face interaction by engaging the *hyperpersonal*—relationships that emphasize intimacy due to the more planned nature of the composition (Walther, 1995).

Either of these extremes presents problems that would undermine the goals of a writing group. On the one end, those who allow the technology to alienate them from interacting with their peers might be disengaged and not motivated to contribute the kind of meaningful feedback that is prerequisite to a writing group; and on the other, those who thrive primarily on the relationship-building potentials of the medium might miss the practical point of the community—improved writing strategies. The middle ground between these poles is perhaps the optimum territory within which to locate an institutionally supported writing group. Yet, within all of these discussions of the potentials and pitfalls of CMC, one issue remains unresolved: how do you locate a community in the middle ground? How do you facilitate its success? Who mediates the computer mediation?

Little research currently exists on the schemes and strategies for facilitating healthy communities—on-line or otherwise. Those of us who function well in groups often do so intuitively, rarely knowing exactly what it is that we do or say or how it is that we present ourselves that makes a difference to the success of the group we inhabit. As we move our ambiguously articulated arts of teaching and tutoring into a medium that seems to encompass the full range of possible human responses, what senses will we use to guide our students to a better understanding of themselves as writers? What cues will indicate the need to add words and ideas to calibrate the conversation so that it remains inclusive and productive?

Clearly these questions do not lend themselves to pat answers. But as Andrea Lundsford reminds us, solving problems is only part of the battle; identifying them is perhaps the more consequential challenge (1991). *LJ-S*

6. Are there good reasons to shift to electronic portfolios for writing assessment?

Whenever we hear people who are not using electronic portfolios talk about them, one of the first issues raised is storage. Early in the portfolio movement, we often heard storage issues raised as a powerful logistical barrier to using portfolios at all. "Where," these voices asked, "will we find money for all the filing cabinets?" As the history of portfolios since the mid-1980s has shown, storage has not been a problem. Schools are not buried in piles of portfolios, nor have they broken their budgets paying for storage space. Just as storage was a red herring for paper portfolios, it is not a primary reason—or even a *good* reason—to experiment with electronic portfolios. Indeed, people who are using electronic portfolios do not typically mention this issue at all. Instead, they focus on the ways that electronic portfolios enhance and extend the already recognized advantages of portfolio-based writing assessment.

If we take a look at Figure 14.1 (Hamp-Lyons & Condon, 2000), we can see what those advantages are; then we can look briefly at how cyberspace provides a supportive environment for the portfolio.

Figure 14.1 reveals that three principal characteristics of portfolios, collection, reflection, and selection, govern how the other six come into play. Collection stems from the teacher and the curriculum; it is the corpus of work a student has been asked to produce over a given period of time. The other two, reflection and selection, allow the student to shape the corpus into an exhibition that addresses a given occasion for undergoing an assessment.

In a writing classroom, that purpose is almost always exit assessment, the portfolio almost always selected to demonstrate that the student has achieved specific outcomes, acquired specific abilities as a writer. Typically, as assessments move outward in scope or larger in scale, the targeted abilities or competencies contract; therefore, WSU's writing portfolio seeks to identify students who need extra support as they enter their upper-division Writing in the Major courses—an important function, but on the whole, a less complicated, less wide-ranging decision than whether a student should pass out of first-year composition. The larger scale and scope of the assessment seems to reduce the kinds of conclusions we can draw about the writer to whether that writer's competencies are significantly lower than his peers' or significantly higher (needs work or pass with distinction). In both cases, too, the focus is on writing abilities.

Electronic portfolios provide an effective tool for assessing writing too, of course, but the nature of the electronic portfolio allows it to fill multi-

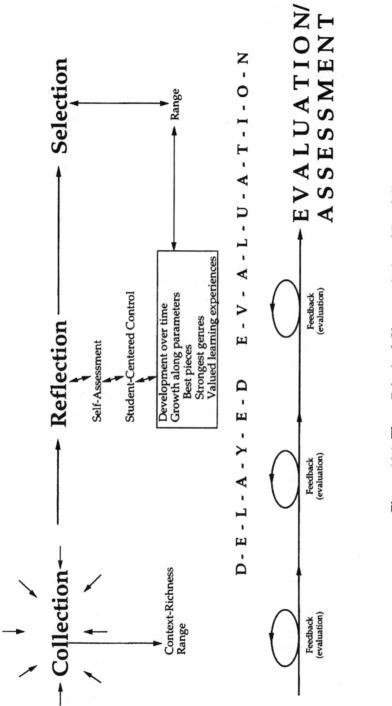

Figure 14.1 Three Principal Characteristics of Portfolios

ple assessment roles. All our old friend *storage* means, in the end, is that the learner's *collection* can be much more extensive than a paper-based portfolio can allow. The electronic portfolio can incorporate more kinds of text, and it can include more texts. It can also be accessed by students, teachers, administrators, parents—by whomever, at a given time and for a given purpose; the learner needs to show competence, achievement, etc. Indeed, those institutions already using electronic portfolios tend to use them for more purposes than mere writing assessment. Students collect their work products on-line and then shape that collection from time to time for various purposes, only one of which may be writing assessment. For instance, several small colleges use electronic portfolios for advising. The student prepares an exhibit that demonstrates to what extent the learner has accomplished the college's General Education objectives, for example, and the learner and the advisor look at that exhibit together as a way to decide, based on past performance, what courses or other learning experiences would most clearly benefit that learner (Mount Olive College uses a system like this one—or it did at the time this section was written). A list of colleges using electronic portfolios can be accessed at the following URL: http://owl.webster.edu/eportfolio/resources.html. The rapid change possible with electronic resources renders moot any attempt to provide a reliable list in print.

As we look forward to a time when assessment and instruction are more intertwined and interrelated than they are today, we can easily see that electronic portfolios provide a platform for *Fourth Generation Evaluation* (Guba & Lincoln, 1989), or, if we prefer, a response to Kathleen Yancey's call for "third-generation" writing assessments. Here, then, as we see them, are the reasons for pursuing electronic portfolios:

- They open the learning processes, increasing access to success by expanding the ways in which learners can demonstrate their learning. One of the advantages of writing portfolios over other forms of writing assessment is that learners can call on a wider range of texts to demonstrate their accomplishments. Electronic portfolios expand that set to include many kinds of text that cannot be contained on paper.

- They provide learners with opportunities to produce texts that correspond to the kinds of text most produced in the workplace—web pages, e-mail, multimedia, and so on. Perhaps, because of this correspondence, electronic portfolios also encourage students to perceive the continuity between college curriculum and the workplace, therefore increasing the learners' motivation in the classroom.

- They can collect all a learner's work products; therefore, the learner can easily and economically assemble a variety of portfolio exhibits, at different times and for different purposes. For each different occasion, the learner must reflect on her collection and select the items for the current audience and purpose. The electronic portfolio, therefore, is potentially more useful for promoting—and tracing—a student's metacognitive development. The act of reflecting at different points and for different purposes would itself provide a significant record of learning and of progress.

• They enable access for multiple stakeholders. Just as students could put together an on-line portfolio to demonstrate writing ability, so could they put another one together to establish that they have addressed any of their school's other educational objectives. In addition, they could put together selections to show their parents; they could make some of their work available to the institution for program assessment purposes; they could identify pieces for awards committees to read. Learners could at any point and for any purpose reflect on their corpus of work, select items that demonstrate a particular ability or an array of competencies, and make that selection available to whoever is supposed to review it. Finally, learners can use the collection to reflect on what is not there, using that information to plan further study.

So far, these are the principal reasons we see for pursuing electronic portfolios. These reasons are clearly enough to make that pursuit worth the effort. Electronic portfolios give the person with the largest stake in an assessment—the subject being assessed—the greatest measure of control over the work being assessed. Increasing the learner's control, as we have seen with writing portfolios, increases the learner's confidence in the results of the assessment. In turn, greater faith in the result boosts the learner's investment in learning itself. BC

7. But do the advantages outweigh the difficulties in making electronic portfolios work?

Recent technological developments for submitting, evaluating, archiving, and distributing information open possibilities for structuring writing assessment programs that would have been unthinkable even five years ago. There are several advantages to using the electronic medium:

• Students can submit portfolios from any location, therefore, providing convenient access to students who have been admitted but have not yet arrived on campus (from high school and community colleges) and to future distance-learning students who may never set foot on the campus.

• Students can submit work that integrates writing with other media— film, video, graphics, audio, websites, etc. Increasingly, technology is creating an on-line world where all these media are used. Currently, however, this may prove especially advantageous for disciplines in which writing is regularly used with other media.

- The portfolio can include drafts and other supporting documents that may be of use to faculty and students but would be unwieldy in hard-copy portfolios.

- Electronic portfolios, once submitted electronically, are difficult to lose and backup copies easily made.

- Faculty can access electronic portfolios from a variety of locations—on campus or at home—and can conduct evaluations in ways that may better fit their schedules than large-scale assessment sessions in which everyone must be in the same room.

- In the case of portfolios that are problematic or need to be read by second or third readers, access is immediately available.

- Depending on how the system is set up, students and their advisors can access their results as soon as the faculty members have submitted them, therefore saving time in distribution of data.

- Large numbers of portfolios can be stored inexpensively. Hardcopy portfolios are unwieldy and take up valuable space, yet keeping records over a period of years is necessary for longitudinal studies (which are especially useful for program evaluation).

- Individual portfolios, once filed, can be sorted in multiple ways for research and archival purposes.

- Portfolios can be made readily accessible to faculty, administrators, students, and external parties (researchers, program evaluators) as appropriate and determined by campus policies. This means that students can look at models of successful portfolios, the public can view award-winning portfolios, faculty members can see other writing samples from a student they may be trying to advise, etc.

- Students can use selections from their portfolio for seeking jobs, applying to graduate schools, etc. Institutions can archive websites for students as part of an alumni program or give students compact disk (CD) copies of their portfolios.

- Electronic portfolios also allow colleges and universities to connect with their community college and high school partners, because student work can be shared, evaluated, analyzed, and discussed among students, teachers, and administrators in a way that hard copy never could.

Electronic portfolios also provide opportunities for problems to develop that can complicate the lives of students, teachers, and administrators in new and unexpected ways.

- Not all students have convenient access to or comfort with technology. The students who struggle with academic writing for reasons of social inequity will likely be the same students who struggle with electronic systems that others assume are fully accessible.

- Additionally, students with the best access to leading technology (the latest software, the best equipment) will be able to submit work that is more sophisticated than students with outdated technologies, which may inadvertently prejudice readers.

- Faculty will find that the combination of assessment and technology doubly intimidating. They may undercut programs or refuse to participate because they themselves feel uncomfortable with the demand on their technological skills.

- New legal issues will develop concerning ownership, reproduction, and use of electronic texts.

- Assessment programs will become more costly, as technical and administrative support will be needed at more sophisticated levels than hardcopy assessments required.

- Accessibility of texts will create new opportunities for plagiarism and hacking.

- Local assessments may develop the facelessness of commercial enterprises as students need not have contact with faculty or writing program personnel to submit their work or receive their evaluations.

- Faculty, working in isolation, may lose valuable opportunities for the development and community building that occur when they read and discuss student work together.

- Administrators will face new challenges in training, norming, and tracking faculty readers if all contact is virtual.

These are not inevitable problems, but they are certainly possible problems with which administrators interested in electronic portfolios must grapple. Like the electronic vehicle, electronic portfolios may work best if mixed with existing practices for the foreseeable future. Faculty could come together in person for training before conducting assessments over the web (though there is no reason that training, too, can eventually be delivered electronically). Students could have hardcopy options, to mitigate against hardship cases.

Moving writing assessment into virtual spaces requires a cultural shift that all parties—students, faculty, and administrators—need to negotiate carefully. The advantages are worthwhile, but virtual space creates new relationships and new expectations that are sometimes hard to live up to, especially in the early stages. Servers crash, students get frustrated because the computer shuts them out if they don't follow directions exactly, faculty don't want to admit that they can't log on because they've forgotten their system password. Virtual space also creates expectations for 24-hour service. If students have trouble submitting work at 2 A.M., they want help then and not two days later when the student tech assistant comes into work. These are changes that benefit from worst-case-scenario planning and a thick skin. Once the technological wrinkles get identified and worked out, however, the possibilities are exciting. *SW*

8. Daniel J. Royer and Roger Gilles advocate a method of first-year writing placement that they call "directed self-placement" (1998). In orientation, entering students read a brochure describing the basic and the regular composition courses and profiling typical basic and regular students with precollegiate test scores. With this information, students place themselves into the courses. Is directed self-placement the method of the future?

Directed self-placement can be described with more assurance as a method of the past. Royer and Gilles' system at Grand Valley State University in Allendale, Michigan has been tried in the past by institutions as diverse as San Francisco State University, Washington State University, and Yale University. In the late 1970s Yale, which had done away with its writing requirements a decade earlier, still had three versions of a first-year writing course on the books. They also had average scores on national tests such as the SAT and the Test of Standard Written English for students whom teachers thought had been placed well in each of the courses. They sent the averages to incoming students and let the students decide which, if any, course to take (Hackman & Johnson, 1981).

Yale, of course, had nothing like a basic writing course, and a crucial issue about directed self-placement is whether it will work for schools that do. Or more exactly, will it work for students who might (or might not) need a basic course. Before 1991, WSU had no first-year writing placement system. We sent entering students who had scored in the lowest quartile of the verbal composite of the Washington State Pre-Collegiate Examination a letter informing them of that fact and suggesting they might be better off in basic writing (see Chapter 8). As might be expected, this form of directed self-placement put a good many students into regular composition who needed basic work to pass the course.

But worse, according to many teachers, it put into the basic course students who were perfectly qualified to handle the regular course. The problem is that self-placement is based on self-evaluation, and self-evaluation is based in part on self-esteem, which with some people can be "low" because it does not match reality. Once in the basic writing course, such a person will find his or her self-evaluation confirmed. Directed self-placement, then, runs the danger of becoming directed self-fulfilling prophecy.

At issue, then, is who should assume the risk for making such a potentially damaging placement, the teachers or the student. Directed self-placement puts the burden on the student. "Our [basic writers] saw *themselves* as poor readers and writers. In the past, we had done the seeing for them" (Royer & Gilles, 1998, p. 62). Royer and Gilles argue that the student's judgment is more reliable than the teachers'. For instance, they note the poor interrater reliability of the readers of their summer placement essay and say that with self-placement "there is no 'interrater-reliability' problem since there is only one rater" (p. 63). This is a curious argument, akin to William Blake's chimney sweeper being told that he shouldn't cry over the shaving off of his hair because now it won't get sooty. The student's decision, of course, does have a reliability, which is whether the student would make the same decision under different circumstances, for instance after talking it over with an advisor rather than with a new roommate. So also at issue is knowledge. I wouldn't deny that most students know more about their determination and willingness to earn the grade than do the teachers. But who knows more about the course that the student is about to enter? In essence, placement is always a judgment about the future, and in this case the future is a course the student hasn't taken taught by a teacher the student doesn't know.

This brings up a final consideration. Along with the student and the faculty, also at risk with directed self-placement is the curriculum. As all teachers know from experience, the students who end up in a course help determine what the course will be. There is no doubt that self-placement has a certain expediency. The student does not have to put together a placement portfolio or spend two hours writing placement essays, and the teacher does not have to read them. When Yale turned to self-placement, "one or two teachers" no longer had to search through student records in August for test scores (Hackman & Johnson, 1981). Administrators at Grand Valley State University had seen that their readers were harassed with the need to score essays during orientation within a short turn-around time, and they decided that to turn to portfolio placement during a time of increased enrollment "would place quite a burden on our already overburdened summer faculty" (Royer & Gilles, 1998, p. 60). It may be that as enrollments and student-to-faculty ratios go up around the nation, systems of self-placement will also increase. But curriculum has its own expediency. Hackman and Johnson note that self-placement "is likely to work best when students' self-esteem and curricular plans are not urgently at stake." The message from WSU is that we have tried self-placement and, for us, it was finally more expedient to solve placement problems with new and better writing samples, new and better reading systems, and new and better courses. *RHH*

Appendix A

The Writing Program at Washington State University: A Time Line

Pre–1985   For graduation, students are required to take one semester of freshman composition. Some departments require a second writing course of their majors. There is no university writing-placement examination at any point in a student's career. Entering students selected to the Honors College take honors composition. Students scoring in the bottom quartile in a state-run standardized verbal examination are advised but not required to take basic writing. There is a drop-in Writing Center. The English Department offers an M.A. in Composition.

1985   WSU sends a team to a Lilly Foundation workshop to develop a revision of the core curriculum. The team includes two members of the English Department, Richard Law and Richard Haswell.

1986   New president Samuel H. Smith, with the approval of the faculty senate, creates an All University Writing Committee (AUWC) to address perceived lacks in writing competence of undergraduates (with Thomas Barton, Director of Composition, as Chair) and the President's Commission on General Education. The two committees work collaboratively to establish a policy basis for a writing program and a reform of the General Education Program. Vice Provost Donald Bushaw and Associate Dean Richard Law are members of both committees and attempt to coordinate emerging policies.

1986   National Endowment for the Humanities (NEH) grant (written by Richard Law and Vice Provost T. L. Kennedy) awarded to implement a revision of the humanities core curriculum, which includes extended writing assignments in all lower-division core courses.

1986   A specialist in writing across the curriculum is hired (Susan McLeod), to be the next director of composition.

1987   The WSU faculty senate and Board of Regents adopt the seven-point AUWC Writing Program policy, establishing a freshman placement examination, "a writing component" in a "designated number" of general education courses, "significant writing experience" as a requirement in the course work in the student's major, and successful performance on a "writing qualifying examination" as a requirement for graduation. The President's Commission on General Education adopts a plan to reform the general-education program, organizing the curriculum in tiers and adopting a core curriculum.

1987   The new Director of Composition (McLeod) installs a first-year composition portfolio examination, similar to Pat Belanoff and Peter Elbow's system at State University of New York (SUNY) Stony Brook.

1987   A composition specialist in computer-assisted instruction is hired (Barbara Sitko) to create and run computer classrooms.

1989–90 The AUWC runs placement and "qualifying" examination pilots, both consisting of one impromptu essay, holistically scored. For the first year placement examination, the

Committee establishes the concept of three placements: English 101 (regular composition), English 102 (a tutorial required of some students to be taken with English 101), and English 100 (basic writing).

1990   Reaffirming and refining its 1987 action, the Faculty Senate votes to "upgrade and monitor" English freshman composition courses, to support "staff development," to apply the placement exam to all students matriculating Fall, 1991, to require two upper-division, writing-intensive courses for all majors, to assign the design of the "qualifying examination" to "representative department and program personnel from across campus," and to require that the exam be taken by students "no later than the end of the first semester of upper-division standing."

1990   A specialist in basic writing is hired (Susan Wyche). Implementation of General Education Program begins; Law becomes Director of General Education Program.

1990–91   Under pressure from writing specialists in the English Department, the All University Writing Committee turns the development of the placement and junior examinations over to a "Testing/Assessment" subcommittee chaired by a specialist in writing and evaluation (Haswell) and including the director of Composition (McLeod), the director of Basic Writing (Wyche), the director of the Writing Center (Robin Magnuson), the vice provost for Instruction (Donald Bushaw), and administrators from university advising, testing, admissions, and the registrar's office.

1991   The Testing/Assessment Committee reshapes the "qualifying examination" into a junior-year placement examination, portfolio-based. Students will write sit-down, impromptu essays, but also submit three course papers validated by the instructors. Students submitting portfolios rated in the top 10 percent will have that fact recorded on their transcripts. The exam will replicate the first-year placement examination to facilitate studies of program and writing growth.

1991   The first-year placement examination is implemented during summer orientation, with essays read following a time-saving, two-tiered method (devised by Haswell). The assessment is administered out of the Writing Center.

1991   English 102 (directed by Lisa Johnson-Shull) is reconceived as problem-specific, group tutorials. The second semester, enrollment doubles as many students not placed there sign up for the course.

1992   International students are required to take the first-year placement examination. A validation study of the first-year placement examination is written (by Haswell, Wyche, and Magnuson)

1993   Implementation of Writing in the Major involving review of around 250 courses proposals over three years and extensive faculty development activities.

1993   In an assessment/instructional move designed by the director of Basic Writing (Wyche), all first-year students placed into the basic course are enrolled for regular composition and the one-hour tutorial.

1993   Late in the fall, the first junior portfolios are submitted. Student fees for the first-year and junior-year examinations are charged directly to the student's account instead of received in cash during the examination sessions.

1993   Writing Program components outside of the English Department, such as Writing Across the Curriculum, are assigned to the General Education Office. Writing Program acquires first permanent budget. A university Writing Assessment Office is established, separate from the Writing Center, reporting to the Director of General Education. The Assessment Office takes in submitted portfolios, enters data, and otherwise handles the two placement examinations (directed by Haswell and assisted by Sue Hallett and Diane Kelly).

1994   A new director of Composition is hired (Victor Villanueva). English faculty members now occupy the positions of associate dean of Arts and Humanities (McLeod), director of General Education (Law), coordinator of the University Writing Assessment Office (Haswell), and Director of the Writing Center (Magnuson).

1995   The office for University Writing Assessment is moved back into the Writing Center space.

1995   A new course is installed, General Education 302, a one-hour tutorial parallel to English 102, taken in tandem with upper-division, writing-intensive courses and administered by the Writing Center (now directed by Lisa Johnson-Shull). The Center supervisor position is established on a permanent basis.

1995   A registration block is put on second-semester juniors who have not taken the junior portfolio, requiring them to sign up for an examination session. Cash awards from donations are established for best junior portfolios.

1995   The first of annual progress reports on the junior portfolio examination is submitted to central administration (Haswell). The first of two-year internal studies of the examination is written (Haswell).

1996   A new administrative position is created, director of University Writing Programs, reporting to the General Education Office, and the position is filled (William Condon). An assessment of compliance with Writing in the Major policy is conducted by McLeod and Law.

1996   Norming sessions are conducted at the beginning of examination rating sessions. After two years of quiescence, basic writing is reinstated. It averages two to four sections a year.

1997   The English Department inaugurates a PhD Degree in Rhetoric and Composition.

1998   The three-course writing sequence for international students is revamped (by Lisa Johnson-Shull and others) into a two-course sequence, with credit earned in the second fulfilling the general university three-hour composition requirement for graduation. A study is conducted into placement essays and basic writers (directed by Steve Smith).

1999   The appeals process for the junior examination is revamped, allowing students three courses of action: submit a new portfolio, recirculate the old portfolio through the rating corps, or appear before an appeals board. Students given a needs-work placement of the one-hour General Education 302 tutorial must take it in conjunction with a writing-in-the-major course; otherwise it reverts to a three-hour, stand-alone writing course.

1999   Norming procedures are expanded at the beginning of the junior portfolio rating sessions. Plans are under way to institute a stretch English 101 to replace English 100.

Appendix B

Writing Placement Essay Prompts— Washington State University

RHETORICAL FRAME 1

Read the following passage carefully. It expresses a point of view with which many people may well disagree.

> I was talking with an Alaskan hunting guide who had killed some thirty-odd wolves himself from a plane, alone, and flown hunters who had killed almost four hundred more. As he described with his hands the movement of the plane, the tack of its approach, his body began to lean into the movement and he shook his head as if to say no words could tell it. For him the thing was not the killing; it was that moment when the blast of the shotgun hit the wolf and flattened him—because the wolf's legs never stopped driving. In that same instant the animal was fighting to go on, to stay on its feet, to shake off the impact of the buckshot. The man spoke with awed respect of the animal's will to live, its bone and muscle shattered, blood streaking the snow, but refusing to fall. "When the legs stop, you know he's dead. He doesn't quit until there's nothing left." He spoke as though he himself would never be a quitter in life because he had seen this thing. Four hundred times.

Here is what I should have said to this guide: It does not demean men to want to be what they imagine the wolf to be, but it demeans them to kill the animal for it.

—Barry Lopez, "Wolfing for Sport"

Clearly, on this complex issue there are other reasonable viewpoints. How do you, personally, resolve the differences among these views?

As you answer that question in your essay, we would like you to include a description of the main issue, a summary of Lopez's view of it and a comparison of that view with at least two other views.

RHETORICAL FRAME 2

Read the following passage carefully. It introduces a complex problem that may have many solutions.

Clearly, this complex issue involves a number of problems. Center on *one* of the problems. How would you suggest solving it in a workable way?

As you answer that question in your essay, we would like you to include a description of the main issue, a summary of Lopez's view of it, and a discussion of the various problems involved.

RHETORICAL FRAME 3

Read the following passage carefully. It may well give a misleading picture of the issue.

Clearly, it is easy to simplify this complex issue. How would you analyze the issue more accurately or honestly or fully?

As you answer that question in your essay, we would like you to include a description of the main issue, a summary of Lopez's view of it, and a discussion of the aspects his passage distorts or omits.

RHETORICAL FRAME 4

Read the following passage carefully. It deals with an issue that may have more sides to it than just the one presented.

Clearly, there are other ways to approach this complex issue. Which angle would you argue is the most useful to take?

As you answer that question in your essay, we would like you to include a description of the main issue, a summary of Lopez's view of it, and a discussion of at least two other ways it can be approached.

Appendix C

Information Rating Sheet

Name _____, _____ _____
                 (last)   (first)   (middle initial)

WSU Identification Number _____ Current phone number _____

Is English your first language? Yes o   No o
    If no, what is your first language? _____

Total college credit hours earned to date _____

The name of your advisor _____

Your declared major _____

Have you transferred credit to Washington State University? Yes o   No o
    From where? _____
    Did you transfer with an AA degree?   Yes o   No o

For which courses did you write the papers that you are submitting in your portfolio?

Course (Prefix/No.)	Semester/Year	Instructor's name	Acceptable or Outstanding
1. _____,	_____,	_____,	_____
2. _____,	_____,	_____,	_____
3. _____,	_____,	_____,	_____

May we use your writing for research? Your work will be anonymous. Yes o   No o

•••••• •••••• INFORMATION TO BE FILLED OUT BY THE WRITING ASSESSMENT OFFICE •••••• ••••••••

Timed Writing Date _____   Topic 1 _____   Topic 2 _____

	Tier-1 Reader	(initials)	Tier-2 Reader (initials)	Needs Work
Distinction?	_____	Pass with Distinction _____		
Pass	_____	Pass	_____	One hour of course work
Needs work?	_____	Needs work	_____	

Tier-1 Reader	Tier-2 Reader	
o conception of topic	o conception of topic	GE 302 + M-Course
o focus and direction	o focus and direction	_____
o logic of argument	o logic of argument	
o support and integration	o support and integration	Three hours of course work
o clarity of ideas	o clarity of ideas	
o beginning & ending	o beginning & ending	_____
o fluency & idiom	o fluency & idiom	
o mechanics	o mechanics	
o other _____	o other _____	

o   Needs-work form has been given to student and advisor _____ (last name) _____ (date)

o   Needs-work requirement has been satisfied by student _____ (last name) _____ (date)

References

Amiran, M., Schilling, K. M., & Schilling, K. L. (1993). In T. Banta (Ed.), *Making a difference: Outcomes of a decade of assessment in higher education* (pp. 71-86). San Francisco: Jossey-Bass.

Anson, C. M., & Brown, R. L., Jr. (1991). Large-scale portfolio assessment. In P. Belanoff & M. Dickson (Eds.), *Portfolios: Process and product* (pp. 248–269). Portsmouth, NH: Boynton/Cook.

Arlin, P. (1984). Adolescent and adult thought: A structural interpretation. In M. L. Commons, F. A. Richards, & C. Armon (Eds.), *Beyond formal operations: Late adolescent and adult cognitive development* (pp. 92–119). New York: Praeger.

Armstrong, C. (1988). Re-examining basic writing: Lessons from Harvard's basic writers. *Journal of Basic Writing, 7*, 68–80.

Astin, A. W. (1993). *What matters in college: Four critical years revisited*. San Francisco: Jossey-Bass.

Banta, T. W. (1997). Moving assessment forward: Enabling conditions and stumbling blocks. In P. J. Gray (Ed.), *The campus-level impact of assessment: Progress, problems, and possibilities* (pp. 79–91). San Francisco: Jossey-Bass.

Barritt, L., Stock, P. L., & Clark, F. (1986). Researching practice: Evaluating assessment essays. *College Composition and Communication, 37*, 315–327.

Basseches, M. A. (1984). *Dialectical thinking and adult development*. Norwood, NJ: Ablex.

Bateson, G. (1972). *Steps to an ecology of mind*. Northvale, NJ: Jason Aronson, Inc.

Belanoff, P., & Elbow, P. (1986). Using portfolios to increase collaboration and community in a writing program. *WPA: Writing program administration, 9*, 27–40.

Bizzell, P. (1986). Composing processes: An overview. In P. R. Petrosky & D. Bartholomae (Eds.), *The teaching of writing*. Chicago: National Society for the Study of Education.

Bloom, L., Daiker, D., & White, E. (Eds.) (1996). *Composition in the 21st-century: Crisis and change*. Carbondale, IL: Southern Illinois University Press.

Bonnema, D., Haswell, R. H., & Norris, J. (1997). *The WSU Writing Portfolio: Second findings (May 1995–May 1997)*. Office of Writing Assessment Internal Report #3. Pullman, WA: Washington State University.

Boyer, C. M., & Ewell, P. T. (1988). *State-based case studies of assessment initiatives in undergraduate education: Chronology of critical points*. Denver: Education Commission of the States.

Brereton, J. C. (1995). *The origins of composition studies in the American college, 1875–1925*. Pittsburgh: University of Pittsburgh Press.

Brewer, J., & Hunter, A. (1989). *Multimethod research: A synthesis of styles*. Newbury Park, CA: Sage.

Bruffee, K. (1984), Collaborative learning and the "conversation of mankind." *College English, 46*, 635–652.

Burnham, C. (1986). Portfolio evaluation: Room to breathe and grow. In C. Bridges (Ed.), *Training the teacher of college composition*. Urbana, IL: National Council of Teachers of English.

Calpas, G., & Smith, W. L. (1995). The expert model of placement testing. *Composition Chronicle*, February, 4–6.

Camp, R. (1996). New views of measurement and new models for writing assessment. In E. M. White, W. D. Lutz, & S. Kamusikiri (Eds.), *Assessment of writing: Politics, policies, practices* (pp. 135–147). New York: Modern Language Association of America.

Capra, F. (1996) *The web of life*. New York: Anchor Books/Doubleday.

Chiseri-Strater, E. (1991). *Academic literacies: The public and private discourse of university students*. Portsmouth, NH: Heinemann.

Clark, F. (1987). Studying the longitudinal study: Do impromptu essays show changes in critical thinking over the span of college? Bloomington, IN: ERIC Clearinghouse on Reading and Writing Skills (ED 293 120).

Cohen, E. (1989). Approaches to predicting student success: Findings and recommendations from a study of California community colleges. Bloomington, IN: ERIC Clearinghouse on Reading and Writing Skills (ED 301 808).

Condon, W. (1997). Building bridges, closing gaps: Using portfolios to reconstruct the academic community. In K. B. Yancey and I. Weiser (Eds.), *Situating portfolios: Four perspectives*. Logan, UT: Utah State University Press.

Condon, W., & Hamp-Lyons, L. (1991). Introducing a portfolio-based writing assessment. In P. Belanoff & M. Dickson (Eds.), *Portfolios: Process and product* (pp. 231–247). Portsmouth, NH: Boynton/Cook.

Curry, W., & Hager, E. (1987). Assessing general education: Trenton State College. In D. F. Halpern (Ed.), *Student outcomes assessment: What institutions stand to gain* (pp. 57–65). San Francisco: Jossey-Bass.

Daniel, N., & Ludgewalt, W. (1988). *Report of The English Department survey of spring 1988*. Fort Worth, TX: Texas Christian University English Department.

Elbow, P. (1991). Foreword. In P. Belanoff and M. Dickson (Eds.), *Portfolios: Process and product* (pp. ix–xvi). Portsmouth, NH: Boynton/Cook.

Elbow, P. (1996). Writing assessment in the 21st century: A utopian view. In L. Z. Bloom, D. A. Daiker, & E. M. White (Eds.), *Composition in the 21st century: Crisis and Change* (pp. 83–100). Carbondale and Edwardsville: Southern Illinois University Press.

Ewell, P. (1985). The value-added debate continued. *AAHE Bulletin, 38,* 12–13.

Fiske, D. W. (1982). Convergent-discriminant validation in measurements and research strategies. In D. Brinberg & L. H. Kidder (Eds.), *Forms of validity in research.* New Directions for Methodology of Social and Behavioral Science no. 12. San Francisco: Jossey-Bass.

Fiske, S. T., & Neuberg, S. L. (1990). A continuum of impression formation, from category-based to individuating processes: Influences of information and motivation on attention and interpretation. *Advances in Experimental Social Psychology, 23,* 1–74.

Freedman, S. W., & Robinson, W. S. (1982). Testing proficiency in writing at San Francisco State University. *College Composition and Communication, 33,* 393–399.

Gebhard, A. O. (1978). Writing quality and syntax: A transformational analysis of three prose samples. *Research in the Teaching of English, 12,* 211–232.

Glau, G. (1996). The "Stretch Program": Arizona State University's new model of university-level basic writing instruction. *Writing Program Administration, 20,* 79–91.

Gleason, B., & Soliday, M. (1997). *The City College Writing Program: An enrichment approach to language and literacy: Three year pilot project, 1993-1996, final report.* New York: City College FIPSE Grant #P116A30689.

Gleick, J. (1987). *Chaos: Making a new science.* New York: Viking.

Gomm, R. (1981). Salvage evaluation. In David Smetherham (Ed.), *Practising evaluation* (pp. 127–144). Chester, England: Bemrose Press.

Graham, J. G. (1987). *A comparison of the writing of college freshmen and college seniors with a focus on indications of cognitive development.* Unpublished dissertation. University of Maryland.

Grego, R., & Thompson, N. (1996). Repositioning remediation: Renegotiating composition's work in the academy. *College Composition and Communication, 47,* 62–84.

Guba, E. G., & Lincoln, Y. S. (1989). *Fourth generation evaluation.* Newbury Park, CA: Sage.

Haas, C. (1994). Learning to read biology: One student's rhetorical development in college. *Written Communication, 11,* 43–84.

Hackman, J. D., & Johnson, P. (1981). Using standardized test scores for placement in college English courses. *Research in the Teaching of English, 15,* 275–279.

Hamp-Lyons, L., & Condon, W. C. (1993). Questioning assumptions about portfolios. *College Composition and Communication, 44,* 176–190.

Hamp-Lyons, L., & Condon, W. (2000). *Assessing the portfolio: Principles for practice, theory and research.* Cresskill, NJ: Hampton Press.

Harrington, S. (1998). New visions of authority in placement testing. *WPA: Writing Program Administration, 22,* 53–84.

Haswell, R. H. (1983). Minimal marking. *College English, 45,* 600–604.

Haswell, R. H. (1986). *Change in undergraduate and post-graduate writing performance (Part I): Quantified findings.* Bloomington, IN: ERIC Clearinghouse on Reading and Writing Skills (ED 269 780).

Haswell, R. H. (1991). *Gaining ground in college writing: Tales of development and interpretation.* Dallas: Southern Methodist University Press.

Haswell, R. H. (1994). Testing of a two-tier system: Categorizing of obvious. Paper delivered at the Annual Conference on College Composition and Communication. Nashville, TN.

Haswell, R. H. (1995). *The WSU Writing Portfolio: First findings (Feb. 1993–May 1995).* Office of Writing Assessment Internal Report #2. Pullman, WA: Washington State University.

Haswell, R. H. (1998a). Final outcomes from a value-added study of WSU undergraduate writing. Pullman, WA: Writing Assessment Office.

Haswell, R. H. (1998b). Multiple inquiry in the validation of writing tests. *Assessing Writing, 5,* 89–108.

Haswell, R. H. (1998c). Rubrics, prototypes, and exemplars: Categorization and systems of writing placement. *Assessing Writing, 5,* 231–268.

Haswell, R. H. (1998d). Searching for Kiyoko: Bettering mandatory ESL writing placement. *Journal of Second Language Writing, 7,* 133–174.

Haswell, R. H. (2000). Documenting improvement in college writing: A longitudinal approach. *Written Communication, 17,* 307–352.

Haswell, R. H., & Wyche-Smith, S. (1994). Adventuring into assessment. *College Composition and Communication, 45,* 220–236.

Haswell, R. H., & Wyche, S. (1996). A two-tiered rating procedure for placement essays. In T. W. Banta, J. P. Lund, K. E. Black, & F. W. Oblander (Eds.), *Assessment in practice: Putting principles to work on college campuses* (pp. 204–207). San Francisco: Jossey-Bass.

Haswell, R. H., Wyche-Smith, S., & Johnson-Shull, L. (1994). Shooting Niagara: Making assessment serve instruction at a state university. *WPA: Writing Program Administration, 18,* 44–53.

Haswell, R. H., Wyche-Smith, S., & Magnuson, R. (1992). *Follow-up study of the Washington State University writing placement examination: Academic year 1991/2.* Office of Writing Assessment Internal Report #1. Pullman, WA: Washington State University.

Herrington, A. J., & Curtis, M. (2000). *Persons in process: Four stories of writing and personal development in college.* Urbana, IL: National Council of Teachers of English.

Homa, D. (1984). On the nature of categories. In G. H. Bower (Ed.), *The psychology of learning and motivation: Advances in research and theory,* vol. 18 (pp. 49–94). Orlando, FL: Academic Press.

Hughes, G. F. (1996). The need for clear purposes and new approaches to the evaluation of writing-across-the-curriculum programs. In E. M. White, W. D. Lutz, & S. Kamusikiri (Eds.), *Assessment of writing: Politics, policies, practices* (pp. 158–173). New York: Modern Language Association of America.

Huot, B. (1994). A survey of college and university writing placement practices. *WPA: Writing Program Administration, 17,* 49–65.

Huot, B. (1996). Toward a new theory of writing assessment. *College Composition and Communication, 47,* 549–566.

Hurtgen, J. R. (1997). Assessment of general learning: State University of New York College at Fredonia. In P. J. Gray & T. W. Banta (Eds.), *The campus-level impact of assessment: Progress, problems, and possibilities* (pp. 59–69). San Francisco: Jossey-Bass.

Jacobi, M., Astin, A., & Ayala, Jr., F. (1987). *College student outcomes assessment: A talent development perspective.* ASHE-ERIC Higher Education Report No. 7. Washington, DC: Association for the Study of Higher Education.

Kahneman, D., & Miller, D. T. (1986). Norm theory: Comparing reality to its alternatives. *Psychological Review, 93,* 136–153.

Kail, H., & Trimbur, J. (1987) The politics of peer tutoring. *The Writing Center Journal. 11,* 5–12.

Kenny, R. W. (1998). *Reinventing undergraduate education: A blueprint for America's research universities.* New York: Boyer Commission on Educating Undergraduates in the Research University.

Kipling, K. J., & Murphy, J. M. (1992). *Symbiosis: Writing and an academic culture.* Portsmouth, NH: Boynton/Cook.

Kitzhaber, A. R. (1963). *Themes, theories, and therapy: The teaching of writing in college.* New York: McGraw-Hill.

Labouvie-Vief, G. (1982). Discontinuities in development from childhood to adulthood: A cognitive-developmental view. In T. M. Field (Ed.), *Review of human development* (pp. 447–455). New York: Wiley.

Law, R. G. (1989). Improving student writing: An institutional approach. *Issues in Writing, 1,* 120–133.

Leviton, L. C., & Hughes, E. F. X. (1981). Research on the utilization of evaluations: A review and synthesis. *Evaluation Review, 5,* 525–548.

Light, R. J. (1992). *Exploration with students and faculty about teaching, learning, and student life.* Harvard Assessment Seminar, 2nd. Report. Cambridge, MA: Harvard University.

Linde, C. (1997). Narrative: Experience, memory, folklore. *Journal of Narrative and Life History, 7,* 281–289.

Loacker, G., & Mentkowski, M. (1993). Creating a culture where assessment improves learning. In T. Banta (Ed.), *Making a difference: Outcomes of a decade of assessment in higher education* (pp. 5–24). San Francisco: Jossey-Bass.

Lucas, C. (1988). Toward ecological evaluation. *The Quarterly, 10,* no. 1, 1–3, 12–17; no. 2, 4–10.

Lundsford, A. (1991) Collaboration, control and the idea of a writing center. *The Writing Center Journal, 12,* 3–10.

Magruder, J., McManis, M. A., & Young, C. C. (1997). The right idea at the right time: Development of a transformational assessment culture. In P. J. Gray & T. W. Banta (Eds.), *The campus-level impact of assessment: Progress, problems, and possibilities* (pp. 17–29). San Francisco: Jossey-Bass.

Mark, M. M., & Shotland, R. L. (Eds.). (1987). *Multiple methods in program evaluation.* New Directions for Progam Evaluation no. 35. San Francisco: Jossey-Bass.

McLeod, S. (1992). Evaluating writing programs: Paradigms, problems, possibilities. *Journal of Advanced Composition, 12,* 373–382.

McLeod, S. H. (1991). Requesting a consultant-evaluation visit. *WPA: Writing Program Administration, 14,* 73–77.

Messick, S. (1989). Meaning and values in test validation: The science and ethics of assessment. *Educational Researcher, 18,* 5–11.

Messick, S. (1995). Standards of validity and the validity of standards in performance assessment. *Educational Measurement: Issues and Prcatice, 14,* 5–8.

Morgan, G. (1986). *Images of Organization.* Beverly Hills, CA: Sage.

Moss, P. A. (1994). Validity in high stakes writing assessment. *Assessing Writing, 1,* 109–128.

Moss, P. A. (1998). Testing the test of the test: A response to "Multiple inquiry in the validation of writing tests." *Assessing Writing, 5,* 111–122.

Moss, P.A., Beck, J.S., Ebbs, C., Matson, B., Muchmore, J., Steele, D., Taylor, C., & Herter, R. (1992). Portfolios, accountability, and an interpretive approach to validity. *Educational Measurement: Issues and Practice, 11,* 12–21.

Murphy, S., & Ruth, L. (1993). The field testing of writing prompts reconsidered. In M. Williamson & B. Huot, (Eds.), *Validating holistic scoring for writing assessment: Theoretical and empirical foundations,* (pp. 266–301). Cresskill, NJ: Hampton Press.

Mutnick, D. (1996). *Writing in an alien world: Basic writing and the struggle for equality in higher education.* Portsmouth, NH: Boynton/Cook.

Norris, J., & Webber, S. (1999). *The Washington State University Writing Portfolio, Third findings: June 1997–May 1999.* Internal Report #4. Pullman, WA: Office of Writing Assessment.

North, S. (1984) The idea of a writing center. *College English, 46,* 433–446.

Nystrand, M. (1993). Addressing reliability problems in the portfolio assessment of college writing. *Educational Assessment, 1,* 53–70.

Palomba, C. (1997) Assessment at Ball State. In P. Gray & T. Banta (Eds.), *The campus-level impact of assessment: Progress, problems, and possibilities,* (pp. 31–45). San Francisco: Jossey-Bass.

Pascarella, E. T. (1987). Are value-added analyses valuable? In Educational Testing Service, *Assessing the outcomes of higher education.* Proceedings of the 1986 ETS Invitational Conference, (pp. 71–91). ETS: Princeton, 1987.

Pascarella, E. T., & Terenzini, P. T. (1991). *How college affects students: Findings and insights from twenty years of research.* San Francisco: Jossey-Bass.

Patton, M. (1986). *Utilization-focused evaluation* (2nd ed). Newbury Park, CA: Sage.

Perry, W. (1970). *Forms of intellectual and ethical development in the college years: A scheme.* New York: Holt, Rinehart and Wintson.

Postman, N. (1976). *Crazy talk, stupid talk.* New York: Delacorte Press.

Rest, J. R. (1979). *Development in judging moral issues.* Minneapolis: University of Minnesota Press.

Rodby, J. (1996). What's it worth and what's it for? Revisions to basic writing revisited. *College Composition and Communication, 47,* 107–11.

Roemer, M., Schultz, L. M., & Durst, R. K. (1991). Portfolios and the process of change. *College Composition and Communication, 42,* 455–469.

Rosch, E., & Mervis, C. B. (1975). Family resemblances: Studies in the internal structure of categories. *Cognitive Psychology, 7,* 573–605.

Royer, D. J., & Gilles, R. (1998). Directed self-placement: An attitude of orientation. *College Composition and Communication, 50,* 54–70.

Russell, D. (1991). *Writing in the academic disciplines, 1870-1999: A curricular history.* Carbondale: Southern Illinois University Press.

Ruth, L., & Murphy, S. (1988). *Designing writing tasks for the assessment of writing.* Norwood, NJ: Ablex.

Schaie, K. W., & Parr, J. (1981). Intelligence. In A. W. Chickering and associates (Eds.), *The modern American college* (pp. 117–138). San Francisco: Jossey-Bass.

Scharton, M. (1989). Models of competence: Response to a scenario writing assignment. *Research in the Teaching of English, 23,* 163–180.

Scharton, M. (1996). The politics of validity. In E. M. White, W. D. Lutz, & S. Kamusikiri (Eds.), *Assessment of writing: Politics, policies, practices* (pp. 53–75). New York: Modern Language Association of America.

Sims, S. J. (1992). *Student outcomes assessment: A historical review and guide to program development*. Westport, CT: Greenwood.

Smith, E. E., & Medin, D. L. (1981). *Categories and concepts*. Cambridge, MA: Harvard University Press.

Smith, M. L. (1986). The whole is greater: Combining qualitative and quantitative approaches in evaluation studies. In D. D. Williams (Ed.), *Naturalistic evaluation. New directions for program evaluation*, no. 31 (pp. 37–54). San Francisco: Jossey-Bass.

Smith, W. L. (1992). The importance of teacher knowledge in college composition placement testing. In J. R. Hayes, M. Matchett, M. McCaffrey, C. Cochron, & T. Hajduk (Eds.), *Reading empirical research studies: The rhetoric of research* (pp. 289–316). Hillsdale, NJ: Erlbaum.

Smith, W. L. (1993). Assessing the reliability and adequacy of using holistic scoring of essays as a college composition placement technique. In M. M. Williamson & B. A. Huot (Eds.), *Validating holistic scoring for writing assessment: Theoretical and empirical foundations* (pp. 142–205). Cresskill, NJ: Hampton Press.

Sommers, N. (1994). *A study of undergraduate writing at Harvard*. Cambridge, MA: Expository Writing Program.

Sosnoski, J. J. (1997). Grades for work: Giving value for value. In L. Allison, L. Bryant, & M. Hourigan (Eds.), *Grading in the post-process classroom: From theory to practice* (pp. 156–175). Portsmouth, NH: Heinemann.

Spack, R. (1997). The acquisition of academic literacy in a second language: A longitudinal case study. *Written Communication, 14*, 3–62.

Speck, B. W. (1998). *Grading student writing: An annotated bibliography*. Westport, CT: Greenwood.

Sternglass, M. S. (1997). *Time to know them: A longitudinal study of writing and learning at the college level*. Mahwah, NJ: Lawrence Erlbaum Associates.

Stock, P., & Robinson, J. L. (1987). Taking on testing: Teachers as tester-researchers. *English Education, 19*, 93–121.

Stoll, C. (1995). *Silicon snake oil*. New York: Doubleday

Swidler, A. (1986). Culture in action: Symbols and strategies. *American Sociological Review, 51*, 273–286.

Tinto, V. (1987). *Leaving college: Rethinking the causes and cures of student attrition*. Chicago: University of Chicago Press.

Torrance, R. (1994) *The spiritual quest: Transcendence in myth, religion and science*. Berkeley: University of California Press.

Townsend, M., Werder, C., & Wyche, S. (2000). Dismantling and revamping mandated writing tests. Presentation at the Annual Convention of the Conference on College Composition and Communication. Minneapolis, MN.

van Gennep, A. (1960) *The rites of passage*. Chicago: University of Chicago Press.

Walther, J. B. (1995, May 25–29). Computer-mediated communication: Impersonal, interpersonal, and hyperpersonal interaction. Paper presented at the annual convention of the International Communication Association, Albuquerque, NM.

Warren, J. (1984). The blind alley of value added. *AAHE Bulletin, 37*, 10–13.

Wheatley, M. (1992). *Leadership and the new science: Learning about organization from an orderly universe*. San Francisco, CA: Berrett-Koehler.

White, E. M. (1985). *Teaching and assessing writing: Recent advances in understanding, evaluating, and improving student performance.* San Francisco: Jossey-Bass.

White, E. M. (1990a). The danger of innovations set adrift. *Bulletin of the American Association for Higher Education, 43,* 3–5.

White, E. M. (1990b). Language and reality in writing assessment. *College Composition and Communication, 41,* 187–200.

White, E. M. (1991). Shallow roots or taproots for writing across the curriculum? *ADE Bulletin, No. 98,* 29–33.

White, E. M. (1993). *Report on the WSU writing program,* Pullman, WA: Washington State University.

White, E. M. (1994a). *Developing successful college writing programs.* (2nd. ed.). San Francisco: Jossey-Bass.

White, E. M. (1994b). *Teaching and assessing writing: Recent advances in understanding, evaluating, and improving student performance.* (2d ed.). San Franciso: Jossey-Bass Publishers.

White, E. M. (1995). The importance of placement and basic studies: Helping students succeed under the new elitism. *Journal of Basic Writing, 14,* 75–84.

White, E. M., & Polin, L. G. (1984). *Research in effective teaching of writing.* Bloomington, IN: ERIC Clearinghouse on Reading and Writing (ED 275 007).

Whitla, D. K. (1977). *Value added: Measuring the impact of undergraduate education.* Cambridge, MA: University of Harvard Office of Students.

Witte, S. P., & Faigley, L. (1983). *Evaluating college writing programs.* Carbondale, IL: Southern Illinois University Press.

Wolcott, W. (1994). A longitudinal study of six developmental students' performance in reading and writing. *Journal of Basic Writing, 13,* 14–40.

Yancey, K. B. (1999). Looking back as we look forward: Historicizing writing assessment. *College Composition and Communication, 50,* 483-503.

Index of Authors Cited

Amiran, Minda R., 192
Anson, Chris, 1, 167
Arlin, Patricia K., 108
Armstrong, Cheryl, 93
Astin, Alexander W., 109, 115, 122
Ayala, Frank, Jr., 109, 115

Banta, Trudy W., 81
Barritt, Loren, 19
Basseches, Michael A., 108
Bateson, Gregory, 81
Belanoff, Pat, 141
Bizzell, Patricia, 20
Bonnema, Douglas, 71, 134, 142
Boyer, Carol M., 108
Brereton, John C., 53
Brewer, John, 127
Bruffee, Kenneth, 88

Brown, Robert L., Jr., 1, 167
Burnham, Christopher, 63

Calpas, Gary, 55, 162
Camp, Roberta, 126
Capra, Fritjof, 84
Chiseri-Strater, Elizabeth, 110
Clark, Francella, 19, 121
Cohen, Elaine, 47
Condon, William, 1, 65, 66,196
Curry, Wade, 122
Curtis, Mary, 110

Daniel, Neil, 139
Durst, Russel K., 1

Elbow, Peter, xiii, 56, 65, 98, 141, 157
Ewell, Peter T., 108, 110

Faigley, Lester, 125
Fiske, Donald W., 127
Fiske, Susan T., 60
Freedman, Sarah W., 141
Fulweiler, Toby, 159

Gebhard, Ann O., 110
Gilles, Roger, 56, 201, 202, 203
Glau, Greg, 95, 104
Gleason, Barbara, 104
Gleick, James, 33
Gomm, Robert, 168
Graham, Joan G., 122
Grego, Rhonda, 103, 104
Guba, Egan G., xv, 145, 154, 155, 156, 194, 198
Guterson, David, 118

Haas, Christina, 110
Hackman, Judith D., 56, 202
Hager, Elizabeth, 122
Hamp-Lyons, Liz, 1, 65, 66, 196
Harrington, Susanmarie, 68, 79
Haswell, Richard H., xi, xii,10, 18, 42, 44, 47, 48, 49, 56, 57, 70, 71, 74, 75, 78, 79, 90, 94, 97, 109, 110, 111, 113, 116, 122, 130, 134, 142, 144, 156, 164, 173
Herrington, Anne J., 110
Homa, Donald, 58
Hughes, Edward F. X., 137
Hughes, Gail F., 126
Hunter, Albert, 127
Huot, Brian, xii, 39, 68
Hurtgen, James R., 81

Jacobi, Maryann, 109, 115
Johnson, Paula, 56, 202
Johnson-Shull, Lisa, xi

Kahneman, Daniel, 60
Kail, Harvey, 25
Kenny, Robert W., 4, 7
Kipling, Kim J., 2
Kitzhaber, Albert R., 110, 122

Labouvie-Vief, Gisela, 108
Law, Richard, 12
Leviton, Laura C., 137

Light, Richard, J., 109, 122
Lincoln, Yvonna S., xv, 145, 154, 155, 156, 194, 198
Linde, Charlotte, 2
Loacker, Georgine, 82
Lopez, Barry, 116
Lucas, Catherine, 140
Ludgewalt, Wendy, 139
Lunsford, Andrea, 88,195

Magnuson, Robin, 44, 47, 94, 97
Magruder, Jack, 82
Mark, Melvin M., 127, 128
McLeod, Susan H., 98, 167
McManis, Michael A., 82
Medin, Douglas L., 60
Mentkowski, Marcia, 82
Mervis, Carolyn B., 59
Messick, Samuel, 65.168
Miller, Dale T., 60
Morgan, Gareth, 32
Moss, Pamela A., 65, 127, 128, 144, 156
Murphy, Richard John, 2
Murphy, Sandra, 141
Mutnick, Deborah, 97

Neuberg, Stephen L., 60
Norris, Joel, 70, 71, 89, 134, 142
North, Stephen, 25
Nystrand, Martin, 126

Parr, Joyce, 108
Palomba, Catherine, 142
Pascarella, Ernest T., 109, 115, 122
Patton, Michael, 137, 168
Perry, William, 85
Polin, Linda G., 19, 52
Postman, Neil, 84

Rest, James R., 110
Robinson, Jay L., 20
Robinson, William S., 141
Rodby, Judith, 103, 104
Roemer, Marjorie, 1
Rosch, Eleanor, 59
Royer, Daniel J., 56, 201, 202, 203
Russell, David, 159
Ruth, Leo, 141

Schaie, K. Warner, 108
Scharton, Maurice, 122, 126
Schilling, Karen Maitland, 192
Schilling, Karl L., 192
Schultz, Lucille M., 1
Shotland, R. Lance, 127, 128
Sims, Serbrenia J., 107, 108
Smith, Edward E., 60
Smith, Mary Lee, 168
Smith, William L., 15, 55, 56, 74, 79, 162
Soliday, Mary, 104
Sommers, Nancy, 109, 122
Sosnoski, James J., 122
Spack, Roberta, 110
Speck, Bruce W., 18
Sternglass, Marilyn S., 110, 111, 116, 122
Stock, Patricia, 19, 20
Stoll, Clifford, 195
Swidler, Ann, 168

Terenzini, Patrick T., 115, 122
Thompson, Nancy, 103, 104

Tinto, Vincent, 110
Torrance, Robert M., 85, 86
Townsend, Martha, 1
Trimbur, John, 25

van Gennep, Arnold, 81

Walther, Joseph B., 195
Warren, Jonathan, 109
Webber, Susan, 70, 89
Werder, Carmen, 1
Wheatley, Margaret, 30, 31
White, Edward M., 16, 19, 49, 52, 65,
    67, 82, 98, 109, 115, 116, 125, 159
Whitla, Dean K., 109, 110, 122
Witte, Stephen P., 125
Wolcott, Willa, 110
Wyche, Susan, xi, 1, 18, 42, 44, 47,
    94, 97

Yancey, Kathleen B., xv
Young, Candace C., 82

Subject Index

Administration, central: audience for reports on assessment-instructional programs, 167–83; budget cycle, concern for, 174; provost, 177–78; role of, 171–72; silence about testing, 139; stakeholders in examination system, 129, 132, 134–36; validation studies, effect on, 114–15; vice-provost, 176

All University Writing Committee (AUWC), Washington State University, 3, 4, 6, 14, 15, 18, 22, 66. 107, 159, 161, 165, 173, 174, 175, 178, 215, 216, 217

Assessment/instructional program at Washington State University: circular relationship between instruction and assessment, 9–12, 81–82, 83–85, 108, 115, 125, 131–32, 156–57, 190, 198; computer mediated, 194–201; critical thinking, rubric for, 10; ecological nature of, xv, 2, 3–4, 12, 20–21, 40, 47, 51–52, 62–63, 126–28, 139–40, 191–92, 194; faculty, involvement in, 162–63; future of, 189–203; general organization of, xiv, 160–61; history of, 1–2, 3–12; innovative nature of, xii; local, interdependence with the, 16–18, 39, 50; longevity of, 41, 51, 189–91; maintenance, advice on, 185–87; narrative as mode for, 1–2; principles of, seven, 4–11; reporting about, to administrators, 167–83; research on, 67, 78–79, 191–92, resistance to, 192–94; review of, outside, 98; rights of passage within organization, 85–91. *See also* Studies of the assessment/instructional program at Washington State University; Value-added studies

Basic writing: abolition of, 93, 97–98; course description, 94–5; legislation about, 97, 102; mainstreaming, 97, 99–101, 101–2, 104; "rehearsal approach," 94–95, 96–97; "stretch program," 95, 104; tutorial workshops, 96–97, 99–104. *See also* Courses, English 100

Categorization theory, and placement, 57–63
Center for Teaching, Learning, and Technology, Washington State University, 11
Chaos theory, 30, 33; Butterfly effect, 32–33, 35
Courses, writing at Washington State University: English 100 (basic writing), xii, 14,16–17, 23, 42, 46, 47, 52, 63, 93–105, 110, 129–30, 132–33, 202–203, 215, 216, 217, 218; English 101 (regular composition, first year), 17, 46, 47–48, 72–73, 94–95, 96, 99, 130, 133, 159, 216; English 102 (tutorial in writing, first year), 5, 16, 42, 45–46, 47, 129–30, 132–33, 194, 216, 217, 218; English as a second language (ESL) sequence, 131–33, 219; General Education 302 (tutorial in writing, upper division), xiii, 71–72, 143, 144, 146, 147, 155, 194, 218, 219; writing in the major, xiii, 5, 7, 8, 9, 70, 142, 146, 147, 155, 160, 162, 196, 217 (upper-division "M" courses)

Evaluators of assessment-instructional program, role of, 169–171
English as a second language (ESL). *See* Non-native writers of English

Faculty, composition: effect of validation studies on, 115–22; stakeholders in assessment program, 132–33
Faculty, campus: apathy toward testing, 139; data on, as examination raters, 179; development of, 8–9, 165; effect of assessment on, 165; involvement in assessment, 159–60; opinion of assessment program, 161–65; rights of passage, 88–90; stakeholders in assessment program, 133–34; subjects for research, 192

General Education Program, Washington State University, xi, xiii, 3, 4, 6, 7, 8, 9, 10, 11, 70, 94, 160, 164, 215, 217, 218
General Education, Commission on, 6
General Education, Lilly Foundation Workshop on, 6

Higher Education Coordinating Board, 9, 11, 115, 173, 190

Junior portfolio. *See* Placement examination, junior year, at Washington State University

Non-native writers of English, 5, 20, 22–23, 61–62, 110, 176, 177, 217; special population, as, 22–23; raters dealing with, 47–49; mainstreaming, 48–49; performance on junior portfolio, 70–74
Northwest Association of Schools and Colleges, xii, 3, 4, 9

Placement examination, first year, Washington State University: basic writing, effect on, 94; changes in, 45–49; construction of, 13–24; exemption from, 133; history of, 4, 5, 216, 217; housing of, 25; outcomes of, 44–46; piloting of, 23, 216; summer orientation, during, 17–18, 19, 217; validation of, 9–10, 46–47, 129–30, 133
Placement examination, junior year, Washington State University: appeals process, 138, 156, 219; authentic nature of, 191; changes in, 49–50, 155–56; characteristics of, 196–97; construction of, 14–15,

Placement examination, junior year,
    Washington State University
    (*continued*)
    21–22; data intake sheet, 49, 223;
    electronic, 195–201; faculty opin-
    ion on, 160–64; history of, 2, 3–4,
    7, 16, 217, 218; impact on the
    Writing Center, 25–26, 28, 30–32;
    needs work placement, 49, 52,
    143, 144, 219; outcomes of, 44–46;
    pass with honors placement, 49,
    133; portfolio, use of, xi, 126; reg-
    istration, block on, 218; relation-
    ship to writing-assessment pro-
    gram, xiii; reports on, 9–10, 173;
    storage for, 195–96, 200; student
    judgment on, 144–55; technical
    writing, placement into, 49; timed
    writing for, 72; validation of, 66,
    67, 70, 73, 130–37
Portfolio. *See* Placement examination,
    junior year, Washington State
    University

Raters of writing examinations, at
    Washington State University:
    apprenticeship, 44–45; changes in,
    50–51; electronic portfolios, expe-
    rience with, 200; esprit du corps,
    50–52; experiences of while rating,
    37, 43; expertise groups, 48–49;
    handbook for, 23; novice and
    experienced, 60–61; reliability,
    47–48, 51–52, 66–68, 79, 178, 202;
    selection and recruiting of, 17, 23;
    subjects of research, 191; teachers
    as, 15, 19, 48, 51–52
Rating method, of writing examina-
    tions, at Washington State
    University: basic features, 41–43,
    68–70; changes in, 43–51; check-
    list of criteria, 50; costs, 42; direct-
    ed self-placement, 55–56; gray-
    area hypothesis, 74, 76, 78–79;
    history of, 41–42, 217; holistic, 18,
    55–57, 58; literature on, 19; norm-
    ing sessions, 219; outcomes of,
    37–38, 74; research into, 65–82;

rubric, 58; teacher option, 55–56;
    tier one ("the obvious place-
    ment"), 54–63; tier two, 60–61;
    training for, 162; transference to
    other sites, 61–63; two-tiered sys-
    tem of, 39–52
Regents, Board of, 115, 129, 136–37,
    173, 175–76, 216

Students: transfers, 67, 70–71, 130–31;
    basic writers, 129–30, 202–203;
    stakeholders in assessment,
    129–32, 156–57; English as second
    language writers, 130–31; opin-
    ions and feelings about testing,
    139, 141–57; subjects of research,
    191–92; reliability of, 202
Studies of the assessment/instruc-
    tional program at Washington
    State University: faculty opinion,
    161–65; mainstreaming of basic
    writers, 99–101; placement and
    end-of-course grades, 132; place-
    ment, student opinion of, 94,
    129–30, 145–54; placement,
    teacher opinion of, 132; portfolio
    outcomes for ESL students, 71–74,
    130–32; portfolio outcomes for
    transfer students, 70–74, 130–32;
    portfolio, performance of aca-
    demic majors, 134–36; portfolio,
    rater reliability and academic
    discipline, 76–78; portfolio,
    recirculation of tier-one passes,
    74; portfolio, recirculation of tier-
    two decisions, 74–78; portfolio,
    student opinion of 131; prompts,
    equivalence of, 47; prompts, gen-
    der effects of, 47; student writing,
    analytic, 112–13; student writing,
    holistic, 112; student writing,
    paired comparisons, 112–13; stu-
    dent writing, teacher evaluation
    of, 133–34; time-to-examination,
    132; transference to other sites,
    122–23; writing folder in first-
    year composition, midsemester,
    46–47, 130

Testing of writing (general): analytic, 18; authentic, 66, 144; Collegiate Assessment of Academic Proficiency (CAAP), 189; College Level Examination Program (CLEP), 18, 39; cost of, 53–54; diagnosis, for purposes of, 19, 52, 55–57, 179; direct, 65; California State University English Placement Test (EPT), 104; Educational Testing Service (ETS), 40, 66; history of, 53; indirect, 18–19, 55–56, 189–90; locally made, 13–24; maintenance of, 39–52; models for, 1; multiple samples of writing in, 19; outcomes, 40, 66; performance, 66; portfolio, midsemester, 216; ready-made, 17, 18–19, 39–40; Scholastic Aptitude Test (SAT), 18, 39, 56, 94, 126, 189, 202; self-placement, directed, 201–203; Texas Academic Skills Program (TASP), 40; theory of, 53–63; Test of Standard Writing English (TSWE), 202; validity, 53–54, 66–68, 79; Washington State Pre-Collegiate Examination (WSPCE), 94, 202

Testing systems for undergraduate writing (general): articulation of, 16, 21–22, 107–108; literature and research on, 18–21; maintenance of, 16; prompts for, 18–20, 21–22; reliability of, 17, 126; social process, as, 126–27; stakeholders, 127–37; teachers' influence on, 20–23; validity of, 17, 126

Testing systems for undergraduate writing at Washington State University: databank, 108; history of, 13–16, 107–108, 202–203, 216–19; prompts, and example of, 221; prompts, and gender effects, 47; prompts, and piloting of, 40–41; prompts, and retesting, 20; prompts, and rhetorical frames, 108, 221–22; prompts, and validation of, 23-24, 125-38. *See also*

Placement examination, first year, Washington State University; Placement examination, junior year, Washington State University

Universities and colleges: Alverno College, 82, 109, 190; Ball State University, 82, 139; Berea College, 98; Brigham Young University, 139; California State University, 93, 139; California State University, Chico, 98; California State University, Monterey Bay, 103–104; California State University, San Bernardino, 82; Catholic University of America, 139; City University of New York, 93, 97; Eastern Oregon State University, 139; Grand Valley State University, 202, 203; Harvard University, 53, 63, 82, 109; Miami-Dade Community College, 82, 109; Mount Olive College, 198; New Mexico State University, 63; San Francisco State University, 141; State University of New York at Fredonia, 81; State University of New York at Stony Brook, 141, 190; Trenton State College, 82; Truman State University (Northeast Missouri State University), 82, 109, 139; University of Arizona, 95, 104, 139; University of California, 93; University of Connecticut, 109; University of South Carolina at Columbus, 98; University of Southwestern Louisiana, 139; University of Tennessee at Knoxville, 82; University System of George, 139; Virginia Military Institute, 82; Western College of Miami University, 82, 192; Yale University, 202, 203

Value-added studies, 10, 107–223; attitude toward, evaluators and administrators, 182–84; cross-

Value-added studies (*continued*)
 checking (triangulation), 128; longitudinal design, 110–14, 191; multimethod, 125–38; problems in, 108–109; recommendations on reporting, 184–85

Writing across the curriculum (WAC), xii, 7–9, 22, 129, 159, 169, 190–91, 216
Writing Assessment Office, 9, 28–35, 167, 218

Writing Center, xii, xiii, 5, 6, 9, 22, 66, 96–97, 102, 160, 215, 217, 218: communication problems, 27–32; crisis, financial, 29; crisis, leadership, 29–30; history of, 25–30, 34–35; impact of assessment on, 25, 26, 28, 30, 31, 32; organization: structural, 26, 27; egocentric, 30, 32; space problems, 28

About the Editor
and Contributors

William Condon came to WSU in fall of 1996, when WSU brought together three campus-wide writing programs—Writing Assessment, Writing Across the Curriculum, and the Writing Center—under one director of Campus Writing Programs. For nine years before becoming director at WSU, he was first associate director for Instruction and then director of the University of Michigan's English Composition Board. Coauthor of *Writing the Information Superhighway*, with Wayne Butler (1997), and *Assessing the Portfolio: Principles for Theory, Practice, and Research*, with Liz Hamp-Lyons (2000), Bill has also published several articles in the areas of writing assessment, program evaluation, and computers and writing.

Fiona Glade has conducted research in faculty responses to WSU's WAC program and has participated in a study examining upper-division non-native writers of English at WSU. She is currently focusing on genre theory.

Richard H. Haswell came to WSU in 1967 as a specialist in British Romantic literature, and served as director of Composition at WSU from

1972 to 1982. He attended the 1985 Lilly workshop to revise the University core curriculum and chaired the 1990 to 1991 Testing and Assessment sub-committee that developed the Junior portfolio examination. From 1991 to 1996 he supervised placement and portfolio readings and from 1993 to 1996 directed the University Office of Writing Assessment. Since 1996 he has been Haas Professor of English at Texas A&M University–Corpus Christi. He is author of *Gaining Ground in College Writing: Tales of Development and Interpretation* (1991), coeditor with John Ehrstine and Robert Wilkinson of *The HBJ Reader* (1987), and coauthor with Min-Zhan Lu of *Comp Tales: An Introduction to College Composition through its Stories* (2000).

Lisa Johnson-Shull came to WSU in 1988 as a graduate student in Composition and Rhetoric when the initial conversations about a campus writing program were beginning to crystallize. She focused her graduate scholarship on Writing Center theory and administration, eventually assuming the assistant directorship and responsibility for the administration of English 102, a brand new, credit-based, small group tutorial program for at-risk writers. In 1995, after four years of nurturing the English 102 program into a course that served the needs of honor students as well as those at risk, she assumed the Writing Center directorship , a position she presently holds. Lisa has coauthored articles on WSU's Junior Writing Portfolio.

Diane Kelly-Riley has directed the Writing Assessment Program at WSU since 1996. She came to WSU in 1993 as a graduate student in literature and, coincidentally, was misadvised to enroll in an internship in the WSU Writing Center. As a result, she participated in the first evaluation sessions of the Writing Portfolio, and in 1994 Diane was hired to help Rich Haswell establish the first office of Writing Assessment. She has worked in all components of the WSU Writing Program.

Richard Law, a member of the English faculty at WSU since 1970, served as associate dean of the College of Liberal Arts from 1983 to 1991 and director of General Education since 1990. A member of the original faculty group that planned the joint Writing and General Education initiatives at the Lilly Conference in 1985, Law was a member of both the All University Writing Committee, which established the principles underlying the WSU Writing Program (1988), and the President's Commission on General Education, which established the goals and curricular structure of the General Education Program. Law has directed implementation of the General Education reform since 1990 and has overseen the Writing Program since 1993. In addition to producing scholarly work on the literature of the American South, he has written, coauthored, or collaborated in a number of projects related to curriculum development, technological applications to instruction, and faculty development at WSU, including projects funded by National Endowment for the Humanities, National Science Foundation, the Ford Foundation, American Association of Colleges & Universities, U S West, Apple, AT&T, Weyerhaeuser, the William and Flora Hewlett Foundation, and Washington Higher Education Coordinating Board's Fund for Innovation and Quality in Higher Education.

Galen Leonhardy attended graduate school at WSU from 1996 to 1998. His major areas of interest were writing assessment and critical pedagogy. Currently, he is a public school teacher who enjoys working with and learning from incarcerated juveniles. He also volunteers at Crosswalk, a shelter for street youth in Spokane, WA.

Susan McLeod came to WSU in 1986 to direct the composition program; she was hired, in part, because of her expertise in writing across the curriculum. In 1987 she instituted a portfolio system for first-year composition, based on the program developed by Elbow and Belanoff. Serving on the General Education Committee and the All University Writing Committee, she worked closely with others who have contributed to this book and with various administrators to help develop and implement various pieces of WSU's comprehensive WAC program; up until Bill Condon was hired to oversee the program, she also directed yearly seminars for faculty who wanted to learn how to assign and evaluate student writing in productive ways. From 1992 to 2000 she served as associate dean of the College of Liberal Arts, and presently serves as Chair of the Department of English. Her publications include *Strengthening Programs for Writing across the Curriculum* (1988); *Writing Across the Curriculum: A Guide to Developing Programs* (1991); a multicultural textbook for composition, *Writing about the World* (1991, 2nd ed. 1995); and *Notes on the Heart: Affective Issues in the Writing Classroom* (1997), as well as articles on writing across the curriculum and writing program administration. Her current project is a coedited collection tentatively entitled *Writing Across the Curriculum for the New Millennium*.

Jennie Nelson is an associate professor of English and former director of writing at the University of Idaho, where she teaches undergraduate writing and graduate courses in composition theory, pedagogy, and research methods. She began her career in composition studies at WSU, where she earned an MA in Teaching Writing and taught first-year composition under the directorship of Rich Haswell. Her research and publications reflect her continuing interest in examining writing from the students' side of the desk: for example, "Reading Classrooms as Text: Exploring Student Writers' Interpretive Practices" published in *College Composition and Communication* and "The Library Revisited: Exploring Students' Research Processes" in *Hearing Ourselves Think* (1993).

Susan Wyche was hired by WSU in 1989 to be the first director of Basic Writing, and from 1992 to 1995 served as director of Composition. She now directs the University Writing Program at California State University Monterey Bay, where she has developed a four-year tutorial workshop system of writing support and is currently at work on a university-wide electronic portfolio. She is the author of numerous articles on writing rituals, peer-based writing groups, and portfolio assessment and is a cocreator of Wordshop Productions' writing group videos.